FIRE
SEASON

Published 2015
Printed in the United States of America
ISBN: 978-1-63152-974-0
Library of Congress Control Number: 2014957847

Book design by Stacey Aaronson

For information, address:
She Writes Press
1563 Solano Ave #546
Berkeley, CA 94707

She Writes Press is a division of Spark Point Studio, LLC.

fire
season

MY JOURNEY FROM RUIN
TO REDEMPTION

HOLLYE DEXTER

[swp]

SHE WRITES PRESS

Contents

AUTHOR'S NOTE

In my extended family, arguing over versions of our history is practically a blood sport. My relatives will wrestle each other to the mat about the way it all went down. In reality, there is no such thing as absolute truth, only our personal interpretations of it. The best way I've ever heard it described was by a woman I met in a writing group. She said as her mother lay dying, she and her sister sat on either side of the hospital bed, holding their mother's hands. At the moment of her passing, the sisters spoke simultaneously. One said, "She's gone cold!" The other said, "She's still warm." And both statements were true to the women who made them.

Anyone who writes memoir will tell you it is a grueling, gut-wrenching task. Drudging up the past to examine your mistakes and weaknesses and relive old wounds is not for the faint of heart. Not to mention the cloud hovering over you every second; the fact that some of the people in your story may be hurt by words you've written. Some may even take offense at details you thought were small and innocuous. For that reason, I have changed some of the names in this book to protect their privacy and out of love, because I do love them all.

I have done my best, as a flawed and complex person myself, to write with compassion and understanding. There are no heroes or villains in this book, only imperfect humans each doing the best they can. That being said, I believe that we own the rights to our own life stories, and if we were born with the compulsion to write, we must do it. I wrote this book based on journals I've kept throughout my life. It is not the elusive "absolute" truth, but it is my truth.

WHAT DOESN'T KILL YOU

❦ ❦ ❦

"We all live in a house on fire, no fire department to call; no way out, just the upstairs window to look out of while the fire burns the house down with us trapped, locked in it."

— TENNESSEE WILLIAMS

Y ou'd think there would have been more leading up to it, this moment when everything changes forever, but November 18, 1994 is just an average night. Fresh out of the bath, I zip our four-year-old son, Taylor, up into his footie pajamas. We have a Peter Pan versus Captain Hook sword fight with toothbrushes, then I chase him to bed. Outside his bedroom window, a full harvest moon hangs low in the sky, grazing the mountaintop. Huge and blindingly blue white, it shines like an icy sun, giving me an ominous feeling. I sidle next to Taylor in his bed, an extra down comforter piled on top us, while I read his favorite book *The Grouchy Ladybug*, acting out the voices of all the bugs.

On the six o'clock news, they'd said temperatures would drop tonight to the low thirties, a record-breaking cold for Southern California. Bonfires blaze in citrus groves all over the state, as farmers try to save their crops from freezing. We are not accustomed to this kind of cold.

I close the book and sing Taylor the same song I'd sung every night since he was born, the song that saddled him with the unfortunate childhood nickname of La-la.

La la lu, la la lu, little wandering angel
Hold up your wings, close your eyes
La la lu, la la lu, and may love be your keeper
La la lu, la la lu, la la lu

He is sound asleep by the last line. I kiss his forehead and tuck the covers in around him, even though he will kick them off within minutes. Turning out the light, I hesitate in the doorway, looking between his and Cissy's beds, hers empty tonight. I don't know that I will ever get used to sharing her with my ex.

In the next room, my husband Troy and our friend Donna tune their guitars, getting ready for our rehearsal. I poke my head into the recording studio, "I'm just going to check on the dogs, okay? I'll be up in five minutes."

Outside, I wrap my arms around myself to quell my shivers. Whitney and Lady romp and play on the patio, unfazed by the weather. A layer of ice floats on the surface of their water dish.

"Come on, girls!" I shout, ushering them inside. I will spend years regretting this.

A fire burns in the living room hearth, illuminating the walls with a soft glow. I lay blankets on the kitchen floor, in the nook where Lady and Whitney like to sleep. My neck is tight. Mounting the stairs, I stop every few steps, eyes closed, hand to my heart. *What am I feeling?*

In the recording studio, Troy, Donna, and I rehearse for an upcoming gig. We sing together in three-part harmony, Donna and Troy strumming their guitars, while I pace back and forth.

"Everything okay, honey?" Troy asks.

I wave my hand, "I'm good . . . keep going." My vocal chords are tight, my breathing shallow. I shift my weight from one foot to the other, shaking my shoulders, rolling my neck to release the tension building inside. Donna is not only a musician, she's a life coach, so I can act crazy in front of her. And Troy, well, he knows I've been like this all day.

My rib cage is tight. I'm not hitting my notes. Donna tilts her head, her soft chocolate-brown eyes registering concern. "What's up, girl? You're not yourself."

I tell her why.

That morning I woke from a horrible, vivid dream. I jolted straight up in bed, heart pounding, my face wet with tears. Troy sat up, startled, and put his arm around me.

"What's wrong?"

"I was falling backward down a hill . . . in this huge avalanche," I sobbed, "and everything I owned, everything I'd ever accomplished in my life was tumbling over me, pounding and crushing me until there was nothing but dust."

"It was just a dream, honey." He pulled me to him, wrapping his arms around me.

"Everything was gone! Everything . . ." My tears rolled onto his chest.

"You're awake now, it's not real."

"But it felt so real!"

He held me tighter. "You're safe, you're safe."

Cissy and Taylor were downstairs eating Cheerios that morning as I laid out their clothes for school. Cartoons hummed cheerily in the background. The dogs were under the dining room table, waiting to catch any stray crumbs or scraps. I threw myself into my routine, trying to shake the residual feelings from the dream. *Everything's fine, every-*

thing's fine, I repeated out loud to myself, all day long.

I chaperoned a field trip for Cissy's fourth-grade class in the afternoon. As we made our way through the Autry Museum, the docent told stories about the Wild West. I smiled, while still grinding my teeth and wringing my hands.

After the field trip, I dropped Cissy at her dad's house for an overnight visit, feeling that familiar pang as I watched her slip behind his front door. Driving home, my chest muscles seized, pulling tighter the closer I got to home. I wondered what the hell was wrong with me. Maybe I need to go back to therapy. Maybe I need medication. Maybe it's just that I'll never get used to sharing my daughter with my ex-husband.

By the time I walked through the front door of our house, I could barely breathe—a weight on my chest, my pulse drumming in my ears. I dropped my head between my knees, grabbed a paper bag, and breathed into it. This kept me from passing out—I knew the drill. I slowed my breathing, but was no calmer. I thought, maybe if I lie down and nap I'll feel better after, like hitting the reset button on my day. I brought my dogs Whitney and Lady, my cats Angel and Munchkin, and my bunny, Bunny, into my bedroom and closed the door. It was an odd thing I had never done before. They surrounded me on the bed and we all fell into a deep sleep. When I woke later, nothing had changed. I was still edgy as the sun set on this strange day, even more agitated when I saw the full moon rising.

I CONTINUE PACING THE STUDIO, squeaking out my parts, back and forth, back and forth. Donna touches my arm as I breeze past her, "Hols, we don't need to do this now. We can reschedule."

I exhale, "I'm so sorry. I don't know what's wrong with me!"

"Whatever it is, just honor your feelings, okay? Ask your intuition what it's trying to tell you."

"I've been asking all day, and getting no answer." I collapse into a chair, my head in my hands. "I'm sorry, you guys."

"It's okay, you don't have to apologize to us," she says.

Troy puts his guitar in its case and an arm around me. "Everything's okay, honey. You're safe." He knows these are always the best words to say to me. Safe—all my life that's all I'd ever wanted to feel—but tonight his words can't reach me.

I'm supposed to be the girl who has it all together. I own a national business, volunteer at my kids' school, am a Daisy Scout leader, and still manage to do gigs on the weekends. I can spin a hundred plates at once—it's my specialty. But this bad dream rattles me. I see the plates falling in slow motion, about to shatter.

At about 10 p.m., we give up on rehearsing and walk Donna downstairs. "Want to try tomorrow night, same time?" she asks.

"Absolutely. I'll be fine tomorrow. All I need is a good night's sleep." Even as I say this it doesn't feel true.

At the bottom of the stairs, smoke from the fireplace stings our eyes. Donna coughs, waving her hand in front of her face. The living room is dark. I was sure I left the lights on for the dogs, but seeing how whacked out I am tonight, anything is possible. I flip the light switch, but nothing happens. I try another, nothing.

"That's weird," I say.

"Must've blown a fuse," Troy says, and sets off to find a flashlight.

By the glow of the fire I see smoke backing out of the

chimney, filling the room with an eerie haze. I squint, making my way across the smoky room to crack a window.

"We heard crows making a racket in the chimney the other day . . ."

Donna pipes up, "Ah. They probably built a nest up there—that's why the smoke is trapped. That's happened to me before." The side of her face is strangely shadowed by the flames.

"Nothing we can do but wait for the fire to die out, I guess." My entire body thrums, my pulse so loud I wonder if everyone can hear it.

Donna stands by the front door, one hand on the knob. "You guys want me to stay?"

I wave my hand, "No! No, everything's fine."

"Get some rest. Love you." She envelops me in a long, wordless hug.

"Love you, too," I say. "Thanks for being so understanding."

In the hallway, Troy shines a flashlight on the breaker box. The smoke swirls in its beam. As he flips the override switch, a deafening buzz sends us both hurling backward. "What the hell . . ." He catches his balance, one hand to his heart.

"Honey, don't touch it," I warn.

He steps closer to inspect, rubbing his eyes. "It's gotta be a fuse . . . I can fix it."

"Please! I have a bad feeling. Let's get an electrician here in the morning."

"Okay, okay."

Cold air blows in through cracked windows. I cross my arms, shivering. "This day is really freaking me out."

"Sweetie," he takes my hand, "everything is okay. Don't worry." His touch is warm, his voice soothing, but his words leave a frost cloud in the air.

We climb the stairs together, peeking in on Taylor. I love to sneak a few glimpses of my children while they're sleeping, their faces so like little cherubs when they aren't arguing or being willful. Taylor is snuggled with his favorite blankie.

"See?" Troy says, putting a reassuring arm around me, "Everything's fine."

Our cat Angel jumps on the bed, pouncing on Taylor's toes beneath the covers. I swoop Angel up, tucking him under my arm. "Come on, you crazy maniac." I ruffle his sleek black fur and take him into our bedroom.

Our room sits three stories above the street, our house built into a hillside. At street level is the converted garage where my kids' clothing business is centered. I'm down there Monday through Friday, on the phone, packing orders, typing up invoices. UPS pulls up at three o'clock each day to load orders and ship them all over the country. Above my office is our living room and kitchen, with an alcove we turned into a playroom for Cissy and Taylor. On the third level are our bedrooms and Troy's recording studio. Because our room sits so high above the neighbors, it's completely private—an eagle's nest. We don't cover the windows. The light eases through the trees every morning as our natural alarm clock.

I wash my face, brush my teeth, and slip on the pink satin nightgown Troy bought me for Mother's Day. All ordinary things on an ordinary night, but I am still anxious, warily eyeing the full moon outside our window. I sit cross-legged on our bed, attempting to meditate, while Troy falls asleep beside me. I wish I could feel safe in the world like he does, but he and I grew up in very different worlds. Angel and Munchkin curl on either side of me, purring contentedly. I run my fingers through their fur, trying to center myself, while my mind prattles on with possibilities to rationalize my behavior. I come to the realization: maybe an aftershock is about to hit.

In January, an earthquake struck in the middle of the night. We thought it was the end of the world. The earth let out a terrifying roar. Power lines outside snapped and transformers blew, lighting the sky like flash pot bombs. The house shook with such violent force we thought we were under attack. As Troy and I ran for our kids' room, we were tossed around like rag dolls, bouncing off walls. Fires erupted all over the city, water mains broke and flooded the streets, freeways crumbled. Fifty-seven people were killed. The sounds of sirens and helicopters filled the air. We had no power or phone lines for weeks. It's taken months for the four of us to be able to sleep through the night again. Strong aftershocks have rocked California all year. Many of us are attuned to the signs. Like animals, we feel the shifts in weather, the particular stillness in the air.

So maybe that's it, I think. Maybe I'm feeling the onset of another aftershock. Or maybe an emotional aftershock. Or maybe it's my childhood rising up to haunt me again. I lie back in bed, staring at the ceiling. *What is wrong with me?*

Too agitated to find inner peace, I give up and walk the house in the dark, checking for . . . for what? I don't know. I wander into the kids' bedroom. Although we have four bedrooms, my kids share a room. I like the idea of them giggling in the dark, telling stories, having each other to turn to when they're afraid, at least until they're older. But Taylor sleeps alone tonight, stretched out in his Winnie the Pooh pajamas, lightly snoring, his sweet little face smushed against the pillow. I pull the covers around him and kiss his forehead.

I walk downstairs, running my hands along the oak banister. The fire in the hearth is almost out, the smoke dissipating. Whitney and Lady snooze in the kitchen, curled up on the blankets I put down for them. I lean over the safety gate to scratch Lady behind her velvety ears, causing Whitney to jump up on her short hind legs and hop around like a circus dog.

"Oh Whitty, don't be jealous." I pat her head. "Go lie down, girl." She snuggles into Lady's side, the two of them spooning like an old married couple.

I climb the stairs and fall back in bed, my wheels turning until thinking exhausts me into sleep. An hour later, panic wakes me. My stomach churns. It is still in the house, too still. The cats have disappeared. A thin veil of smoke still lingers in the air, and I hear the words in my head, *check the baby.* I walk down the hall that connects our rooms. Taylor is sound asleep, as is Troy. Everything is okay, so why can't I rest? I force myself back to bed, tossing and turning until I'm too groggy to keep my eyes open.

Within an hour I am awake again, my pulse racing . . . *check the baby.* I get up, wander the halls, check the baby. He's fine. I stand still in the center of the kids' room. *What am I feeling?* The house is still smoky, in fact it seems worse but how can that be when the fire burned out hours ago? Maybe the smell is trapped because the upstairs windows are closed, I reason. I crack a window and lie down beside Taylor.

The kids' room is illuminated by the full moon. Cissy has been learning about the rainforest in school. She and Taylor have lemonade stands to raise money, with hand-scrawled signs saying Save the Rainforest. In support of this new interest, I bought them bedspreads with brightly colored cheetahs and macaws, and draped their beds in mosquito nets. Over the windows I mounted wooden branches we'd found on our family hikes, and wrapped them in vines and silk flowers. I bought thirty butterflies made from bird feathers, all different species and colors, and hung them from the ceiling with clear fishing wire. When the breeze comes through the open windows, they dance and sway as though they've come alive. The kids love those butterflies. But tonight, they hang still and somber.

I kneel at Taylor's bedside, my face just inches from his. Everything is okay. Our life is good—everything I ever dreamed of—so why can't I just relax and be happy? I breathe him in, brushing his blond hair off his sweaty forehead. It astounds me that he can sweat while my hands are so cold my bones could snap.

"Must be hard work growing so much while you sleep." I whisper, tucking the covers up around his chin.

I crawl back into bed, exhausted. Without waking, Troy throws an arm over me.

The third time I wake, I can hardly open my eyes but the words won't stop. *Check the baby . . . check the baby.* I'm groggy, trying to emerge but sleep pulls me back like undertow. *Check the baby.* I feel drugged. My breathing is shallow. With all the strength I have I push my woozy self onto one elbow, forcing myself up. My feet are leaden as I drag myself down the hall to the kids' room. I move through a grey haze, like a dream. *Am I dreaming?* I lean over, put my cheek against Taylor's, feeling his warm, soft, baby breathing. Still sound asleep. I push his bedroom door closed to keep the smoke out. I shuffle over, my eyes at half-mast, and collapse into bed with him. I don't remember the moment I fall into a comatose sleep.

I HEAR SCREAMS.

It's Troy. Troy is screaming.

I open my eyes—this is not a dream.

"Hollye! Get out of the house!"

Hearing the panic in his voice I instinctively bolt upright and run to him. I swing open the bedroom door and am blown back, knocked to the floor. Backdraft, I'll later learn, is what it's called. Searing heat and black smoke overtake me, burning my skin. Through the deafening roar of fire, the shrill, distant sound of a smoke alarm whines like a mosquito. In one second, the fire sucks all the oxygen out of the room. I gasp for breath, taking in only smoke. I crawl across the floor, gagging, and then I collapse.

The smell of that fire is something I will never forget. It is not the warm, cozy smell of a campfire, but the putrid stench of synthetic carpeting and drywall plaster and household appliances melting, the toxic cloud of our life disintegrating.

For a moment, I lie motionless on the floor. I am strangely calm. Everything moves around me in slow motion, like walking underwater. I am transfixed by the butterflies on the ceiling, and for what seems like a very long time, that's all I see —those butterflies. They dance feverishly, and start to spin as if they're panicked, struggling to break free. As the heat melts the fishing wire, one by one they curl, wilt and drop to the floor. A few at first, then a deluge of charred butterflies rain down on me. I am detached, floating inside my own head: *Oh, I'm going to die. I guess this is my time.* I see my son, lying still. His arm hangs limp over the edge of the bed.

What happens next, I can't be sure. Maternal instinct startles me awake? Without knowing how, I have Taylor in my arms and am at the window, kicking out the screen. Taylor hangs deadweight, as I suspend him from the ledge. The moment I open the window, the firestorm rushes toward the oxygen like a tsunami. Ashes and black smoke blow through us into the night sky, as the fire and heat are pulled toward us.

A gutteral, instinctual wailing fills the air—a voice I've never heard before. It is my voice.

Fire behind me, a thirty-foot drop to concrete below.

Troy shouts from our bedroom window, "Hold on! I'm coming—I'm gonna jump!" Following his words is the loud *thwack* of his body, the sickening sound of bones against cement. I scream his name over and over but he doesn't respond. I start to cry, but there is no time for panic.

Taylor and I hang out the window, engulfed in smoke, suffocating. I lower him as far as my arms will stretch so he can breathe. I hold only his tiny hands, his body dangling midair. I am in the center of the firestorm. My body betrays me by instinctively gasping for breath, pulling in heat that sears my lungs. I choke, spitting out black grease. Sparks and ashes dance around my head. Blisters rise on the backs of my legs, the pain becomes unbearable. I have to do something. Now. No one is responding to my screams. Troy may be unconscious or worse. Without oxygen, I will soon lose consciousness. But there is no grass below, no trees or bushes, no soft place to fall.

My brain searches for options. If I hold Taylor while I jump, I could crush him. I have to let go of his hands. I know that if I do this, he may break bones, or suffer a brain or spinal injury. But if I do nothing, I will burn to death, and he will fall. There are no options. Years later I will watch men and women jump from the twin towers on 9/11. I'll know the horror that drove them to the ledge.

Stretching my body over the windowsill to make Taylor's drop as short as possible, I lower him as far as I can, until I'm holding just the ends of his chubby fingers. The smoke is so thick around me I can't see him anymore. I beg God to protect him. Blind faith.

I let go.

At that very moment Troy shouts from below, "Drop him! I'm here!" I throw my legs over and scramble out the window. Hanging onto the window casing by my fingertips, I take a deep breath then let myself free fall. I hear the loud thump of a hip against concrete but it's as though it happened to someone else. I feel nothing; my body is in deep shock. Troy grabs my hand, yanking me to my feet. Taylor is clutched tight against his chest. "I caught him," Troy says, wild-eyed. We look at each other in disbelief. We are alive.

Clinging to each other, we run. I look over my shoulder at our life engulfed in flames. The children's Little Tikes playhouse on the front patio has melted in a puddle like ice cream. Neighbors run toward the house with a garden hose, but stop short at the sight of it. All three levels are consumed, flames shooting out the windows we'd just jumped from. My body trembles violently. I can't speak or move, until the sight of the burning doghouse snaps me to my senses. "Oh God! The animals!!" I wail like a mad woman. Troy thrusts Taylor into my arms and runs back. A few neighbors follow him. "No!" I scream, but he doesn't hear me. As they near the house, the windows blow out. Maybe a gasline exploding, or another backdraft. Shattered glass is everywhere, apocalyptic flames rage. There is no way to get back in. All is lost.

All is lost.

Our neighbor Melissa throws a blanket around me and Taylor, then runs in hysterical circles, crying, "I don't know what to do! I don't know what to do!" She screams, "Her little girl is in there!"

Still in shock, my brain goes into a frenzy. *Cissy. Cissy.* What is real? Troy runs toward me. I hear him shouting, "We can't get in!"

Someone grabs my shoulders, shaking me, "Where is your daughter?"

I am disoriented, doubting my own memory. I grab Troy's arm, "Cissy's not in there, right? She's not there!" I become hysterical, squeezing my son, who is silent and dazed.

Troy grips both my arms and says in a firm voice, "Hollye, she's not in there. She's at her dad's house."

"*Are you sure?*"

"Look at me, Hollye!" He gets in my face, "She's safe! She's not here!"

Troy will later tell me that I repeated this panicked scenario many times that night. There is mayhem in my head, mayhem in the street. The property next door has caught fire and still no fire department. I stand at the edge of the road, clutching my son, watching our life go up in flames, knowing our animals are dead. This horror is too gruesome to be real. It can't be real. Our neighbors pace, some are crying. Everyone on the street knows our dogs. No one knows what to do, how to help. Troy wraps his arms around Taylor and me, his eyes filled with tears. He whispers, maybe to himself, maybe to me, maybe to God, "We will come back stronger."

I look up to meet his eyes, wanting so much to believe him, my sunny, optimistic man. But the morning before, he was the one who told me my nightmare was just a dream. Now I am wide-awake, and the nightmare is real.

Inside I sense this is only the beginning of the avalanche . . . just as I dreamed it.

MY ROMANCE

❧ ❧ ❧

My journey with Troy began in 1987, a time of skyscraping Aqua Net hair and Hammer pants, when Michael Jackson was moonwalking, and Governor Dukakis was mulling over his decision to run for president. I was twenty-three years old. I took college classes in the mornings, spent afternoons with my baby daughter Cissy, and worked nights at a French café. A relationship was the last thing on my mind. My loveless three-year marriage had just crumbled, and I was determined to make it on my own, hoping to find the self I lost in the rubble. I wasn't looking for any company. I still wore my wedding ring. Living in the aftermath of my mother's relationships, I swore I'd never divorce. I held a thin thread of hope that, for my daughter's sake, maybe I could make my marriage with Gary work. A foolish hope, when you consider that I left him because he suggested that I have an affair. Gary was a good guy, but he didn't, and couldn't, love me. He found me needy, because I needed something from him that he was never given —love. But I walked into that marriage set on fixing everything. When you're young, you cling to the delusional belief that you can change people.

I worked at L'Express Cafe, the hot spot in the San
Fernando Valley where all the hipsters hung out drinking
espresso until 2 a.m. One night, picking up orders at the bar, I
felt someone staring at me. I met his gaze and he quickly
looked away. *I know him,* I thought. *Where have I seen him
before?* Later I caught him staring again. I smiled and waved.
Again, he looked away. I remembered meeting him the week
before—a friend of a friend. I tried to make eye contact, but he
avoided me. I walked straight up and smiled widely. "Hello!" I
said.

"Hey," he nodded, barely glancing at me.

I crossed my arms. "You really don't remember me?"

"No," he said, sitting back in his chair.

"We met last week. I'm Mitzi's friend. Remember?"

He shook his head. "I don't know anyone named Mitzi,
and I was in Australia so I definitely didn't meet you last
week," he said.

My face flushed. "Oh . . . sorry." I turned and sped away,
thinking, *What the hell? I'm sure I know that guy!*

His friend followed me. "Hey! Wait a minute, come back!"

Humiliated, I turned around.

"We may not know you, but we *want* to know you. How
about we get to know you now?" I offered a weak courtesy
laugh, wanting only to slink away. He kept on about us all
getting to know each other. He was funny and sweet. Dave
was his name, and his snobby friend, the one I thought I knew,
was Troy. They hung out all night at the bar trying to make
me laugh, flirting relentlessly.

Finally I said, "Look guys, you're sweet, but I'm married." I
flashed the ring. "But I have a couple cute girlfriends who
would love to meet you." I told them to come back the next
Saturday to meet my friends Mitzi and Deirdre.

A week later, I was making my way through the café with a huge tray over my head, when Dave and Troy walked in. I ducked behind the wall. *Shoot—I forgot to tell the girls!* I delivered the cappuccinos and casually waved to the guys from a distance, then ran to the payphone in back to call Mitzi and Deirdre, who knew nothing about this and were home in sweats watching *Dynasty*.

"Please come! They're really cute and funny, I swear!" I pleaded with them. They were less than enthusiastic about it.

Dave and Troy tossed back a few beers at the bar, teasing me about my stellar matchmaking skills whenever I'd rush past. An hour later, Deirdre walked in alone. Mitzi refused to come. My badly arranged double date turned out to be a super-awkward disaster. Deirdre's loud nervous laugh pierced through the café buzz and hum. When my shift ended at 1 a.m., the trio was still there. To make up for my colossal blunder, and to rescue Deirdre, I stood in for Mitzi and joined them at Denny's for coffee. Dave and Troy held court at our Formica table, telling animated stories that doubled me over with gasping-for-breath laughter. This kind of joy had been absent from my life, after three years trapped in a loveless marriage, my days spent alone, changing diapers and pacing the halls with my colicky baby daughter. But over bitter coffee and stacks of cold, half-eaten pancakes, I was awake, uncaged. I felt like the young woman I was. We drained three pots of coffee before I realized it was four in the morning, and even then I could hardly pull myself away. Cissy would be waking up and needing me in just a few hours.

FOR THE NEXT SIX MONTHS, the four of us were insep-arable. Troy's band *Race To L.A.* played all the best clubs in the LA circuit. He played guitar and keyboards and wrote the songs, and I was his biggest fan. He had that pop-star look, too. Sort of a cross between Don Johnson and Shawn Cassidy. Dave, Deirdre, and I went to most of Troy's gigs. During the week we'd head off to the gym, lunches, late-night dinners, game nights, and barbeques. We were the four musketeers, and Cissy, who everyone adored, was our little mascot.

Troy and I had a weekly ritual of going to the gym and then taking Cissy to lunch at Sizzler—it was her favorite place. As we were leaving, Cissy would often take both our hands and beg us to swing her back and forth between us. It wasn't something we ever discussed, but it felt easy and natural. Sometimes when I had to work an extra shift and Gary couldn't watch Cissy, Troy and his drummer roommate Russ babysat her—a scenario that would have made a good sitcom. From Cissy, they learned how to change a diaper, cut crusts off sandwiches, and rock a baby to sleep. One night at Troy's apartment, Cissy got the stomach flu. I expected Troy to bolt but instead, he brought towels and a wet washcloth, and sat next to me on the cold bathroom tile, rubbing Cissy's back with concern. I studied his hands, the question in my head— *Who is this man?*

Troy would often stop by the café after a gig, and hang out long after everyone else had gone. We'd talk while I emptied ashtrays and wiped down tables. Sometimes about silly stuff— *Saturday Night Live* characters, and inside jokes. Sometimes he'd be starry-eyed, telling me about some girl he had a crush on, or he'd listen as I unloaded the mess of my divorce, my fears about being a single mom just like my mom had been. "You don't have to figure it all out now," he'd say. "Just a little bit today."

One night, he was keeping me company as I cashed out, divvying up my checks. That damn MTV video played on the overhead TV again, and I clicked it off.

"You don't like that song?" he asked.

"That girl?" I gestured to the TV. "I used to be in a singing duo with her when we were teenagers. We were best friends since second grade. We performed all over LA and were making a name for ourselves . . ."

"Really? I never knew that about you. That's so cool!"

"Not really. We got a chance at a record deal and she ditched me. And that was the end of our friendship."

"Man, that sucks."

"What sucks is working here every night while her video is playing. I mean . . . this isn't what I imagined for myself." I slumped down into a chair. "I didn't plan to be divorced, working nights, a single mom, you know? I was an honors student and . . ."

I put my hands over my face and sighed, "whatever . . ."

"Hey, let's write a song together," he said, "You and me." He smiled, hopeful.

I waved my hand, "Eh, that ship has sailed."

"I won't ditch you," he said, with sweet sincerity.

And because I am notorious for lame comebacks during a tender moment, I responded with, "You say that *now* . . ."

A few days later he brought me a tape with a tune he composed on his keyboard. At night, after Cissy was in bed, I worked on the lyrics and melody. This was the eighties, the era of light, dance-pop. So I wrote a light, dance-pop song.

The next week, Cissy and I went to Troy's apartment. You could tell two guys lived there. The furnishings were black and chrome, with not a single personal touch. No framed photos. No throw pillows. Anvil speakers served as end tables in the living room. I set Cissy up with crayons and paper. Troy sat at the piano, "Ready?"

I got out my lyric sheet, my stomach tight with nerves. He

played while I sang. At the end, he stopped and didn't look at me for a minute.

I broke the silence with, "Well? What do you think? Catchy?"

"To tell you the truth, I kind of expected more from you."

I could feel the air escaping as I deflated. "What do you mean?" I asked, trying to sound as though I wasn't dying inside.

"I mean, I *know* you. You're capable of writing much deeper lyrics than that."

My face flushed with the heat that comes from being found out. *He sees me.* I wasn't used to being seen, but there was a part of me that liked it. *Find me out.* My pulse pounded all through my body, but not a nervous pounding. This was something else. Like when you've been searching for something all your life, and finally it's right in front of you.

"Well, I'll work on it some more, later . . ."

He paused, but looked like there were words forming in his head and I didn't want to hear them.

"You know what, I really have to go," I said, fumbling with my lyric sheets. I heaved Cissy onto my hip and walked to the door. He tried to half hug me but Cissy made a good barrier. As my cheek brushed against his neck I felt electricity, a burning revelation in my solar plexus. *Another woman will one day occupy that space. She will lay her head against his chest in the dark.* And then I shut it down. *What a ridiculous thought! Why am I even thinking that?*

I never told anyone and was careful not to let it show, but I felt pulled to Troy. How could I help it? He was practically irresistible with that great head of dirty blond hair, highlighted by the sun (and his hairstylist). He wore trendy clothes in bright colors that matched his personality. He was happy and seemed to have no anger toward the world. And he believed in me. But he was also a touring, professional guitar player, which may have been a strong elixir for some young girls, but not for me. Although I was only twenty-three, I was not a young girl, and never had been. I came with heavy baggage, and a child.

The last thing I needed in my life was a flaky musician, just like my stepdad had been. Eventually they take off on the road and never come back. *Stay away from that one,* I said to myself. I already knew where that road led. And yes, I'd learned enough in college Psych 101 classes to know that there were Freudian implications that I was eager to avoid.

About six months into our friendship, summer arrived, and with the weather, everyone's love lives began to heat up. Deirdre was dating an actor. Dave became entangled with a waitress friend of mine from the café. Troy, the doe-eyed romantic, had an unrelenting crush on his downstairs neighbor, and I eventually let the news slip out that I was separated, and began dating a man named Terry, although I still wore my wedding ring.

I also met Terry at the café, where he was a regular customer. We had friendly banter here and there, but nothing more. One day he was watching me as I worked, and when I met his gaze he didn't look away. His face rested against his palm, his deep-set blue eyes searching me. He sighed heavily while raising the other hand in a balled fist to his chest, pantomiming being psychically stabbed with every beat of his heart. (He had been a Shakespearean actor, so he knew how to work this.) His eyes pleaded with me across the room. Whatever it was those eyes wanted, I was sure I could not deliver. But my resolve buckled with my knees. I was too weak to resist feeling loved. I agreed to one date with Terry, but just as friends.

At the end of our first date, we stood in front of the restaurant under a streetlamp, my hands clasped around the pole.

"You don't want to get involved with me, Terry. I'm not like other girls," I warned.

"That's exactly why I want to get involved with you," he said, unblinking.

"I'm a disaster zone . . ."

"I'll take my chances," he said.

"It's just that . . . you've put me on a pedestal."

"What's wrong with that?"

"I'm afraid of heights."

"Wow. That's a great line," he said.

Terry was a filmmaker, always writing a screenplay in his head. He was handsome and romantic and kind, and we had much more than one date. Through the lazy summer months, I lay in his lap while he read me passages from Rilke's *Letters to a Young Poet*. He carefully chose gifts for me that required more thought than anyone had given me in my whole life. He called me Sunshine, and basking in his gaze, I began to live up to that name. He awakened everything I had forgotten I was. I sparkled again. I was alive and vibrant and happy. It was too easy to forget my vow of not getting involved. But I still wore my ring as a reminder to myself, and to him, that I was not ready for any kind of relationship.

After dating for a couple months, Terry took me to Santa Barbara for a much-needed getaway. We held hands as we strode through the art walk, where California artists gathered to show their works. The exhibit stretched for a mile on a strip of grass above the Pacific shoreline. The towering palm trees swayed above us like hula dancers as we walked along, absorbing the creativity and natural beauty that surrounded us.

But I was carrying a heavy weight. Escaping the busyness of my daily routine gave me the space to think, and soon my thoughts consumed me. Terry led me down to the shore, where we took our shoes off, letting the water roll over our feet. The tide pulled back, the ground below me eroding.

"This I how it feels," I said. "My life. No solid ground. Like everything is washed away . . ." I fell quiet. Sensing I needed some time, Terry went for a run on the beach. I sat on the shore, digging my toes into the cool damp sand, feeling the warmth of the waning sun on my skin. My thoughts tumbled over themselves like waves, churning up the foundation beneath them, the waters murky. What was I doing, falling for this guy when I still had a wedding band on my finger?

A chill overcame me as the evening fog rolled in off the ocean. Fishermen headed to the far end of the pier with rods and buckets. Terry was a distant dot on the horizon, probably reconciling thoughts of his own. Terry was so kind to me, despite the distance I kept between us. I was a broken doll he'd found, but he was so sure of my value, so sure he could put me back together, just like the films he wrote and directed where he's got the happy ending already mapped out in Technicolor hues. But I was wrongly cast. No matter how he wrote it in his head, he couldn't fix it, he couldn't fix me. I had to fix myself.

The truth was my marriage was irreparable, and I couldn't understand why. I didn't want to be a divorced woman, but my husband didn't love me. How did this happen? It's not like it all fell apart in an instant. Losing Gary was like discovering a tiny crack in your windshield. You wonder how it got there. Days later, the crack has grown and you never saw it happening, until one day, the man who once sent you roses at work and hounded you with twelve-page love letters doesn't even see you standing in the doorway, your eyes begging him to love you again. I was unlovable to Gary, and I could not face the rest of my life as an unlovable woman. What twisted me inside was the image of Cissy growing up the child of a broken marriage, just like I did. I swore I'd never do that to her. But growing up with miserable parents in a loveless marriage was no better.

As I wiped tears from my cheeks, a sweet memory broke through, a moment I'd had with Cissy earlier that year. She and I were home in our dingy, dark apartment. I held her in my arms and put on my favorite Roxy Music album. Swaying with her, I sang, "As free as the wind . . . maybe I'm learning why the sea on the tide has no way of turning . . ." I pressed the side of my face against hers and sang the chorus, "More than this. You know there's nothing more than this . . ." I spun with her in my arms, the music carrying us. I was giddy and free in the revelation. Cissy erupted into that deep belly laugh that only babies know, a music all their own. It was just the two of us, spinning and laughing. From the moment she was born I knew I would throw my body in front of a train to protect her, and in that moment I knew, no matter what happened with Gary, Cissy and I would be okay.

Looking out over the ocean, I repeated those words to myself, *Cissy and I will be okay*. I slipped my wedding ring off my finger. It wasn't so hard to do. Terry was walking back to me. "Hello, sunshine," he said.

WHEN I RETURNED FROM MY TRIP, I met my friends for breakfast. Troy noticed the white un-tanned spot on my ring finger right away. "Wow. That's a new development," he said.

"Yep." I nodded. My heart pounded wildly, awaiting the judgment that never came, except from me. Dave, Deirdre, and Troy told me it was the right thing. Cissy will be okay, they assured me. If you're happy, she'll grow up happy, they said.

A few days later, Troy called about our weekly lunch. "Sure. Meet at Sizzler?" I asked.

"Actually, let's meet at La Fiesta. And just this time, could you come alone?"

"And not bring Cissy? Why?"

"I just want to talk to you about something," he said.

"What's wrong?"

"Nothing's wrong. Just . . . just come."

I hung up, perplexed. Had something happened while I was gone?

AT THE RESTAURANT, after Troy ordered us margaritas, he took a deep breath and said this, "I think you know by now, I've developed strong feelings for you." I was floored—this being the absolute last thing I expected. Needless to say, no, I did not know. He continued, "When I heard you were going to Santa Barbara with Terry, I knew I had to talk to you. If you're putting yourself on the market, I want a chance with you."

My mouth hung open, no words coming out, but the voice in my head was jabbering away. *Putting myself on the market? Wait a minute—Troy talks to me about girls he likes, and none of them look like me. I'm already involved with Terry, and he wants a chance with me, now?* "What about your neighbor . . . I thought you had such a crush on her?"

"That's just a distraction. It isn't real. What I feel for you is real."

This set me spinning between stress, a strange kind of elation, and panic. I searched the smoky room for the waiter. "Good lord, how long does it take to make a *margarita?*" I looked back at Troy. He met my eyes, and didn't look away this time, but I did. My face flushed.

"I've never seen that little smile on your face. That's a new look," he said.

I stared down at my silverware. "What look?"

"That sweet, shy smile. I like it." He'd never made comments like this before. We joked around. That was our thing.

"When did you start to feel this way?" I met his brown eyes, then looked away.

"Since the day I met you."

I felt woozy, and maybe a little bit like puking. "I don't understand. Why didn't you say anything?"

He looked down, and seemed to be gathering his thoughts. "As long as you were wearing that ring . . . you know . . . and still had hope for your marriage, I just . . . I wasn't going to jeopardize that. I mean, you have a child with him."

My thoughts turned back to Terry. I'd told him I wasn't ready for a relationship. But that weekend, Terry told me that he loved me. He wanted to fly me down South to meet his dad. "I . . . I really don't know what to say."

"You don't have to say anything. I just had to get this off my chest or I was going to explode. I'm not asking anything of you right now," he said.

The waiter finally arrived with our margaritas and I practically dove in to mine. I left the restaurant dazed.

AUGUST WAS OPPRESSIVELY HOT. The days dragged on forever, the air heavy with the decision I had to make. I was honest with both Troy and Terry, and they, being extra-ordinary men, each took a step back to give me space. My whole life up until then had been devoid of love, and then, as a sudden storm after a long draught is needed but can also cause great damage, it came rushing at me too fast.

I had always felt that pull to Troy. But he was young: twenty-six to my twenty-three. I'd always been with older men who were established, had homes, stable careers, responsibilities. Troy was a carefree guy who traveled on a whim. He was on the road half the time, gigging nights, going out to jazz clubs until 2 a.m. I was up every morning at seven to feed my daughter breakfast and get her ready for nursery school. Our lives couldn't have been more incongruent.

Troy told me stories from his Brady Bunch childhood. His parents were all-American high school sweethearts. His dad was class president, his mom a cheerleader. They had three kids, a house in the suburbs. Dad worked, Mom stayed home and raised the kids. His grandparents and great-grandparents were all married forever—divorce was unheard of. His life was full of family vacations, camping and fishing trips, bike rides, and block parties.

Me? I longed for a Brady Bunch life, but I grew up with a single mom who worked nights in a bar, and a father in prison. I ran the household and raised my younger brother, who had psychological problems after being shot in the head by a neighbor at seven years old. I never knew what it was to be young and carefree. I'd already lived a lifetime more than this happy-go-lucky guy who never had to be responsible to anyone.

But there was something about Troy. He was good. Good to the core. And whether I wanted to or not, I loved him.

My head and logic told me to stay with Terry. He was stable, seven years older than I was. He was co-owner of a film production company. He was tall and charming and handsome.

He cherished me, and I had never been cherished before. Terry made me happy. And yet, something inside was telling me that although I couldn't see it then, and on paper it didn't make sense, Troy was the one.

Late in August, I made the gut wrenching decision. After the awful, tearful break up with Terry, I needed time to be alone. I hated being responsible for hurting him, and I needed time to mourn what was a terrible loss for both of us. My time with Terry was enchanted and sparkling and unbelievably romantic, and I just let him walk out of my life. Was I insane?

The next week, Troy and I met a couple times to talk. I was jumpy, nervous. When he kissed me for the first time, a sweet, tender puppy-love kiss, he gently stepped on both my feet. Maybe it was his way of saying, *Don't run away.* My body trembled as I struggled to tamp down whatever it was inside me that was trying to emerge.

He set up a real "date" that weekend. Not that we hadn't been out together a million times—but this was to be a romantic date. I'd made my decision and was committing myself to him. Kind of. The truth is: I was terrified and unsure.

He took me to dinner in the Marina del Rey harbor, where sailboats glided past. The sky held an orange-and-crimson fire as the sun slipped behind the Pacific Ocean. We toasted to a new beginning. I smiled weakly, with butterflies in my stomach, and not the lovey-dovey kind. I worried I was making a huge mistake. *He is so young. Will he be strong enough for me?*

As he took my hand across the table, I studied his. They were sturdy, his palms rough and calloused from lugging heavy amps and speakers, fingertips permanently hardened from years of playing guitar. At times he groped me with the enthusiasm of a full-grown puppy, bruising me, not yet aware of his size and strength, clumsy and awkward in his own skin, and with his words. He would sometimes bruise me with those, too. But when his hands flew across the fretboard of a guitar and over the keys of a piano his passion came alive. He played like a starving man being served his first meal. He never met an instrument he couldn't master, and made music with everything he touched—rims of glasses, spoons, blades of grass. He sat at his piano one day and casually plunked out one of the most gorgeous, haunting melodies I'd ever heard. My eyes filled with tears upon hearing it, because it seemed impossible that someone could just sit down and rock the world off its axis like that. "You like it?" he said. "I wrote it for you." His hands were strong, but unsteady. Loving, but untested.

After dinner, he took me to the beach and built a fire. I was shivering—he took off his jacket and wrapped it around my shoulders. He played guitar for me, his eyes closed, his head tilted slightly. I studied his face, his perfect profile, the creases in his eyelids. I had to know everything about him. I searched for clues, or reasons to run. His face was unlined, untouched by the world. I, on the other hand, had been touched by the world, sometimes in dark and unspeakable ways. *He won't be able to handle being with someone like me.* I drank in his every feature; his full bottom lip, the light stubble on his chin, the heavy Paul McCartney eyebrows. He opened his eyes to meet mine, set the guitar down, and pulled me toward him. We kissed and I shivered again. Looking out over the black water of the Pacific, the moon's reflection on its surface, I asked the question that had been plaguing me all year. "Are you sure we never met before that first night at the café?"

"Pretty sure. I definitely would've remembered you."

"Then, why were you staring at me like that?"

"I was drawn to that bright smile of yours," he said, kissing my cheek, "and I was attracted to your posture."

"My *posture?*"

"You carry yourself nicely. You stand tall and confident. It's attractive . . ."

I laughed, "I've never been called tall before," having a slight, five-foot-four frame.

"You know what I mean . . . you look like . . . like you know who you are."

I let that comment soak in for a moment. *Do I know who I am, or do I just walk like I do?* "But . . . why were you so snobby and standoffish to me?"

He ran a hand through his hair, "I guess I was shy. And then I saw your ring. When you walked away, I told Dave, that ring's gotta be fake."

"Why would you think it was fake?"

"I don't know. I guess I wanted it to be."

We stared up at the sky together, and Troy pointed out a shooting star. To this day, he still has a knack for that. It was a perfect night, as though the scene had been set especially for us. All the signs were there, but I didn't trust them.

Later when the beach got too chilly, we headed to a restaurant up the road for a drink. We ordered martinis, settling into a quiet corner table, when a man approached us.

"Hey you guys . . . I'm a psychic, and I'm getting a really shhtrong vibe about you two." His breath reeked of alcohol. We rolled our eyes, laughing. "No shheriously guys, I'm not kidding. Here, I'll prove it. I'll guess both yer weights." He pointed at me, over-enunciating, "You. One-fourteen. And him . . . uh . . . one-forty-seven."

I looked at Troy, my eyebrows raised. We'd weighed

ourselves at the gym a few days before. He was right on the money.

"Okay, you've got my attention," I said.

He pointed at us, wide-eyed and wobbly, "Aha! I knew it!"

Troy humored him, "Okay, buddy. What else ya got?"

He went on, slurring, "Listen, you two have something really shhhpecial. You're gonna get married, and will be together for life." He put a hand on each of our shoulders, maybe to make a point, or maybe just to steady himself, "You're also gonna have two kids together."

We laughed maybe a little too loudly at this.

"Whoa, settle down! We're only on our first date!" I protested. I vowed to myself as I dressed that night, *I am not sleeping with him.* To ensure this, I wore my dorky every day bra and my schoolmarm cotton underwear.

Troy paid the bar bill, and as we reached his car in the parking lot, he pushed me against the side of his SUV and kissed me like he meant it. Suddenly I found myself wishing I'd worn better underwear. I can think of a million clichés to explain what happened to me then, but I can think of no real way to say what it really was. I only know that as of that moment, there was no sleep, no food, no drink that would suffice. All I needed and wanted was him. *I'm not going to sleep with him,* I reassured myself. But as that evening turned to morning, kissing for hours became making love for the first time, and all my fears and worries dropped away.

Lying in Troy's arms at dawn, my head on his chest, I listened to the steady beat of his heart and felt completely safe for the first time in my life. He lifted my chin with his hand, looking into my eyes, and I realized that his eyes were not brown. They were green like mine, with a burst of golden-amber in the center. There were many facets to this man I didn't yet know. He held his gaze steady. He didn't look away, and I didn't either. "I love you, Hollye," he said, and something broke inside me. That's when I knew that crazy drunk was right. Ready or not, this was the beginning of a beautiful and complicated love story.

Exactly two years from our first date, we were married, and flying away for a honeymoon in Jamaica. A month later, I was pregnant with our son Taylor. Cissy embraced her new-born baby brother with love and protectiveness as though he were her own, and began, of her own accord, to call Troy, "Daddy." I finally had the family I'd always ached for. This was my happily ever after.

When the fire hit, we'd only been married five years. Cissy was nine and Taylor four. We thought the actual fire was the worst of it. *You've lost everything . . . It can only go up from here,* people say. But it turns out there are more things you can lose, more than you can possibly imagine.

YOU CAN GO HOME NOW

❧ ❧ ❧

Running from the flames, Troy leads the way up the steep driveway across the street to our neighbors' house— Larry and Cathy, good friends of ours whose two boys play at our house every day. Troy pounds on the door. Larry peeks through the curtain and screams, "Go away or I'll call the police!"

Troy shouts, "It's us, Larry! Troy and Hollye! We need help!"

The porch light flickers on. Larry, looking disheveled, cracks the front door and peers through, squinting at these people who are coughing and crying on his front porch.

"It's us, Larry!" Troy implores.

His eyes widen, "Oh my God!" He throws the door open, "Come in, come in! What in the name of God happened to you?" He looks over our shoulders and catches a glimpse of the flames. "My God . . ." He hurries us into the kitchen, fumbling for the phone. He presses numbers frantically. I can hear the operator, "411. What city, please?"

"Send an ambulance!" he screams, his voice cracking.

She flatly repeats, "This is information, sir. What city, please?"

Larry's wife Cathy, my good friend, rushes into the kitchen with the boys trailing behind her. When she sees us she quickly turns around, pushing them back. "Go to your room, boys! Go out!" They dart around her, and stand slack-jawed upon seeing us.

Larry stoops down to their eye level. "It's okay guys, don't be afraid. It's just Hollye and Troy, and look, there's your buddy Taylor! Everything's okay," he says, his voice shaking.

Cathy paces back and forth, crying with her hand over her mouth. She steers clear of us, as though being victims of a fire were something she could catch. The boys, Brendan and Ryan, usually squirrelly and full of energy, stand silent. They stare at Taylor, who is also silent in my lap. After Larry successfully dials 911, I call my mother, and then Sarah and Scott, our best friends. I can only imagine what a terrifying call this is at two in the morning. Knowing they are on their way to us grounds me. Sarah and Scott will know what to do. Sarah and Scott always know what to do.

When the fire department arrives twenty minutes later, there is nothing left to save. They apologize for taking so long and say they couldn't find us. Living in the hills off a narrow mountain road had once seemed so dreamy, but now is our undoing. The fire is so intense they can't get anywhere near the house, can only blast their hoses from the street. The small hope we held for our animals is lost.

Our best friend Scott bursts through Larry and Cathy's kitchen door, breathless. He takes one look and falls to his knees in front of me, his eyes filled with tears.

"Oh my God!" He takes my hand, deep grief in his face. "I'm so sorry," he whispers. Eying the burns on my hand, he says, "Oh my God, my God . . . thank God you're alive." We hold hands in silence, sniffling, wiping tears. Staring death in the face strips away the need to fill space with words. He leans away from Taylor and whispers, "What about . . . Whitney and . . . ?" I shake my head as a sob catches in my throat. He claps a hand over his mouth, squeezing my hand tighter.

Sarah is with Troy at the bottom of the hill, talking to one of the EMTs who she somehow knows from high school. She doesn't come into the house to see us. Maybe she can't bear it, but Scott stays by my side until the EMTs reach us.

The EMTs check our vitals then usher us to the waiting ambulance. I wobble along the gravel driveway, stopping to look down upon the scene. My eyes and lungs burn from the stench that hangs like a heavy blanket over the street. The flames rage on, the fire hoses no match for their fury. A long line of fire trucks clogs the narrow lane. Firemen run to and from the wreckage. I put my hands over my ears to muffle the sounds of helicopters circling overhead, voices screaming and shouting, sirens, the whoosh of water being dumped from the sky. Neighbors huddle together, watching the horrifying spectacle. Sarah waves to me from the street. I am a ghost hovering above it all.

Troy, Taylor, and I are loaded onto stretchers in the ambulance. Just as they are closing the doors, my mother arrives, jumping in the back.

"Ma'am, you can't come in here," the EMT starts to say.

"She's my daughter!" she screams, "I'm going in this ambulance!" He backs down from my mother, as does everyone.

The stretchers rock, wheels squeaking as the ambulance takes hairpin turns down the hill. I hear the strange sound of the siren from the inside. The drivers look back with their headphones on, giving the thumbs up to Taylor. *What movie am I in? What is happening?*

They wheel us into the ER, my mother and her husband

Eric running alongside our stretchers. Fluorescent lights above me flicker and hum. I breathe in the dead hospital air, the antiseptic smell. My senses flood with all-too-familiar memories; *the panic, the blood, my little brother Kyle being wheeled away behind the double doors. I'm not the one who arrives on a stretcher. It's not supposed to be me.* Scenes flash through my head —reels from a chapter of life long pushed away. *Kyle, seven years old, a baby bird in a nest of sanitary white sheets, his head shaved and bandaged like a mummy, his body twitching involuntarily from the brain damage. A bullet lodged so deep in his brain they had to leave it in.* I sit up, panicked, searching for my son. The nurses and administrators stop what they're doing and stare silently at us. Why? Haven't they seen everything?

Under the harsh glare of hospital light, I understand why they're staring. Taylor's skin and blond hair are jet black except for the tear tracks on his face. Troy is covered in what looks like black war paint, his beard and hair scruffy, sticking out. They look like survivors of Armageddon. People who look like us don't come through the ER. They are wheeled into the morgue.

I look down at my own arms and hands, completely blackened. My pink satin nightgown is now black, charred at the edges. The jewelry I'm wearing has burned into my skin. The charm bracelet I share with Cissy; a heart split in half that reads, "Lord, protect me and thee when we are apart," has branded the words into the underside of my wrist. The scar will remain there for months.

The ER is machines and beeping and flurry as nurses hook us up to oxygen and take blood samples. We each have carbon monoxide poisoning, which explains the grogginess and the deep sleep. But what explains how were we able to wake up? Troy has the worst case of it, along with an injury to his leg that leaves him on crutches. I have second-degree burns on my back and legs, and one of my ears is charred like a hot dog left on the grill too long. There is a black-and-purple bruise that runs from my hip to my knee. My tailbone is fractured and my hip from now on will be out of alignment. Except for the carbon monoxide poisoning that could have killed him, Taylor is otherwise unharmed. I saved him from the fire. Troy saved him from the fall. There but for the grace of God. After treating our wounds and burns, we are kept on oxygen and fluids until our blood is pure again, the carbon monoxide flushed from our systems.

In the morning, arson investigators arrive to question us. They tell us it took fifty firefighters and three water-dropping helicopters to finally extinguish the inferno at daybreak. People just don't walk away from a fire like that, they say. It was an unusually intense fire, and they want to know if we have any enemies. All I can think of is . . . God?

We explain the chain of events of that night, and they conclude it began with a short in the electrical wiring of our house, that a spark had flown inside the wall, landed on a wood beam, and began to smolder.

"The smoldering could have been going on for hours," he says. "You basically went to bed in a burning house."

His partner eyes the burns on my wrist and ear, "A house-fire burns at a temperature above 1,000 degrees Fahrenheit," he says. "We investigate a lot of these kind of fires, but . . . there's never anyone left to interview." I don't want to hear it, or think about it. "It's a miracle you're alive. You're very lucky," he says.

I do not feel lucky. Maybe a stronger woman would focus only on the fact that we are alive, but in this moment, the loss is too overwhelming. Whitney, Lady, Munchkin, Angel, and Bunny—all animals we rescued over the years—are dead. This time, we couldn't rescue them. We failed. They are gone. Our livelihoods are gone. Our life is gone. Why is this happening to us? We're good people. We don't deserve this. But this is only lesson one that life is not about fairness. It's about how we rise to meet the mess and the chaos that we are each guaranteed. I have nothing in my emotional toolbox to handle this, and neither does Troy, I am sure.

After the arson investigators leave, a nurse breezes in. "All of your blood levels are back to normal. You can go home now," she says cheerily. I sit on the hospital bed, unmoving. Home? What does that mean? Where will we go in our hospital gowns? We have no clothes to change into. No shoes, no underwear. Nothing. No toothbrush, no wallets, no ID of any kind. We are refugees.

"Knock, knock?" Sarah and Scott peek their heads around the door. I am relieved to see their faces. Sarah and Scott are my touchstone—the one constant I know I can count on.

Sarah walks in and sets a large shopping bag at the foot of my hospital bed. "Okay, we've got sweatpants in all your sizes, we've got T-shirts, and we picked up some flip-flops for you guys at Rite Aid." She begins distributing them to Troy, Taylor, and me. It's just like Sarah to think of everything.

Along with the sweatpants, Scott and Sarah also brought my business partner, Deirdre, who trails in behind them. She gives me a gloomy hello, then paces my hospital room, anxious. My stomach tenses. I don't want her here.

Over the thirteen years of our friendship, Deirdre has hijacked most of the happiest moments of my life; my bridal shower, my bachelorette party, even my wedding day. Moments before I walked down the aisle, as my mother steamed last minute wrinkles out of my dress, Deirdre was on the payphone having a fight with her boyfriend. She slammed down the receiver, breaking into huge sobs. Everyone gathered around to comfort her, while I stood alone in my wedding dress, my stomach tight with nerves. My bridesmaid Keri stood with her arms crossed, shaking her head. She never had any patience for "Deirdre-drama." Deirdre never showed up to my baby shower. Two hours into it she called, hysterical, crying. She left the gate open—her five dogs were missing, blah, blah, blah. It was summer, I was eight months pregnant, hot, cranky, fed up. Of course she would find them right after we hung up.

But today, my family is in crisis, and Deirdre sits in a chair in the corner, looking worried and wounded, as though she is the one who should be in the hospital bed. Deirdre is the last person you call when things are falling apart. I know she must be worried about our children's clothing line, and ultimately how this loss will affect her. I get it, but I can't fucking deal with it. Not now.

Sarah sits on the edge of my hospital bed and takes my hand, "How are you feeling this morning?"

"Honestly, I don't even know. Numb," I say, "and they just told us we could leave but I don't know what . . ." My voice breaks.

"You know you can always stay with us. There's not much room but we'll make do," Sarah says.

Scott nods in agreement, "Absolutely. You're all welcome in our home."

"Thanks you guys, but we couldn't impose on you like that." Scott and Sarah have a beautiful house but it's only two bedrooms and one bath for their family of four. Eight people would be too much. "My mom and Eric said we can stay with them for as long as we need. I appreciate the offer, but the thought of it . . ."

"I know," Sarah squeezes my hand. "It's not forever," she says. When I left my mother's house at eighteen years old, I vowed never to return. Our relationship is so complicated, it will one day take a host of therapists to unravel it all. But just like the window last night, I have no choice. Sarah continues, "Right now it's about making the kids feel as safe as possible. They feel safe at their grammy's house, right?"

I nod, grateful for Sarah's clear and sensible thinking. Safe. Safe is what we need.

Troy and I wash our hands and faces over the hospital sink. I catch a reflection of us in the mirror, dressed in other people's clothes. Outside, my mother and Eric wait at the curb for us. We hug Scott and Sarah good-bye, and walk out of the hospital into the light of a new day, a day that holds no promise, no direction, and yet the sun rose, as it does every morning. *Everything will be okay*, I reassure myself. *Everything will be okay.*

Pulling out of the driveway, I watch the hospital recede in the rearview mirror. Troy and I ride in silence in the backseat of my mother's Mercedes. He has his hand on my leg the whole time, as though he might keep me from slipping away. He knows that, although outwardly I'm a strong woman, I have fragile fault lines that have surely been compromised now.

I stare numbly out the window, stroking Taylor's hair as he sleeps in my lap. People pass us on the freeway—talking to each other, singing along to the radio, daydreaming. But the sky overhead is dark and oppressive. Can't they see that? I want to scream at them: *Don't you understand? Don't you know what's just happened?* While Eric drives, my mother turns around every few minutes, offering a smile as reassurance. Reassurance of what? I avert her eyes and watch the blur of scenery going by . . . scenery I pass every day driving to and from *my* home.

In my head I practice how to tell Cissy. Gary agreed to drop her off so I can break the news myself. I don't know what to say, how to tell her about the animals. The thought of them is a hard kick in the gut. I don't bother to wipe the tears running down my cheeks. Troy takes my hand, whispering, "It's gonna be okay, honey." I offer a weak smile and nod. But having lived through my share of tragedy, I know better. You don't just bounce back the next day. A thing like this changes you forever. I know it will be a damn long time before anything is okay.

My mother turns around again with that irrepressible, hopeful smile but worried eyes. My mother is a devout worshipper of Scarlett O'Hara, her favorite quotable line being, "I'll worry about that tomorrow." I'm worried about it right now. I need someone to walk me through this, tell me how I'm supposed to build a life again starting at square one, how my husband and I are going to support our family, now that both our businesses have burned down with the house. And I am tortured by the fact that will plague me for years: we are not insured for any of it. Weeks before, maybe even months, I called my insurance agent and got the paperwork. Renter's insurance seemed like a good idea now that we were both working from home. I just hadn't sent out those papers yet. I was waiting for some money to come in so I could pay for it. I imagine the forms sitting on my desk, bursting into flames, along with all of Troy's guitars and keyboards and recording equipment, and all the merchandise in my office, the packed boxes of orders yet to be shipped to my customers. Why didn't I fill out those fucking papers? All of this is my fault.

If only I'd filled out the papers.

If only I didn't bring the dogs in the house last night.

If only we never touched that breaker box.

If only, if only, if only.

But there is no turning back the clock. Everything is gone.

Crossing the threshold into my mother's house is a crushing defeat. Life has kicked my ass, and I am dragging my ragged, greasy self to the place I worked so hard to leave behind. I collapse on the bed in my mother's guest room. *Think about the kids—just think about the kids.* I need to see my daughter, feel her, hold her, and know that she is okay. My mother calls Gary, who agrees to bring Cissy right away. While we wait, I put Taylor in the bathtub and gently wash him. Black grease is inside his nose and mouth, in his ears, in every fold. I talk to him in the gentle sing-song voice that usually soothes him, but he is silent, a dull expression on his face. In fact, I can't remember him uttering a single word since last night. I know he's exhausted from being up all night, on top of the trauma he witnessed. "You're a brave boy, sweetheart," I say. He stares blankly at the shower walls. "You okay, baby?" I ask. He nods. Black soot and grease ring the tub, forming a slimy film on top of the water. I snatch him up out of the filth and wrap him in a bath towel. He hangs limp in my arms, like he did the night before. I have nothing, no underwear, no pajamas to change him into. I hold him close to me, burrowing my face into his neck. *What if I hadn't woken up last night? What if I hadn't crawled into bed with him?* I am nauseated at the thought, and quickly shut it down. I can't allow such thoughts into my consciousness, not now, not ever, for that means that losing Taylor was possible. Those words can never be spoken, the thoughts can not be thought. I hug him tight enough to feel his little heart beating against my chest, feeling his aliveness, my every tear a prayer of gratitude. I lie him down in the bed and turn on the TV. The sound of cartoons soothes him in a way I cannot. He falls asleep instantly.

In the shower, I lean my head against the tile, letting water run over me. Shrugging off the last residual of shock, my body awakens to the trauma. Every nerve ending is hyperalert. The hard water stings my burns. My bones ache from the fall, my lungs from the toxins. Black water circles the drain like an oil spill, activating that toxic stench. I scrub vigorously to get the rancid smell off me, like a possessed person trying to eliminate every trace of the monster that beat us down. I can't get the black grime out from my fingernails and cuticles, inside my ears, inside my head. I can't control my coughing fits; my body keeps trying to eject the poison. I wipe my runny nose with the back of my hand. The mucus is black.

I dress myself in the same baggy sweatpants and T-shirt I wore home from the hospital. I have no underwear or bra. No makeup. No hairbrush. I look homeless. And that's when it hits me: I am homeless.

The phone and doorbell begin to ring, and will continue all day as a continuous swarm of friends and family whir through my mother's house. Some offer money, others bring bags of clothes or a few toys for the kids. The one gift that makes me cry is from a woman I barely know who brings packets of cotton underwear for all of us.

Donna soon shows up and throws her arms around both Troy and me, crying, "I knew something was wrong last night. I should have stayed!"

Troy and I comfort her, assuring her that *we're fine*. We are on a weird temporary high, the kind of euphoria you experience when you have just escaped the maw of death. We are grieving, but alternately grateful and hopeful and full of optimism and faith, and it reminds me of doing coke in the '80s when every problem seemed solvable until the coke ran out, as this high soon will. We haven't slept, have poisoned blood, yet we're still "on," telling the story over and over, answering the questions everyone has. So many questions follow tragedy. I guess its human nature to want to distance oneself from it. You tell someone, "My best friend died," and they want to know, *How old was she?* (If she was old then it's justified.) *Was she sick for a long time?* (Because then they can say it's for the best.) *Did she smoke, drink, have poor eating habits?* (Because they would never do that therefore it will never happen to them.) This is how we create the illusion of self-protection. I understand this behavior. I've done it myself. It's like we think we can immunize ourselves from the terrible fates that fall upon others. But this—a random house fire in the middle of the night? People pummel us with questions. They have to understand every detail so they can reassure each other, "Oh, that would never happen to us. We always walk around feeling the walls before going to bed. We would have known if the breaker didn't reset. We would have been able to tell the difference between fireplace smoke and a smoldering inner wall" or whatever it is they're thinking. I don't have the energy to ease their worries. I want to lie in a fetal position and sleep for a month. Wake me when it's over.

When Cissy arrives, she bounds into the house, smiling and cheerful. She sees the people, the food trays, and thinks it's a party. Until she sees me, and her sweet expression drains away. She knows her mama.

Troy and I hold hands and sit with her on the couch. When I tell her, she lets out a sharp cry, then puts her small hands over her face, sobbing. She shakes her head back and forth. "I knew it," she says, "I knew it!"

"You knew what, sweetie?" I move in closer, my arms around her like a shield.

It takes a moment to get her words out. "Last week," she cries, "when we were driving to school . . . in my mind, I kept seeing the house on fire, like a daydream." Her shoulders shake. "I tried to make the dream go away, Mommy."

"Baby, this is not your fault!" I grip her tighter, "I dreamed about it, too. It's nothing to be afraid of." But the truth is I am afraid. What the hell is going on? Cissy never told me anything like this before. And I, too, knew something was about to destroy our lives.

"Where's Whitney and Lady and . . . ?" she asks, fear in her eyes.

I search my brain for the speech I'd rehearsed inside my head. "Honey, it got smoky last night so we opened all the windows, and the animals ran away," I lie. She is nine years old. I will not tell her the gruesome truth.

"We have to find them!" she shrieks through big hiccupy sobs. I rock her in my arms, "Okay, baby. It's okay . . ."

Hours later, Troy's family arrives. His parents and sister huddle in a protective circle around him in my mother's driveway, where they remain. Troy's sister Valerie gives him a book of photos of our family, many I'd sent in Christmas cards over the years. But they don't come inside. Since the first time I met them, I knew I wasn't accepted into their Brady Bunch world. They must have sensed some defect in me, my brokenness. No matter how I tried, I didn't fit. But Taylor and I almost died last night. Isn't a life-or-death situation enough to melt the ice wall between us? Somewhere in my subconscious I'm hoping this is the tipping point, and we'll all come to our senses and end the cold war. But they leave without saying good-bye to me.

As the day finally draws to a merciful close, Troy, Cissy, Taylor, and I huddle together in the spare bedroom of my mother's house. In the stillness, my body relives the trauma. My adrenaline hasn't stopped pumping all day. My nervous system is a wreck. I drink red wine until the sharp edges of reality are dulled. Lying in bed with Troy and my babies, all of us in other people's clothes, in someone else's home, it plays back in my head like a record skipping. In a moment of delirium, overtired, overstressed, a little tipsy, I start laughing.

Troy leans over me with concern, "Are you okay?"

For some reason this makes me laugh harder. "When Larry . . . ," I can barely get the words out, "dialed 411 . . . and the lady said 'What city, please?'" I roll on my side, doubled over.

Troy catches the bug and muffles his laughter, trying not to wake the kids. "And his face!" Troy wraps an arm around his stomach, folds over, "When he saw us on the porch . . . and thought we were the Manson family."

I circle my fingers around my eyes, "His eyes all bugged out . . . *boing-oing-oing.*" The Warner Brothers image of Larry's horror-stricken face, his eyes popping out on springs, puts us both on the edge of absolute, straight-jacket hysteria. Within moments it builds until we are both overtaken by the kind of laughter that squeezes all the oxygen from your system, leaves you gasping, sucking in huge gulps of air. Laughing, wheezing, coughing up black tar like a couple of old chain smokers. We laugh and cough ourselves to exhaustion, and then I cry until I fall asleep.

TAYLOR DOES NOT SPEAK for three days. He sits in front of the television passively watching cartoons, drifting in and out of sleep. I can't get more than a nod or a one-word answer from him. Taylor is a quiet kid, but he's also funny, loves to be silly and play make-believe. Now he has retreated into himself and I cannot draw him out.

Finally, on the third day, he turns to me and breaks his silence, "Mommy?"

"Yes, love?" I respond immediately.

"Why did you throw me out the window?"

For a moment I forget to breathe. It never occurred to me how confusing this whole thing must be for him. He's only four years old. His brain does not yet have the capacity to understand a trauma this big. Hell, even mine doesn't. I explain to him in simplistic terms what happened, and promise him Mommy will never throw him out a window again.

A couple years later, I'll receive a Mother's Day card he made at school, cut into the shape of a wobbly heart. Other kids in the class write things like, "Thank you for buying me toys" or "thank you for letting me watch cartoons." Taylor's says, "Dear Mommy, thank you for saving my life."

Late at night, as I'm dressing Taylor in his pajamas, Cissy sits at my mother's dining room table, a crease in her brow, drawing pictures of our pets. Without looking up, she says, "Mommy, you said the windows broke and the animals jumped out. How could they have jumped out if the screens were still on?"

"Well sweetie," I stall, "animals have really good instincts, and they just somehow found a way out."

"If they did, then they must be out in the woods somewhere and they're scared."

"No, honey. Our animals were so smart and so friendly, I'm sure they found themselves happy homes."

"Then I'm going to make these signs, and we'll post them around the neighborhood and get our pets back. Then everything will be back the way it was."

I rub her back, "Okay, baby." She doesn't look up, just keeps drawing, with a determined look on her face.

The next morning, I go through the ruse of the kids making more signs with scribbled drawings of our five pets. As I drive them to post their signs around the neighborhood, their little faces are so hopeful it destroys me. I agonize over whether I've done the wrong thing in lying to them. We never drive down our street. If I let them see what's left of the house (more accurately, not left) they will know the truth.

The loss of the animals is a constant ache. I can't sleep at night thinking about them lying in the rubble, buried in ash and concrete. I lie in the dark, envisioning their last moments. It runs through my mind like a horror movie I can't turn off. *Were they afraid? Were they trapped?* I have to know the specifics, as if that could change anything. *What part of the house were they in? What was their exact position? How close to the door were they?* After a week of sleepless nights, Troy says he'll go back and find them. Sarah's father, Murray, volunteers to go with Troy. I am overcome by Murray's gesture. There are few people that would be willing or able to face this. Troy and Murray later set off with shovels and blankets, while I stay behind to take the kids to a therapy session arranged by the hospital, where they will draw bright Crayola pictures of our home in flames, our pets jumping out the windows.

That night, Troy walks in to my mother's house, ashen, reeking of that sickening electrical fire. His face looks older. He tells me he found them, and had their bodies removed and properly cremated. He tells me only the location where he found them, but not the condition. I don't ask.

I am relieved to learn that Whitney and Lady were found together in the place where they slept, not against the back door pawing to get out, as I feared. Our cat, Munchkin, was found in the guest room, on top of the springs and ash that were once a bed. We believe they died in their sleep of carbon monoxide poisoning before the flames got to them. I believe this, because surely the dogs would have been barking if they had seen flames. I believe this because I have to believe this.

Bunny was trapped in her cage and never stood a chance. They never found Angel Kitty. I like to think he's the one who actually escaped.

People call, but don't know what to say. Most are kind and empathetic, saying only, "I'm so sorry." To me, this is the only appropriate response. Some say things like, "Wow, you guys must have some bad karma!" Some wave off the enormity of it all by saying, "You're alive and that's all that matters. Everything else is just stuff." We hear that a lot. I'm sure they mean well, but this makes my body flush with red-hot anger. Of course I'm grateful to be alive, and can't even let myself think what might have happened had I not crawled into bed with my son. But what I want to say to them is this: It's just "stuff" unless it's *your* stuff. And by "stuff" I don't mean furniture and clothing and dishes. I mean everything we ever accomplished: my paintings, Troy's compositions, videos of our marriage and our childrens' births. My great-grand-mother's rocking chair that had rocked four generations of babies. The children's book I wrote for Cissy. My blue ribbon for winning the sixth-grade spelling bee. The masters to our first album that we'd spent two years working on. By "stuff" I mean Troy's recording studio and my children's clothing business, our only sources of income.

There is other "stuff" we lost in the fire. Home. Our sense of safety. Our peace of mind. The ability to ever sleep through the night again without getting up to check on our kids five and six times. We lost our identity and place in society because we are now homeless and jobless. I worked in the clothing and fashion industry, where personal style was central to my life. I never cared about designer labels, but I had my own funky, artist vibe that reflected who I was. Now I'm anonymous, walking around in other people's baggy T-shirts and sweatpants every day. We all are. We wear the daily costume of "fire victims." We are a charity case. And the worst of it—five irreplaceable lives were lost that night. They were family members that we ache and grieve for. All of this is the stuff that made our life. And yes, we are alive, but the life we made together is gone.

Just stuff.

And through all this noise, Troy's words are what echo every day: We will come back stronger. At first it is a battle cry in my heart. Later, I will come to understand, coming back stronger requires a rebirth, the gestation long and arduous.

TROY AND I DECIDE the best thing for the kids is to return to a normal routine as soon as possible. My mother lives forty-five minutes away from their schools. This hour and a half loop twice a day is the new normal. Once the kids are back in school, we begin the process of reintegrating into society.

First step: get a locksmith to make keys for our cars. One remains charred in the driveway, the other was luckily parked on the street that night.

Next step: reestablish ourselves as citizens. We start by applying for birth certificates, then social security cards, and on and on, like being a newborn baby all over again. In bandages and on crutches, we spend our recovery time in downtown LA, City Hall, the DMV. It will take a solid month of phone calls and sitting in waiting rooms for the apathetic county workers of Los Angeles to validate our existence.

My mother kicks in to high gear rescue-mode, which should be comforting, but instead, I'm irritated and resentful, feeling that this is an opportunity for her to reinvent herself and become the protective mom she wasn't when I was growing up. I should be more grateful for the support and the fact that we have a place to live. And she should have been there when I was a child. But both of us fall short in the "shoulds."

THE SCORCHED EARTH

ФФФ

November 27, 1994

My first memory of my mother: we are standing on the corner, surrounded by large buildings, grey and brown cement. There are cars and buses, the smell of hot black pavement mixed with exhaust fumes. I am so small that as I look up to her I can only see the underside of her chin and the fabric of her tweed miniskirt. There are many people standing with us. Waves of heat rise up from the hard cement, everyone waiting for the light to change. My mother's hand is slightly outstretched, but she doesn't look at me. I wrap my hand around her pinky finger. Everyone steps off the curb in unison, marching across the street like soldiers. I hold fast to her pinky, never taking my eyes off of her, trying to catch a glimpse of her face. She is unreachable, unknowable to me . . .

THE RAIN HAS POURED nonstop in the days since our house burned to the ground, which seems impossible. It's winter, but winter in Southern California is usually no different than spring or summer. This year it's miserably cold, the skies dark, the rain clouds ominous, hanging heavy over us all. Even larger is the cloud of words unsaid hanging over us as my mother and I move carefully around each other in this house.

People believe we are close, and we play the parts beautifully. But our relationship is not what we project. We present two false, cheerful selves who are always "on" and can never let their guard down, lest one of us trip the wire that connects to our past.

Maybe I should start there. At nine years old, I walked into oncoming traffic. On purpose. My mother had no clue what to do with a suicidal kid. Shortly afterward, I was sent to live with her sister, my Aunt Laura, for a year. I learned then that showing my feelings would lead to estrangement, so I pushed my feelings down, so far that even I didn't know what I felt. This cycle of estrangement would be a repeating motif between us. She kicked me out of the house at fifteen—I had to get a restaurant job to support myself and spent a summer couch surfing. She disowned me again when I was twenty-three. I had stayed up late one night with my roommate Shana, sharing our life stories over a bottle of wine. This was while I was going through my divorce with Gary, and was trying to sort out where I went wrong. I told Shana how I'd witnessed my stepfather "Bullet" beating my mother, and how it had affected my relationships. *It may have been the reason I married a man who didn't love me,* I hypothesized. *Maybe I thought that love was dangerous.* Shana listened, shared her similar stories with me. We hugged, we cried. It was the first time I felt connected in the world—like I wasn't the only freak of nature.

Shana shared my story with someone else. That *someone else* told my mother.

My mother called me, furious, "How dare you talk to anyone about *my life!*" she screamed through the receiver.

"I was talking about *my* life," I said.

"What do you know about it? You were little—you don't remember."

But I did remember.

I remember Bullet sitting on top of her, his face red and sweaty, the veins bulging on his neck.

I remember his big knees pinning my mother's frail, white arms to the ground.

I remember him screaming, "You whore! You bitch!" then lowering his head over her, spitting in her face again and again.

I remember her crying, trying to get away.

I remember her screaming, "Hollye! Call the police!"

I remember standing mute and still because I was four years old and didn't know how to use a phone.

I remember feeling responsible for her beating, because I had been impotent to save her.

I remember her telling me that my grandfather had done the same to my grandmother.

I remember her stabbing Bullet with a fork.

I remember her telling me to keep it a secret.

I remember.

"How could you betray me like this?" she shouted, dropping the receiver.

Her husband Eric picked it up, "Look how you've hurt your mother. You're a terrible daughter," he said, before hanging up on me.

I spent that Easter alone, and later went crawling back again, apologizing. My mother was all I had in this world, so I learned my lesson, and I followed the rules—her rules. I learned to withhold the truth. I learned to keep the peace. I learned to keep all the secrets in our family—secrets about myself, and her; secrets about my grandfather, aunts and uncles and cousins; secrets about violence, drugs, incest. I carried them in silence as they grew ever larger in my head, the tendrils wrapping around my throat, strangling me when I tried to sing. My mother and I were able to have a relationship because we never talked about the past. She appeared to have erased it all from her mind, rewriting the script in her head and becoming someone new, while I was haunted by it.

She became pregnant with me when she was just fifteen years old. My biological father was a bad-boy James Dean look-alike, who became a heroin addict. Her middle-class parents were horrified. My grandfather wanted me aborted, but as far as I can tell, having me was her act of rebellion against him. There was no baby shower, no birth announcement with my tiny footprints, no nursery awaiting me. In my grandparents' eyes, I was the result of a disastrous mistake my mother made, bringing shame to the family.

Through the sixties, I grew up in her shadow. My mother was a bleach-blond beauty, with green cat eyes and a petite frame. To me she was like a beautiful TV star, so much so that I could almost feel the glass of the TV screen between us. She used her beauty to her advantage. Why she didn't set her sights higher, I'll never know.

There was a string of men that lived with us over the years. My father was in jail when I was born. Soon after, my stepfather "Bullet" came along. Others followed, flakes that bailed out, one after the next. Her worst choice was a drug addict with a penchant for guns. Double score.

My father, who robbed to support his heroin habit, ended up in prison, but my mother told me he was dead, because to her, he was. Folklore has it that he kidnapped me for three days when I was an infant, and then there was the restraining order. I never knew him, and we never spoke about him. In fact, on my first day of school at five years old, my mother enrolled me under a false name, and told me that from then on, I was never to tell anyone my real name or who my father was. I never did. But I never stopped wondering about him, and grew up under a mantle of shame for the tarnished DNA that ran through my veins.

Growing up, though I witnessed domestic violence, shootings, and drug use, I was a good-natured and hopeful child. My spirit was like a firefly trapped in a jar, always trying to find its way out. I was intuitive, a skill I honed to survive. Predators are adept at detecting the weakest prey—the ones whose mothers are distracted. I was scrappy—I learned to punch and kick, and was able to escape most of the time. Despite my life circumstances, or maybe because of them, I had strong faith and prayed all the time. I saw God as my true parent and that is why I wanted to go home to him when I was nine.

My mother was a licensed beautician, but chose to work in nightclubs instead. "I'm not going to waste my life setting rollers for little, old, grey-haired biddies," she'd said. She wasn't the type to attend PTA meetings or bake cupcakes for school fundraisers. As we arrived home from school each day, she was off to work in short skirts and high heels, leaving me and my little brother behind with a string of inadequate babysitters. Or sometimes, no babysitter at all. I didn't want my mom to wear short skirts. I wanted Carol Brady to tuck me in at night. I wanted Alice to cook for me. I wanted Mike Brady to give me short, simplistic pep talks about morals and character.

Instead, since I was ten years old I had the responsibility of caring for my brother, Kyle, who was seven years younger. I burned frozen TV dinners in the toaster oven, and yelled at him to go to bed when he resisted. Since the day he was born, Kyle never got a fair shake. His father, my mom's boyfriend Gene, took off when he was two. Kyle became unmanageable, craving attention he would never get. By the time he was three, he had been in the emergency room repeatedly for doing things like swallowing household cleaners and jumping out of moving cars. Suicidal tendencies were all we had in common.

When Kyle was seven, he was shot in the head by a teenage boy who lived down the street. While my mother floored it, running red lights all the way to the ER, I held Kyle in my arms as he lost consciousness. He begged me not to let him die. I was fourteen years old. His blood stained my arms, and my memory. At night, I slept in the hospital because it was my responsibility not to let him die.

Kyle lived. With physical therapy, he learned to hold a fork in his right hand. He learned to talk without slurring. With heavy daily medication, the seizures and nosebleeds eventually slowed. He wore a helmet to school to stop the bullet, still lodged in his brain, from shifting. But part of him died that day. The part that was pure and childlike and trusting. He was young enough to heal from much of the brain damage, but not strong enough to heal from the emotional damage. He has struggled with addiction since his early teens. We cheer his periodic bouts of sobriety, but they are followed by crushing disappointments and betrayals. He is prone to violent outbursts. He has been in and out of jail. He carries the memory of the shooting as close as that piece of bullet in his brain. We never talk about it. We just live it.

His father, Gene, was the only calm in the center of our lifelong storm. Gene floated in and out of our lives, finally bailing out for good when I was sixteen, and Kyle nine. Gene was kind. He was gentle and loving. In the years that he was around, he threw me the lifeline that kept me afloat long after he'd disappeared. I think he is the one my mother tries most to forget. He is the only one who ever broke her heart, and this changed her forever.

In his absence, I tried to make my mother happy. I got good grades. I danced. I sang. I was a child actress—landing a starring role in a film and even was a character on a soap opera for a short time. After I made the movie, my mother bought a rabbit-fur coat. She took Kyle and me and Frankie, a girl who worked with her at the club, to Hawaii. By the time I turned eighteen, all the money from my "trust account" was gone. She said I owed it to her. She showed me a list she had been keeping since I was thirteen years old, where she had written down every time she had given me five dollars to buy a hamburger or see a movie.

Don't get me wrong—my mother loved us. We were always made to feel special on our birthdays—always given parties no matter how broke we were. Christmas was her tour de force. She made everything sparkle so brightly that we'd forget that our grandmother was dying of cancer and Gene was leaving us. It's just that our mother was distracted by the man-drama that swirled around her, and we got left behind in the wake. The loving moments we shared with her were too sparse to string together. Vague, hazy glimpses are all I can resurrect.

My childhood didn't begin well, and it didn't end well. On my last night in my mother's house, she dragged me out of bed in the middle of the night, pulling me across the house by my hair because the cat had shit in the living room. She stood over me bellowing orders about how I was to clean it, while I crumpled in a heap beneath her, leaning over a pile of cat shit, sobbing, scrubbing. My mother had never been a drug addict or an alcoholic, but this was during a period that she was working nights in a nightclub. I choose to believe that drugs are what turned her into a monster that night, because I don't want to think she could hate me that much. After I fled my mother's house, I forgave her everything, not that she'd know. On the rare occasions I found the courage to bring anything up, she would deny it all.

As a teenager, in a grand effort to fix my flawed entry into the world, I set my sights on spiritual perfection. At nineteen, I settled for self-realization, and began following the teachings of Paramahansa Yogananda. I was convinced that I could rise above human suffering. My Aunt Laura wrote me letters trying to deprogram me from what she thought was a cult, hoping instead I'd become a born-again Christian, like her.

But my bumbling soul was not evolved enough to rise above the human condition, and as sainthood eluded me, I stayed tangled in my family pathology. But hey, I tried.

After I moved out of the house, my mother finally married a nice guy, Eric, and settled down. She had moved up the evolutionary ladder from nightclubs to restaurant management, and soon would be given the opportunity of a lifetime—a job in corporate management. From then on, she was a reinvented woman. The days of nightclubs and short skirts were long forgotten. *Sandra the Business Executive* drove a Mercedes, lived on a golf course, and wore designer suits. On the back of her closet door was an elaborate chart detailing every item in her closet and when she wore it. She explained to me her system, how she kept track so that no one would ever see her in the exact same outfit twice. I didn't know this woman.

Now, on the verge of reinventing herself again, *Sandra the Supermom* has got her hand stretched out to me and I don't know how to let her in. I learned early on not to long for my mother's arms. When I had nightmares as a child, I'd curl up on the floor outside her closed bedroom door, but I would never knock.

I'm staying in my mother's guest room, which seems fitting. Every morning I awaken in this room to the fact that I have no foundation. My life was built on quicksand. My strength was a mirage. My relationship with my mother is hollow. The outer trappings of my life are gone, and the shell of who I am, the ambassador self I presented to the world, is beginning to erode. Inside there is nothing. Nothing but the girl with no father, and no name. Nothing but the girl I buried long ago.

GIVING THANKS

❧ ❧ ❧

J ust days after the fire, I wake to the smell of my mother's turkey stuffing baking at 8 a.m., the Macy's Thanksgiving parade on TV in the background. *Is it Thanksgiving?* I've lost track of reality, days, dates. I shuffle out to find Taylor and Cissy in front of the TV eating cereal. I kiss the tops of their heads and sit at the counter in my mother's kitchen, her custom curtains pulled back, the ones that match the couch and throw pillows.

In the house where I was raised, weeds grew thigh high in the backyard, and we sat on tattered vinyl dining chairs that scratched the backs of our legs. We never had the money to fix the water-damaged walls and peeling paint. But everything in my mother's new house is picture perfect.

"Morning sweetie! Coffee's made. Want some?" she offers.

"Yes. Please." I pour cream into the steaming mug, watching it swirl like the black slime circling the shower drain. "Am I supposed to cook something for Aunt Laura's dinner tonight?"

"I think you get a pass this year. I've got it covered, don't worry."

I rub the sleep from my eyes, "Jesus, none of us even have anything to wear."

"Well, take a look at that front entry," she says in what I register as an overly chipper voice. "The bags are piling up! Let's start sifting through it today."

Each day that week, cars pulled up to my mother's house with bags of clothing, toys, and blankets. We were offered furniture, even appliances. At times it feels like we're living our own version of *It's a Wonderful Life*, and I half expect everyone to break into song. Calls come in from old friends, musicians we've worked with over the years who want to help. They suggest a benefit concert, which gives my mom an outlet for her energy. She sets to work, tirelessly organizing and calling in favors.

By night, Troy and I are plagued with nightmares. By day, we're surrounded with love and support. It is simultaneously the worst and the best time of our lives. Through tragedy, we are given the chance to feel something most will never know— to be held by hundreds of unseen hands—a comforting, and yet overwhelming sensation. It's hard to be on the receiving end of charity. At least it is for us. We're the strong ones. We reach out to others, not the other way around. Yet here we are on this day of giving thanks, grateful, yes, and also tired of being grateful and needy.

We spend Thanksgiving day digging through bags of donations, making piles of the clothes that are our sizes, stopping about every hour or so to try them on. Most don't fit and will be passed along to Goodwill, but even being able to do that is repaying a small debt. Some people used our fire as an excuse to get rid of junk, and this, thankfully, gives us the opportunity to laugh again.

Used underwear and nylons? BONANZA!

A bag full of jock straps? You shouldn't have!

A wetsuit? Skis from the 1970s? We're homeless. But thanks!

As we make our way through the piles, we try to have fun with it, for the kids' sake. We put on fashion shows, seeing who can come up with the most ridiculous outfit. Troy saunters into the living room in a baggy tuxedo wearing a snorkel with skis under his arm. "What do you think, too much?" That's my husband, always looking for the comedy in everything.

Later, we shower and dress. The kids are scrubbed shiny and clean, looking pretty sharp in their hand-me-down outfits. Even Troy and I manage to look presentable. Just as we're getting ready to leave for Aunt Laura's, the doorbell rings. My mother answers it while I help the kids get their sweaters on. She peeks her head around the corner and whispers, "There's a guy from the Red Cross here."

"Really?"

"Yes, were you expecting him?"

Troy and I look at each other and shrug. It turns out that the Red Cross had been at our fire that night, doling out food and water to the firefighters. They know about our losses and our hospital stay. We hadn't contacted them, but what I would learn about the Red Cross is that they reach out. They don't wait for you to ask for help.

Our representative Frank is about fifty, stocky with a salt-and-pepper beard and full head of hair. He has thick fingers, heavy hands that look like they could steer a ship. He sits us down on the sofa, and guides us through what to expect. "Right now, you're in what's called the honeymoon phase of tragedy," he explains. I ponder the absurdity of that statement, comparing it to floating in the Caribbean Sea with my husband, drinking rum at noon. "You're surrounded by people showing up to support you. Donations are coming in. You're getting phone calls every day. But soon, those things will taper off, and you'll be left picking up the pieces. That's the hard part, and that's when a lot of this loss will start to hit you," He hands me the card of a therapist, "We've arranged some free counseling sessions for the four of you, and I really hope you'll take advantage of this."

"We will. Thank you so much."

"Here are some immediate items you might need." He hands us four bags with toiletries, combs, brushes, toothbrushes, deodorant, shampoo, etc., and teddy bears and soft blankets for the kids.

"Thank you so much, Frank." Troy says, his eyes on the carpet.

Frank hands me an envelope, "And here are gift certificates for Vons and Target, so you can get personal items like toothpaste, underwear, and socks . . . things like that."

There is something about Frank's ease with all of this that makes my shoulders relax, my breathing become even. He navigates disaster every day, and now he's our guide. We nod our heads, listening with reverence as he gives us the coveted road map. He is the first person we've talked to who really gets it. He knows the depth of this loss. He understands that we have no driver's licenses, no car keys, no social security cards, no insurance policies, no checks, no ATM cards, no birth certificates. He knows we have no way of accessing our bank accounts without ID, and that utilities have to be cancelled and mail rerouted somewhere because there is no longer a house where the charred mailbox stands. He knows there are a million tiny details that most people would never imagine. He gives us direction and advice on how to begin again, starting with those tiny details. We take notes, write down important names and phone numbers, making an appointment to visit Frank at his Red Cross office the next week.

"We've also been in touch with a local talk show, *The Mike and Maty show?*"

I nod, "Oh yeah, I've seen that. It's a morning show, right?"

"Yes. We've told them your story and they will be contacting you. They may be able to help."

We walk Frank to the front door. "I can't believe you came here on Thanksgiving. Really . . . I just can't believe it. Thank you so much."

He smiles, "What better way to spend Thanksgiving than to help your family get back on their feet? And what a great Thanksgiving for *you*. You're alive."

"Yes . . . we're alive." I let that fact sink in for the first time as I hug Frank good-bye.

Troy gives him a firm handshake, looking him in the eye. "Thank you so much. You don't know how much this means to us."

Frank shakes Troy's hand with both of his. "Be well, brother."

After Frank leaves, we pile the kids in the car and drive to my Aunt Laura's house, where we spend every Thanksgiving. This is the aunt I'd lived with as a little girl, when I was suicidal and she lived just far enough away that my mother rarely came to visit me. She now lives just a few blocks away from my mother's house.

Troy takes my hand in the car, "Everything's going to be okay, baby," he says. "You know, everyone has some hard knocks. Now, we've paid our dues. Life can only get better from here." I think about that—all the hard knocks. The tragedies, the drama, the violence. Maybe this is the grand finale, and life will be smooth sailing from here on out.

We arrive at Aunt Laura's, Troy on crutches, and me with a bandaged wrist and visibly burned ear. We're met at the door by my aunts and uncles and cousins who descend upon us with hugs and much sniffling and wiping away of tears. Notably absent is my brother, who is using again, and though he knows about the fire has not called nor shown up to see us. We gather and chat in the kitchen, everyone wanting to know how we're feeling, what our plans are. Every time Troy and I cough from the smoke inhalation, our bodies still trying to eject the toxins in our lungs, we are met with more hugs and choruses of, "Are you okay?" and somehow after meeting with Frank, I feel I am. I really am okay.

At dinner, we hold hands and take turns saying what we're grateful for. Everyone at the table thanks God for looking out for us that night. Then it comes time for the prayer. Aunt Laura and Uncle Bob, born-again Christians, always say grace at Thanksgiving. We fold our hands, bow our heads, waiting for the familiar opening line, "Heavenly Father." Instead, Aunt Laura says, "Troy, would you lead us in prayer tonight?"

We all jerk our heads up to look at him. My husband is a man of deep faith. He has faith in people, faith in goodness, faith in love, and a belief in the unseen. But he has no faith in religion. His own life experiences led him to believe that it is nothing but hypocrisy and lies. After a moment of hesitation, he says, "Yes. I'd love to, actually." And he begins this prayer, "Heavenly Father, we thank you for this meal tonight, and for all the love in this room. We thank you for our family and friends, for the opportunity to be here together," he pauses, steadying himself, "and that we are alive." His voice breaks, "Please God, help me get back on my feet, so that I can give back."

I squeeze his hand tight. If it's hard for me to receive charity, it's ten times harder on him as a man.

There's a loud chorus of "Amen." A few of us wipe tears away with our linen napkins as we pass the mashed potatoes and pour the wine. Good God yes, pour the wine.

Clearing the plates after dinner, my Aunt Diane pulls me aside in the kitchen. She is another of my mother's sisters I lived with when I was young. I've always been very close to her. "I really think you need to get your story out to the media," she says. I shake my head at this, but she adds, "Just watch, more people will come along with even sadder stories closer to Christmas and the public will forget about you." She'd been married to a celebrity whose star had faded so this is how her mind works. "Anyway, my church is gathering some clothes and household items for you, honey, so that will help."

Aunt Laura pipes in, "I contacted my pastor and we're doing a fundraiser for you, too, sweetie."

My mother tops them all with, "I'm organizing a huge musical benefit for them at the Palomino and everyone who's anyone is going to be there." My mother and her sisters, though they love each other deeply, have been competing for top dog all their lives. Our tragedy provides yet another opportunity for them to trump each other.

Aunt Diane pulls me close against her, wrapping me in a tight hug. "Just can't believe how close we came to losing you," she says, her pale-blue eyes misting over. "Love you, baby girl," she says. Before you know it my mom, my aunts, and my cousins Tracey and Tammey are surrounding me, and it's a tearful love-fest in the kitchen.

※ ※ ※

THE NEXT NIGHT, we head to Troy's grandparents house for a second family Thanksgiving with Troy's parents and sisters. Troy is close to his gram and grandad. He and his mom, Shelby, lived with them for the first few years of Troy's life, while his dad Dennis was in the Navy. From day one they insisted I call them Gram and Grandad, and treated me like one of their own. They love our kids, displaying pictures of them around the house, and on the refrigerator door. There's a warmth and comfort in their home that I've always longed for, while in Troy's parents' home I often feel like I'm tiptoeing through an emotional minefield where I'm the only one who doesn't have the map. Once, after a particularly bad visit with Troy's parents, I called Grandad in tears. *Why don't they like me? What have I done wrong?* He only said, "We don't talk about those things," and abruptly got off the phone.

When we arrive at Gram and Grandad's house, Troy drops into his role as the family entertainer. He is lively and jovial, cracking jokes at every opportunity. Through dinner, we muffle our hacking coughs under cloth napkins. No one flinches. No one mentions that our house burned down days earlier. No one expresses thanks that we are alive. Around the table there is laughter and storytelling of days gone by, as though this were just an average Thanksgiving and nothing catastrophic has just taken place. The grandfather clock ticks loud and slow, every second an eternity to me.

After dinner, Cissy and Taylor dig in to the toy basket Gram keeps for the grandkids. On the floor they set up little plastic farm fences to corral their animals, while Troy's parents and two sisters visit at the kitchen table or peruse Gram's copy of the *National Enquirer*. Only Dennis makes reference to our fire, sort of, when after dinner he offers, "You know, if you guys need a vacuum cleaner, we have three."

The rest of the evening is torture for me. I can't pretend that nothing has happened. But it seems to be the unwritten script here that no one is to give Troy and me any attention for what we've been through. Maybe anything we mention about our suffering would be seen as immodest and self-involved. Maybe it's Midwestern stoicism. Or, maybe they just don't know what to say. Troy goes along with the script, laughing as though he didn't have a care in the world and hasn't just lost everything. It never occurs to him to turn to his mom or dad and say what's in his head: *I'm terrified. Where do I go from here?*

I guess the credo of "We don't talk about those things" passes down through several generations. And so at family gatherings, people spend an inordinate amount of time discussing how they got there, what route they took, what the traffic was like, and other times they had taken different routes and how that traffic had been.

In the car, as Troy pulls out of their driveway, I heave a frustrated sigh of relief, but stew over it all the way home. It doesn't bother Troy that no one mentioned the fire. It bothers me that he acted like everything was A-OK when he lies awake all night with worry, and has had nightmares every night since the fire. We fight over it all the way home, and that will be our pattern for years to come. Every visit with his family will be either preceded or followed by a fight between us. My role is to be the little boy in the crowd who cries, "The emperor is naked!"

Troy's response, "What emperor?"

A FEW WEEKS LATER, the phone rings. It's Troy's father, Dennis. "We want to help, but we don't know how," he says, "Tell us what to do." Lying in bed at night, Troy and I have wondered if there was anything left in the rubble, anything at all. Troy tells Dennis this, and Dennis shows up a few days later with a truck, shovels, and two pairs of thigh-high fishing boots. The two of them set off for the house. I imagine the scene, the profundity of a father digging through the remnants of his son's broken life. Not that they'll ever talk about it.

Late in the afternoon, Troy and his father pull into my mother's driveway, sweaty and smudged with that familiar black grime, dragging industrial black garbage bags behind them. Dennis hauls bag after bag, uncomplaining, quiet, sturdy, reliable. After his truck is emptied, we invite him to stay for dinner but he politely declines. He says his brief good-byes, waving as he pulls out of my mother's driveway to make the hours-long drive back in traffic.

As I open the first plastic bag, the electrical-fire stench brings my senses to full attention. My head is swimmy, my heart beating erratically. I calm my breathing, put on my mother's dishwashing gloves and reach in. The first thing I dig out is a black charred square. Troy pries it open with a screwdriver. I gasp, grabbing his hand. There, in vivid color, is a photo of me and Troy on our wedding day. The edges are singed, the colors running together. Like us, our wedding album is damaged, but it survived. I smile and wrap my arms around him, happy tears in my eyes. Of all the things to be saved from the ashes. Is this just a random coincidence? I take it as a sign. Troy is elated that he salvaged several guitars from the rubble. They were in hard shell cases that melted, but he was able to peel the melted cases off, miraculously finding the guitars underneath in good condition.

The next find is a book of my poetry, and several childhood journals. The front and back covers are gone. The edges burned, the words inside unscathed:

I will bend like a willow
I will not fall
I will not break . . .

I find a black, scorched metal tin. Inside is the pink satin bow I'd pasted to Cissy's head when she was a bald baby. Macaroni jewelry she had made me. A lock of Taylor's baby hair. A ticket stub from the first time I saw Troy perform. My grandmother's watch. *My grandmother's watch,* I think. Had she been on watch that night? Was she the voice I heard, *check the baby, check the baby?* Whether there is any sense to it, this much is clear. There was not a shred left of our sofa, piano, dining table. Only the most meaningful things survived. Mementos of my children and my marriage, Troy's musical instruments, my writing. *Pay attention,* I tell myself. *This is what matters.*

I TOSS AND TURN in bed in my mother's guest room, sleep eluding me. After dropping the kids at school, I'd hoped to nap, having been up the night before vomiting. My nerves are shot from bad dreams where I'm being chased, attacked, and beaten. But now, although the light of day feels a safer place to sleep, my mind won't let me rest. I lie on my side, staring at a piece of art my mother hung to cover the hole Kyle punched through the wall. Troy and I raced out here in the middle of the night to save my mother after Kyle pinned her against that wall, his fist to her face. No wonder I can't sleep. There are ghosts all around me in this house.

My mom comes in with the cordless phone. "Sorry to bother you. It's Deirdre . . . She said she needs to talk to you about the business."

I sit up in bed, take a deep breath, and steel myself. These days it requires all my energy and centering to talk to Deirdre.

I take the phone, "Hey . . ."

"Why haven't you called me?" Her voice is tense.

"What?" My voice is groggy.

"You're ignoring me!"

I am caught unprepared for this. "What?"

She continues, her voice becoming shrill, "You think I don't know what's going on? I know. You're pushing me away!"

I keep my voice even and measured, "Deirdre, my kids are in therapy. I'm trying to find a place to live, driving three hours a day to get my kids to and from school." I can't believe I have to spell this out for her.

"How do you think *I* feel? My business burned down, too."

"I know that, and I'm sorry for this whole nightmare. But I have to take care of my family right now. You have to understand, Deirdre." But it's clear she doesn't understand. Although the office burned down, there is still business to do. We had written $100,000 in orders that season, and most of it shipped out before the fire. There is money to be collected, seamstresses to pay, and my credit card loans to pay back. I rerouted all the mail to Deirdre's house, and forfeited my salary so she could hire someone to help her until I was back on my feet.

"Deirdre, we'll get through this. In a month or two, checks will be coming in from last season, and we can figure out our next step. Everything is going to be fine." I cup the phone and exhale. *Just count to ten, count to ten.* My nerves are so frayed it's all I can do not to blow up at her. *Are you fucking kidding me? I'm sitting here consoling you right now?* I have no reserves in my energy bank—not one ounce of anything to give. But I breathe, and I count, and always exercise extra patience with her, because I know how fragile she is, and why.

I met Deirdre when we were both teenagers working at a restaurant together. She was a year older, but emotionally young with a nervous laugh. Later I would find out why Deirdre was so nervous. Her mother was a brilliant artist, and also schizophrenic. Her father was a physician who worked long hours and late nights. He left Deirdre and her three younger sisters at home with their mother, who would be lost in her own paranoid world. Deirdre remembered her sisters pounding on their mother, screaming at her to get a response, but they could never reach her. Her father hired housekeepers to keep the girls in line but they would quit, one after the next. The girls were wild and out-of-control angry. When Deirdre was a teenager, she arrived home from school one day to the news that her mother was gone. Dead. No explanation.

I rub my eyes, "I'm sorry, Deirdre, I have to get off the phone now. I was up sick last night and I'm still queasy."

"Fine. Goodbye," she says curtly, and hangs up.

I fall back in the bed and let out a gutteral, frustrated scream. As if on cue, my mother pokes her head around the door, "Everything okay?"

"I'm fine," I say with a forced smile, waving her away with one hand over my eyes.

She comes in and sits on the edge of the bed.

"Really Mom, I'm just frustrated right now. I'm fine." I sit up, uncomfortable with the nearness of my mother.

She puts a soft hand against my cheek, "Everything's going to be okay." I remember that hand smacking me in the face, pulling my hair as she dragged me across the house that awful night. I shrink away from her touch.

"Thanks, Mom. I think I just need to take a shower and get on with my day." I make a beeline toward the bathroom.

"Okay honey, just know I'm here for you if you need me,"

she calls after me. "And don't worry, you can live here as long as you want. I wish you guys would live here forever!"

In the bathroom, I lean against the shut door, my head throbbing, my stomach clenched. *I have to get out of here.*

I turn on the shower, overcome with frustration, rage, claustrophobia. I try to break down the issues one by one, and process what I'm feeling. Why can't I let my mother be nice to me? What the hell am I going to do about Deirdre? Why am I so angry? Wrapping myself in a towel, I turn to face my reflection. As steam clouds over the glass, I watch myself fade away. The turmoil I'm feeling inside—about Deirdre, my mother, Troy's family—has all been lying dormant inside me, festering. I busied myself with so-called important things— running my business, flying back and forth to New York, and volunteering at the kids' schools. I never had time to feel anything. But now, everything has burned away. There is nowhere to run, nowhere to fly. I am left alone with my inner truth. Feeling it means that soon I will have to deal with it. I don't have a single clue how to do that.

THE NEXT MORNING, I have endless calls to make, questions to ask. Where to start first? I have to cancel the utilities. Cancel the phone service. Call every credit card company and bank to get replacement cards. Automaton-like voices on the other end of the phone—*your account number?* I have no idea. *Address?* I don't know how to answer that. *Ma'am, where would you like us to send the new card?* Where will they send the new cards? Where will we be living? I call UPS to cancel my daily pick up. *Will you be continuing your account with us?* I don't know. (I do run into Bruce, my UPS driver, some months later, who tells me of his shock driving up to our home that

Monday morning to find only a burned out shell of a home, not knowing if we were dead or alive.)

I call our health insurance to make sure they covered our hospital stay. This is where the first few rocks of the avalanche begin cascading down—foreshadowing what we are in for. Our ambulance and hospital bills are not covered. The ambulance delivered us to the closest hospital, which was out of network. I argue this to no avail with an apathetic insurance representative. On top of our losses, we now have astronomical medical bills. Now there's something to keep in mind; if you are ever almost killed, make sure your rescuers only come from in-network facilities.

THE HARVEST

As Troy and I pull up to the Palomino, my palms are sweaty, my stomach nervous with anticipation. For the past few weeks we've spent our evenings calming our children's anxiety at bedtime, then drinking red wine until we beat our own monsters down enough to sleep. But tonight is going to be a good night.

The Palomino is a funky little club in North Hollywood where many of rock and country royalty got their start. Linda Rondstadt, Patsy Cline, and Johnny Cash all graced the rustic stage at one time. I've been here many times before to see artists I loved. But tonight the marquis outside reads:

DEXTER FAMILY BENEFIT
FEATURING TOWER OF POWER AND SPECIAL GUESTS

I never imagined a night like this, nor would I have believed we'd be in a position to need it, but here we are. Miracles seem to only happen in the middle of mayhem.

For weeks, calls came in from musician friends offering to lend their talents to help us. Over the years, we had worked in so many different bands, on so many recording projects, we never paused to take inventory. As my mother compiled her list of offers on a yellow legal pad, I saw page after page of names, and was amazed at the friends our musical journey had brought. Rounding the corner to park, we see the long line of people waiting to get in—every one of them is here for us. Troy stops the car, "Wow. Unbelievable . . ." His eyes are wet. He blinks it away.

Troy and I have done plenty of griping about the fact that, as artists and musicians, we walk a tightrope every day without a safety net. We have no 401(k). No pension plan. No company health care plan. Budget? We can never make a budget. It's a roll of the dice every month as to what we'll be making, what calls might come in. Maybe some corporate entertainment gigs, a few sessions, a tour, a TV gig, or maybe nothing at all. For Troy it's easier as he has so much to offer. He tours as both a guitar and keyboard player, but can also play bass and drums. He sings, composes, can write a complete score for an orchestra then conduct that orchestra. You need a banjo player on a session, or someone who can play a lute, a zither, or a Russian balalaika? Troy's your guy. But me? I just sing, so I'm always scrambling to find other ways to compensate financially, like my children's clothing line.

Troy always says a musician's life is no joke. You've got to have the stomach for it. It's a life of great highs and lowest lows. Just a few years before, Troy and I were on tour in Japan staying in five-star hotels. We were taken out for lavish dinners, carted around Tokyo by a personal driver, treated like rock royalty. A month later I was cutting coupons and working a corporate sales job to make ends meet. Such was our life, and we learned to roll with it.

We both have ancestors who were farmers. When Troy gets fed up with our lifestyle, I remind him to look to them as an example. Our ancestors, just like us, planted their fields, tended them, put all their energy and effort in with no guarantees. And when harvest time came around, they worked. That's how it is for us. When the harvest comes, we never say no to a gig, we don't take a day off. We work. We miss friends' parties and weddings and other events because that harvest is all we've got. For our ancestors, sometimes the harvest paid off in a bumper crop. But some years brought flood, or drought, or the very worst thing—locusts. During those lean years, friends and neighbors often pitched in. And when the planting season came around, they picked themselves up and began again, sowing those seeds, turning that soil.

This is our year of locusts. But tonight at The Palamino Club, like farmers for an Amish barn raising, our relief begins to appear. One by one they walk through the front door, instruments slung over their backs, ready to help us reconstruct the framework of our new life. That's when I realize we were never working without a net. This, our community of musicians, *is* our safety net. *Love* is our safety net. There is no safer pension plan.

The night unfolds like a series of snapshots in my mind. I am dancing with my husband, sawdust on the well-worn floor. He picks me up and spins me; Sarah's pink dress that I borrowed twirls around me. The smiles of friends I haven't seen in years lift me. And the music. That's what I'll remember the most.

Our friends Russ McKinnon (Troy's old roommate who used to change Cissy's diapers) and Carmen Grillo bring their bandmates from Tower of Power. Rick Braun, our neighbor whose deck caught on fire that night, has just gotten off tour with Sade, and comes by to play trumpet with the band. My mom's husband Eric—also a guitar player who had toured with Ray Parker, Jr. and Andy Gibb—plays the blues with his old buddies from Tulsa. Friends whose albums Troy has produced take the stage: Julie Silver, Craig Taubman, all the guys from the Disney album Troy just finished. Many, many musicians we've done corporate entertainment gigs with over the years sit in. There is such immense talent and love in the room. Tonight is the celebration of all that has gone right in our lives.

Music is the powerful force that lures me away from fear. It becomes our first implement of healing—the first stitch of many sutures to come. We let the music lift us, dancing until we are red-faced and sweaty. I feel giddy and free, all the while knowing this moment is fleeting. But I'm squeezing this baby for all it's worth. Lord knows I'm going to need the strength.

There is no cover charge to get in, but everyone makes a donation at the door. By the end of the night we have $3,000 to tuck away for a home. That's a decent amount of money, but what we take from the Palomino is something much more valuable. Our spirits are restored, our faith in the life we've chosen renewed. Driving back to my mother's house, I'm well aware of how rich we really are. I feel like Donald Freekin' Trump.

HOLIDAY

❦ ❦ ❦

This journal entry marks the beginning of my new life. I cry as I write this, because it also means saying good-bye to the sweet life we once had. The fire on November 19 wiped our slates clean, and now we begin again. There is so much that I have not even begun to let myself feel, like the fact that God spared my children and husband. I can't even think about that, because the alternative is so terrifying. It is my most primal fear.

What we experienced was horrifying. There are few people who can understand. They think, Well, it's been a month now. Don't you have your life back together? Doesn't insurance just set it all straight again? Aren't you all back to normal? Our life will never be back to normal. As Troy said, "My life is a do over."

I know that God has a place for us, but I am hurt and angry for what he did to us. In the beginning, I could see mixed blessings. Now, I am sick of it all. The charity, the pity, the stress, the changes, the expectations. I don't want this life. I want my life back.

I WANT MY LIFE BACK! I have been stripped and robbed of everything I ever accomplished. Every creative endeavor I ever undertook is ashes now. All my efforts, my creativity, everything good I ever did—gone. Why God?

*My animals that I cared for and loved so much—gone. The home
that we made and filled with love and music and happiness—gone.
Why God?
Why?*

TROY AND I SQUEEZE each other's hands as the kids bounce
with excitement in the backseat of the parked car. I'm steeling
myself for the next act of immense charity that's about to
come. Troy looks at me, "Well, shall we go in?"

The front of Sarah and Scott's perfectly appointed house is
aglow with Christmas lights, a bushy pine wreath on the front
door. Just the day before, Sarah called and asked us to come
over with the kids because she had a surprise for us.

I joke to Troy, "I'm going to put in a request that Sarah be
canonized the patron saint of charity."

"Are there any Jewish saints?" he asks.

"Yes—and her name is Sarah." Aside from showing up at
the hospital with clothes, Sarah handed out fliers at our kids'
school, listing all their sizes, then contacted all our friends in
the clothing industry, and showed up at my mom's with boxes
full of brand new beautiful clothes for the kids. She then called
our story in to a radio station and won our family a trip to
Disneyland. Saint Sarah.

The front door swings open. "Hi guys!" Sarah throws her
arms around us. "Come in, come in!" Inside, we hear a
booming, "Ho, ho, ho," as we are greeted by a jolly Santa in full
regalia, a large red-velvet sack behind him. Standing next to
him is a middle-age woman in a suit, her hair bobbed and
Clairol blond. She introduces herself as the head administrator of a local hospital. Sarah has arranged for them to
"adopt" us for Christmas. I am conflicted; moved by the
goodness and generosity of people, ashamed to be adopted. I

focus on the grateful part and play up the moment for the kids.

"Look who's here, guys! All the way from the North Pole!" I say in the most cheerful voice I can muster. Meeting Santa with a huge sack of presents is magic—and that's what my kids need right now. Cissy bounces up and down on her toes, her big brown eyes wide with excitement, but Taylor hangs back a little, always discerning, assessing, not sure about this big hairy guy.

I give to charity at Christmas, but I never thought I'd need it. This isn't a Christmas feeling I'm comfortable with. I hope to God no one is planning to show up on Christmas with a turkey and canned food. We have to draw the line of dignity somewhere. Troy says the appropriate thank yous, but his eyes are cast down, arms tightly crossed against his chest. I can tell from his body language he's ashamed. It isn't his fault we're here. I'm the one who didn't fill out that insurance paperwork. I'm the one.

Santa and his administrator dole out beautifully wrapped gifts to each of us. We all receive brand new winter coats and shoes. I try on my fitted, black ultrasuede parka with the fur-lined hood. It is elegant, soft, and warm. It feels good to have nice things, to be able to dress and feel some dignity again. I then try the black leather boots they bought me, which fit perfectly. Sarah has seen to all the details.

"Thank you all so much," I say, my voice cracking. "Really, these are just beautiful."

The woman smiles wide. I can tell it gives her great joy to be able to do this for us. Sarah stands beside her, her eyes glistening and teary. Deep down I understand the act of giving blesses the giver as well. I know because I've experienced it, but still feel ashamed and small and pathetic. Just months ago Sarah, Scott, Deirdre, and I were all in New York together, showing our new spring lines at the Children's Fashion Show. We stayed at the Embassy Suites in Times Square and ate dinners in the finest restaurants in Manhattan. Now I am accepting charity.

After we open our gifts, Santa folds up his empty velvet sack. "Good luck to you, and God bless." He then turns toward the kids, "You two stay on the nice list, okay?"

"We will!" Cissy says cheerily, Taylor hiding behind her.

"Take care," says the nice lady in the business suit as she shakes our hands. She adds, self-consciously, "You know . . . there are a lot of us out here praying for you."

"Thank you," is all I can muster. I want to thank her for the clothes, the toys, the kindness, but mostly for the prayers, because I know we're going to need it much more than winter coats.

Troy is outside packing the car with our new gifts. Cissy and Taylor play on the floor, sharing their toys with Sarah's kids, Lauren and Kayla, as Sarah and I look on.

"You've done so much for us, Sarah . . . really. I don't know how to thank you."

She waves her hand as though swatting a fly. "You would do the same for me in a heartbeat."

"Yes, I would, and it would be so much easier than this."

"Listen," she says, "everyone is happy to do this for you. Just accept it."

Accept it. Stop fighting it. One day, I tell myself, I will pay this forward.

"Oh, I almost forgot," she says, darting over to the kitchen table and returning with a manila envelope. "I finally got some pictures together for you."

I leaf through photos of our faces pressed close together, joyful, smiling. Our kids, so happy together: Cissy and Lauren, best friends holding hands with their toothless little smiles.

Taylor and Kayla kissing as toddlers. Christmas Eve, the kids' birthdays, riding horses at a dude ranch, eating dinner in Chinatown; memories that make me ache for the way life was. On Scott's birthday, Troy and I took him and Sarah on a hike just before sunset. When we got to the top of the mountain, they were shocked to find the table Troy and I had hauled up there earlier, with an ice bucket, wine, and hors d'oevres. We sat up there on top of the world, drinking wine, watching the sunset. We told stories and laughed as the stars came out one by one, and finally hustled down the mountain when the howls of coyotes surrounded us. And then there was the car rally that Scott organized for Troy's birthday—a scavenger hunt with clues hidden all over the West Valley. Scott had crafted homemade trophies for the winning team. What a crazy night of laughter and mayhem—one that fueled us with stories we would tell for years after.

"God, will we ever have times like these again?" I say.

"We will. We definitely will," Sarah says without an ounce of doubt in her voice. I love that about her.

We stand there quietly for a moment. Sarah breaks the silence, "You know, there's something I wanted to tell you, but I wasn't sure if I should . . ." She stares out the window, her fingers pressed against her lips.

"What is it? You can tell me anything."

She exhales like she'd been holding her breath a very long time, "It's just . . . very strange. Last month, Scott and I were leaving your house after dinner one night, and as we drove down the hill I saw a picture in my mind . . . just a quick flash . . . of your house in flames." She turns to look at me, a worried expression. "I didn't say anything because I thought it was just some weird daydream. I'm sorry—I wish I had said something! I just didn't know . . ."

Mildly freaked out, I take her hand. "But even if you had said something, what could we have done? How could any of us have known or understood these strange dreams and flashes?" The more people tell me these things, the more I feel convinced this fire was destined. I have no idea why, but I hope that one day I will.

I give her a long hug good-bye, and corral the kids back into the car. The neighborhood Christmas lights twinkle as the sun wanes. Troy starts the car, and I dial the radio station to Christmas tunes as we make our way back to my mother's house. Frank Sinatra croons in the background. "Silent Night . . . holy night," I sing along in harmony. The kids join in, their little voices so sweet and pure. Troy manages a smile for me, keeping his eyes on the road. I brush away the tear that rolls down his cheek.

DRIVING UP THE ROAD toward what used to be our home, my stomach and rib cage tighten. Troy has already made a few trips back, but this is my first time.

"You okay?" he asks.

I take a deep breath, exhale, "Not too good. How about you?"

"I'm okay." He's got that reassuring hand on my knee.

It is overcast and cold, the clouds overhead threatening rain. As we turn onto our old street, the camera crew from *The Mike and Maty Show,* huddled in the middle of the narrow lane, waves us down.

"Park here guys, we want to get a shot of you walking up to the house." We park and begin the dreaded walk up the street. Troy keeps a protective arm around me as cameras flank us. Walking across what's left of the front patio, I feel dizzy as that putrid smell of electrical fire overtakes me, now made worse by the mold that hangs in the air. Helicopters had doused the smoldering remains with water, and the soggy remnants of our life have begun to mildew.

Cameras shadow us as we step tentatively through what was once our living room, but now is only skeletal charred beams. There isn't a hint of the furniture that once filled these rooms. Not a trace left of the sofa, bookcases, dining room table. No walls where my paintings once hung. And yet, in the black hole that was our staircase, my stockings dangle from a charred rafter, untouched. So strange, the way fire chooses its victims, like a firestorm that torches one house and jumps right over another.

Walking the outside perimeter of the house, I find an old jewelry box lying on the ground. I can still make out the image of Degas ballerinas sashaying across the top. As I open it, a melted plastic ballerina makes a spasmodic series of spins as "Dance of the Sugar Plum Fairy" sadly warbles then stops. Inside I find a locket with Cissy's baby picture. The photo is foggy with smoke damage, but my baby's smiling face is still visible. I put the locket around my neck, and keep touching it to assure myself it's there.

Mike interviews us in front of the house with composed concern. I, ever the chatty one, can't speak. My jaw is clenched, my body shivering. Troy does most of the interview while I stand behind him and nod, Hillary Clinton–style. When the interview is over, I flee the house almost as quick as I did the night of the fire. I will never again go back.

A few days before Christmas, we're off to Hollywood for a live taping of *The Mike and Maty Show*. The kids are excited when they see the studio's limo pull up in front of my mother's house. We take a photo of them in their new clothes, standing in front of the black stretch Cadillac. Scott loaned Troy a nice shirt to wear, and I wear the dress my mother bought me for my birthday. I was up vomiting last night, after having another nightmare about the fire.

When we arrive at the studio, it's a whirlwind. They usher us in, powder puff our noses, and seat us in front of a fifteen-foot Christmas tree. We have no idea what to expect. A man with a headset tapes microphones to our clothes and says, "We're going to roll the montage footage from the house, then we'll ask you a few questions live, okay?"

We nod, mute. He turns to the crew, signals Mike and Maty, "Live in five!" he shouts and counts down silently while holding his fingers up.

Maty does a quick intro about us in her announcer-voice, "Troy and Hollye Dexter started 1994 with everything going great. Two beautiful children and nice house in the suburbs. They seemed to have it all." They roll the footage, and suddenly we are watching film of our house on fire. This is a terrible shock. Apparently the producers got video clips from the local news. We didn't even know we were on the news, or that this footage existed. My heart pounds at the sight of our home in flames, the helicopters circling overhead. Cissy starts to cry. I clutch the kids tight against me.

"Don't look, babies," I whisper in their ears, my voice trembling. *I never wanted them to see this. I should never have brought them here.* Mike tells our story in narration over footage of the house burning, sad music underscoring it. They cut to a scene of us scooping through the ashes, looking for anything salvagable. I turn my head away from the monitor, trying to hold it together.

The montage scene ends and they switch to a live studio shot of us in front of the Christmas tree. My face is red from crying. Taylor is in my lap, Cissy between Troy and me, stunned. Mike is talking to us, reading questions from cue cards—one of them being *So, is everything getting back to normal now?* I have a frozen smile on my face, can't digest what he's saying but it sounds like—*Let's wrap this up and cut to the happy ending—this is television, you know.* My head is fuzzy, my hands cold and numb. They wheel out a shiny new pink bike for Cissy, and bags full of Ninja Turtle toys for Taylor. The audience claps wildly. They award Troy and I a $1,000 shopping trip to Target. Maty's bottom lip is trembling, her eyes red and tear-filled. She seems to understand that this television wrap-up is not the end of the story. Then, as quickly as it began, they cut to commercial and it's over. When the cameras stop rolling, Maty hugs me so tight, whispering in my ear, "God bless you." This is a heartfelt, human moment I will always remember. Maty is whisked away by make up, who dab at her tears with Kleenex and powder. Lou Rawls is already on set, testing his microphone. *Chestnuts roasting on an open fire . . . .* Minutes later, we are in the limo driving away, a shiny pink bike sticking out of the trunk. Our lives have become surreal. I feel vacant inside my own body, almost as if I'm watching someone else have these beautiful but strange experiences.

The Target shopping trip is another media blitz. We seem to be the poster children for holiday disaster. Target's PR department sends journalists and photographers to accompany us on our shopping spree, following us up and down the aisles, making notes of the items we choose. In the newspaper article entitled *A Spark of Hope After Fire*, they note, "One of the first items the Dexters grabbed during the three-hour shopping spree was a carbon monoxide sensor—a grim reminder."

December 23, 1994

The Destroyer

The destroyer has come
And left nothing in its wake
Men in plastic coats
Trudge through the ashes
Moving clumsily
Over the corpses of our dreams
That still smolder
And stink up the morning sky

Shell-shocked, charred, and broken
We stand at the side of the road
Adrift
Tears resolve nothing
But only serve to wash away
The last traces
Of what we were,
Changing us forever
But cleansing nothing

What was the meaning
of all that meaning
If only to be stripped from our canvas
Exposing a vast emptiness
Of all possibility and no possibility
Bleak
Open
Beckoning but not inviting
It awaits

I stand motionless, no palette in hand
Silence pervades
Even the angry voices in my head
Are quiet now
False optimism is offered freely
I swallow every last drop

Clutching it like a crucifix
I face the cold and distant unknowing
Wearing it like a warm coat
I take my first steps
Blind and shivering
As a newborn babe
I begin again
I am alive.

IT FEELS STRANGE TO wake up in someone else's house on Christmas morning. My little ones stir beside me, which means it's only minutes before they'll be up. Hard to believe I've woken before them, but I hardly sleep anymore. I'm determined that today will be a happy memory for Cissy and Taylor. My mother threw her annual Christmas Eve party last night, which is always a dressy, elegant affair. She put out a huge spread of gourmet food, and hired a magician to entertain the guests. We never know if my brother Kyle will be sober or even remember to show up. Last night he didn't. We dressed up and went through the motions, visiting with everyone, answering their many questions about the fire, "But how? How? How could a house just combust in the middle of the night?" They'd ask, fear in their eyes as they clutched at their Christmas sweaters and swizzled their holiday cocktails.

After the party, we did our midnight Santa thing, stuffing the kids' new stockings, laying out all the presents just so.

Before Troy and I headed off to bed, my mom and Eric gave us a present wrapped in shimmery gold paper, gold voile ribbon tied at the top. My mother knows how to make things sparkle so brightly it hardly matters what's inside. But inside this package was something that meant a lot to us—a video camera. She smiled, "Starting now, there are new memories to be made." My mom has been great to us, and generous with me in a way she'd never been before. No longer is she keeping lists of what I owe her. Something has changed. I don't know if it's Troy being in my life or the kids, but I'm glad for it. I still keep my walls up, as much as I want to feel differently.

I peer over the edge of the mattress to see my little ones sleeping peacefully, their arms and legs tossed over one another like a pile of puppies. Their bed consists of sleeping bags and comforters layered on top of a foam mattress pad on the floor, which makes me feel inadequate and responsible and guilty. *It's not forever*, I remind myself. *Focus on the good.* I pick up the new video camera from the nightstand, making sure the battery is fully charged. As I turn it on, it makes a weak beep. Cissy's eyes open, registering a sliver of light through the blinds, which signals it is go time. She sits up and looks around. I wonder if it takes her a few seconds every morning to figure out where she is, like it does for me. She turns her face up to look at me, beaming. "It's Christmas, it's Christmas!" She jumps into bed with me and I hold her tight. It doesn't matter that we lost everything and are homeless. Santa came, and that makes everything okay again. Troy and Taylor wake and within moments the kids are out the door charging for my Mom and Eric's bedroom, while bleary-eyed Troy and I stumble across the room to get dressed.

My mother's tree stands twelve feet tall, overflowing with brightly colored packages. Thanks to the generosity of friends who went overboard for our children, there are so many gifts in the living room we have to clear space to sit. We take turns opening gifts, as we always do, and save the stockings for last. We still have our traditions.

A small guitar we bought for Taylor sits in the middle of the room, a big red bow tied around it. Troy wraps an arm around Taylor and points to it, "Look what Santa brought you."

Taylor glances in the direction where Troy is pointing. "What? Where?"

"Right there, buddy. With that big red bow!"

"What big red bow?" Taylor asks, stepping over packages and walking right past it.

Cissy jumps up and physically navigates him toward it, "Right there, Tay-Tay!"

"Huh?"

We all shout in unison, "The guitar!"

"Oh," he says, unimpressed.

"Don't you like it, La-la?" I ask, "Daddy can teach you how to play it!"

"Eh, I already know how."

"Oh great. Maybe you can teach me a thing or two." Troy answers and we all laugh.

Cissy orchestrates the morning. My little ambassador of Christmas passes out all the gifts, making sure no one goes out of order. She is sentimental and emotional about the new dolls we bought her to replace the ones she'd lost in the fire, but I'm the one who is given the most that day. Some weeks before, Cissy and I had been at a craft faire where we saw a beautiful handmade angel. It was a stunning work of art, and I stopped to ogle over it.

"Why don't you just buy it, Mommy?"

"I can't buy frivolous things like that, sweetie. We need a home, and lots of other things. Besides, it's eighty dollars."

But as I open my gift from Cissy, dig through the foam peanuts, unwrap layer upon layer of tissue paper, inside is that angel. My eyes brim with tears as I look up at her. Her face is beaming, as she bounces up and down on her toes with excitement.

"It's the one you wanted, Mommy!"

"I don't understand . . . how?"

"I bought it for you with my birthday and Christmas money. I had my dad take me back there to buy it because I knew you really wanted it," she says, her eyes bright and hopeful. Nine years old, and she's trying so hard to fix everything.

I clutch my baby and hug her tight, my tears soaking her nightgown. "You are such a sweet girl. I love you so much," I barely squeak out.

The goodness of others, the generosity, the kindness, my love for my husband and children, it all becomes too much on Christmas morning. Troy gives me a new stocking with Raphael's angels on the front and I bawl like a baby. Everything, I mean everything, makes me cry. Cards, socks, a pack of gum in my stocking—*You remembered I prefer peppermint to spearmint? Oh thank you, thank you so much . . . sob, sob, sob.* For everything we've lost, we're given hope on this morning. More than food, more than oxygen, this is what we need to live. And though we are homeless and jobless, I am filled with gratitude, and absolutely, deliriously happy.

START AGAIN

❦ ❦ ❦

The sky shifts orange to pink to violet as evening falls on the very last day of this horrible year. "Don't let the screen door hit you in the ass, 1994," I mumble, while Troy and I make the three-hour drive to our New Year's gig in San Diego. As I gaze at the scenery whizzing past us on the 101 Highway, I think of everything that has happened this year. Nineteen ninety-four started with an earthquake, and ended with a fire. It turned my life upside down, and took everything that I thought I was. Troy and I are both quiet, immersed in thought. I mourn all we've lost, yet I'm hopeful for a new beginning.

I break the long silence, "I've been praying to feel joy again. This is our new beginning. I want sadness to be replaced with joy."

"Amen to that," Troy said, eyes focused on the road.

"I mean, not to be superstitious but they say that however you spend New Year's Eve will set the tone for your year. We have to make this the best night ever. We have to start fresh!"

"I know, honey. We will," he says.

"Did you make your New Year's resolutions?" I ask. New Year's resolutions are of heightened importance to me this time around.

He thinks about it for a minute."I want to make music that matters to me, not just that pays the bills. I want to be the musician I studied to be."

"Is that all?"

"Well, of course I want to find us a place to live. I want to get back on my feet, get my kids settled. I want to be able to give back." Charity is a cloud of debt hanging over his head that he needs to eradicate. "What about you?" he asks.

"Same," I say. I am quiet, ruminating on words I'd been trying to say for weeks now. I want to clear out all the negativity so I can have my fresh start. Do I dare bring up the worries that spin through my head as I lie awake night after night? "Deirdre thinks we can somehow save the business."

"Right. *That's* gonna happen," he says, sarcastically.

"It would take a miracle, and I don't have a miracle in me," I say. "We were already in trouble before the fire, struggling to bounce back from the damage the earthquake caused. We haven't even started paying down the government loan from FEMA. So much of our merchandise was lost in the fire; our patterns, all of our customer records, our files, computers." I'm getting myself worked up.

"It's okay," he says, patting my knee. "Do what you have to do. I support you."

I tell him how frustrated I am over everything I've sacrificed for that business, and for what? It became the focus of my life, consuming all my energy and time. But now my family needs me present to build a new life. And also, deep down there is a truth that I fear makes me a bad person somehow: I can't bear the thought of working with Deirdre anymore. I would rather let the business go to spare the friendship, because if I go back to work with her, I will sink into depression.

"It all burned down, babe," he says. "It's over. We have to start again." The three hour drive is therapeutic, a chance for us to be alone and think, and to say all the things that had been building up inside our heads. Sharing a room with the kids in my mom's house made it impossible to talk, so this time is a godsend.

"So you're going to make a pact with me that tonight is our new beginning, right?" I ask him.

"Yep, fresh start," he says.

"At midnight, we leave the nightmare behind, and ring in the new year with only positive thoughts, okay?"

"Yep."

When we arrive at our gig at the posh country club, a beautiful redhead in a sequined gown walks up to me. "Hi, I'm Joy!" she says, taking both my hands, "I'm the one who called you after the fire." Her round blue eyes sparkle.

Joy. Isn't that what I just asked for? Though I don't know her, Joy was recording at our neighbor's house in November, and was horrified to see the burned out shell of our home. She made the effort to find out who we were, track us down, and leave a message saying she wanted to help in any way she could. Synchronicity being what it is, it turns out the Wayne Foster agency that booked us for New Year's had also booked Joy, and standing before me is the face of that sweet voice on the phone, looking just as joyful as her name.

I pick my jaw up off the floor, "What a wonderful surprise! Hi!" We give each other a strong hug, and I fall in love with her on the spot. Of course I would find Joy on the eve of my new beginning. Of course.

Joy and I glitter in sequins, singing and dancing for four straight hours. Aside from music, there is a real harmony between us. We rock the house as the crowd gets roaring drunk. I never tire of seeing drunken CEOs, physicians, and hedge-fund managers dance badly in ridiculous hats. I keep looking over at Troy, whose head is down, focused on the neck of his guitar. For some reason he won't make eye contact with me, but I can see that he's pissed off. He told me during a break that one of the band members said something asinine that offended him.

"No! Not tonight—you can't be mad. Only positive from now on, remember?" But he isn't listening. I can't believe it. He's not the moody type and almost impossible to offend, but tonight, of all nights, he's in a funk. In between songs I look over and flash him the big smile he loves, reminding him of our pact, but he just looks away.

Maybe it's what I said about quitting my business. Maybe it's the hospital bills that are flooding in. Maybe it's living at my mom's house or all my vomiting and crying or the fact that the kids are still in therapy, but probably it's everything. I know he's so stressed he's bursting at the seams but still I'm panicked—he's going to jinx us! I can't take any chances at this point in my life. I don't know what I did wrong to cause all this bad luck, but I am vigilant about praying every night, and equally careful not to break mirrors, or step on cracks in the sidewalk, or blow my chance at a perfect New Year's Eve.

After midnight, Troy packs up his guitar and amp in a fury, as I hug Joy good-bye.

She takes my hand, "Like I said in my message to you, call on me if you need anything."

Troy trudges ten paces ahead of me and throws his equipment in the back of our Honda. The three-hour drive back toward reality at my mother's house is very different from the musing and inspired drive away from it. We fight all the way home. I'm furious at him for cursing us, so terrified that the gods of New Year's Eve are surely going to get us now. That's how ridiculous and fearful I am at this point.

January 5, 1995, 12:01 a.m.

It always hits me late at night, like a tidal wave. The reality of our situation sets in, and I am heavy and alone with the burden. There are times when I know I'm not alone, that I'm being watched over, but sometimes the grief and sorrow is bigger than everything else and it's all I can see or feel. I can't sleep. My soul is agitated. I wonder . . . What next, God?

I do feel a new part of myself has been shaken loose and is starting to spread its wings. I feel more in touch with my inner voice. I am looser, less restrictive with myself and others. I can see it in my painting and my writing. You come this close to losing your babies— it puts everything in perspective. I want to be the barefoot mother who takes her children on fairy hunts and teaches them to finger paint and squish their toes in the mud.

I started a new painting last night. When I began it I almost felt giddy. The paintbrush was loose in my hands, the strokes whimsical, adventurous. My attitude was . . . my life is a blank canvas now. Let me just start painting and see what comes.

FIREFLY IN A JAR

✿ ✿ ✿

I sit exhausted on the floor of my mother's garage, my hands blackened with ash from digging through fire remnants. There are several bags of charred photo albums, the plastic-coated pages melted together, creating a solid block. It's a process to pry the pages apart one by one, to salvage each photo. That will come later. For now, I'm just preserving what I can, throwing out what I can't. There are bags full of donated clothing that doesn't fit us, which I'll now donate to others.

I pile bags for Goodwill at the curb. Dragging the last bag out, I see a painting I gave my mother years before, lying on the garage floor. I spent months working on it. It took so much time to get that fluorescent hue under the waves, to capture the reflection of the moon just so. When I think of the joy I felt when Troy salvaged the keepsake box of macaroni jewelry my kids made—in contrast to my oil painting lying on my mother's dirty garage floor—I feel small and worthless. I pick up the painting and dust it off. The canvas has a footprint on it. Anger wells up inside of me as I dig furiously through boxes of old photos, taking any baby pictures, blue ribbons, awards I'd won, anything of mine I can find.

I discover a cache of black-and-white photos of my relatives; my grandmother and her brothers as children, a newspaper clipping with a photo of my great Uncle Larry signing with the . . . New York Yankees just before being drafted to World War II? How did I not know this? Then I come across a photo of my great-grandmother Kindred, standing behind a sales counter. The sign behind her reads, Kindred's Tot Shop. My great grandmother had her own children's clothing company? Did no one think to mention this to me as I launched my own children's clothing company? Why do I feel like I'm not even part of this family—like I'm some outsider who isn't entitled to my own family history?

I'm agitated, pissed off, surely fueled by anxiety and the cornucopia of other emotions brewing, but it all becomes more than I can take. It's been two months since the fire. Two months of sharing a bedroom with my kids under my well-meaning mother's roof. Two months more than I ever thought I could handle, and now I know I can't live in my mother's house another day.

I spend the rest of the day hunched over the classified section of the paper, circling every rental house in our price range. Staring out the window, memories flood in and render me motionless. I see myself jumping out our window—the flames raging behind me. And then I remember another window I had jumped out of, a long, long time ago. The firefly escaping the jar . . .

IT WAS THE SUMMER OF 1978, the same summer that Kyle was shot. I was fourteen. My mother told me she was going on a business trip for a few days and sent Kyle off to stay with a friend. I was home alone that weekend when I witnessed our neighbor Don put a gun to his head and pull the trigger. My friends dragged his lifeless body onto the lawn, where he bled to death as his girlfriend ran in frantic circles, screaming. I fell to my knees and said the Lord's Prayer over and over because I didn't know what else to do. Police, paramedics, media trucks swarmed our little street, the neighbors huddled together gossiping. He always was a troubled guy, they said.

That night, I was alone in the house, reeling from the shock of what I had witnessed. The day had been stifling hot, oppressive, so thick you could barely move your legs through it, like walking in quicksand. The night brought no relief. The air was still and swampy. I couldn't shake the sound of Don's girlfriend's primal, wounded-animal screams. It replayed over and over in my head. I picked up the phone and tried to track down my mother, but in doing so, I found out there was no business trip. I called her friends. No one knew where she was.

Later that night my mother surfaced, offering no explanation of where she was, never asking how I'd fared while she was gone, or whether, perhaps, I had just watched a guy blow his brains out. She retreated to her room and shut the door. For hours I lay in the dark, eyes wide open, a nest of angry hornets buzzing in my solar plexus louder, louder, until I thought I would lose my mind. I threw the covers off and jumped out my bedroom window. I ran through the pitch black of night until my lungs ached, and then I ran some more. I ended up in a park, where I eventually collapsed with exhaustion.

I remember waking, squinting in the hazy light of dawn. A man in a business suit bent over me, nudging my shoulder, "Miss? Miss, are you okay?"

I bolted up, grass clippings in my matted hair. Where am I?

"Oh, thank God!" he exhaled, clapping his hand over his mouth. "I was driving to work, saw you lying there . . . I pulled over. I thought you were . . ."

"I'm okay. I just fell asleep." I stood up straight, brushed the grass from my clothes, did my best to smooth my hair. "Sorry I scared you."

I turned to walk away, my heart heavy with shame when I looked over my shoulder and saw the look of concern in the man's eyes. "Do you want me to call someone?" he asked.

"No," I said.

I spent that day walking along the wash that snaked through the San Fernando Valley, hiding from truant officers under concrete freeway overpasses where the bums and junkies slept on stained mattresses, because even that felt safer than living in a house with a mother who didn't care about me.

STARING AT MY MOTHER'S kitchen curtains, I am brought back into the present moment by the overwhelming cabbage rose print, the swags with pink-and-white seersucker valances, the ones that match the sofa, that match the throw pillows, that match the fucking dishes and the coffee cup I'm holding, for Christ's sake. I hate these fucking roses. They are a lie!

I turn my attention back to the real estate section. No point thinking about that nonsense now. It's over. I am not that lost girl anymore.

Am I?

I keep searching through listings of low-priced rental homes in the San Fernando Valley, circling every possibility, until one grabs my attention. Even reading the ad for it in the newspaper, I feel tingly. I call Troy, who's at a recording session. "I think I found us a home. I have a feeling . . ." Since the fire, Troy has deep respect for my "hunches" and "feelings." We make an appointment to see it the next day.

❦ ❦ ❦

IT IS COLD, grey, and rainy, as it has been for months, when we drive up the steep winding road not far from where our last home burned down. This one, however, is close to a fire station. There at the top of the hill, like a Thomas Kinkade painting, is a little cottage with wood shingles and a soft warm light glowing in the picture window. Stepping out of the car, I breathe in the hickory smoke that billows from the chimney—not the toxic-fire smell, but the good aroma of hearth, of home. The house sits on a hill above the street, with a lush green lawn and pink ice plant billowing over the front slope. Flowering baskets hang along the front porch.

Mark and his very pregnant wife, Deanna, greet us at the door. "Welcome, welcome, please come in!" It is gorgeous inside, just as I knew it would be. The scent of cookies baking wafts through the house. Deanna takes our coats and brings us hot cider, as Mark shows us around. This is obviously a carefully constructed plan to sell us on the place, and it's working. Every detail, from the plush, deep-rose carpet to the shell pedestal sinks to the Victorian print custom draperies (which they say they will leave for us) are as though I custom ordered them myself. I want to fall into the overstuffed shabby-chic sofas with Deanna's two schnauzers, eat those fresh-baked cookies, and fall asleep for a week. What is it I'm feeling? Safe. I feel safe in this house.

The backyard has an English garden—the kind I've always dreamed of. I close my eyes, breathe in the scent of wet earth, lavender, and pine. I can imagine myself living here. The back door off the master bedroom opens to the backyard where a redwood twelve-seat Jacuzzi sits surrounded by towering pine trees. Citrus trees dot the hillside, and I scope out a perfect place to hang a hammock for Troy. I see us here in spring, sitting on the terracotta patio, watching our kids play tag on the lawn. Troy makes eye contact with me. He smiles and nods. Yes, this is it. This is the place where we can heal, and even be happy again.

We sit at the kitchen table with Mark and Deanna as they explain the paperwork. With their new baby coming, they're anxious to move to Florida, where they have family. Deanna is already seven months pregnant. They don't have time to sell the house, so they offer us a lease option, which means that with a small down payment, and a little extra every month, we're paying into the eventual purchase of the home. It's barely 1,000 square feet, but it's beautiful, it will be ours, and we'll never be homeless again. Troy and I know we've found our home. We call it the "Happy House."

I CAN'T WAIT TO show Sarah and Scott the Happy House. Troy and I respect their opinions so much. Sarah and Scott are so practical and seem to have it all together, while Troy and I, creative types, have always lived on a wing and a prayer. Sarah and Scott bought their home in their early twenties, launched a successful kids clothing business, drive two new cars, and take their kids on vacation every year. We, on the other hand, scramble every month to meet our financial obligations, but always make it somehow. But this is a new beginning.

Sarah and Scott have been my mentors in the kids clothing business, showing me the ropes, sharing all their contacts. They hired a nanny to watch Lauren and Kayla and clean the house while they worked, and had convinced me to do the same, even though I was sure we couldn't afford it. They said it would pay for itself, as I'd get more work done, instead of carrying Taylor around on my hip while I was on calls with buyers in New York. As usual, they were right. I was able to really focus on my work, and the business began to take off. They told me I should enroll Cissy in the same private school that Lauren attends, which I did, and she is thriving there. It just seems Sarah and Scott's way of doing things is always the smart way.

We make arrangements for them to see the Happy House the following week. I am giddy with new hope, anxious to start a new life. Most of all, I'm excited about the prospect of owning our own home, and though it sounds silly I kind of hope they'll be proud of us.

Troy and I meet them on the front porch, waving and smiling. Scott strides toward us in his freshly pressed, creased jeans, shirt tucked in, not a hair out of place. Unsmiling. Sarah follows behind him, her strawberry-blond curls pressed straight into a bob, a concerned look in her blue eyes, peering over the top of her glasses. They follow us through the rooms of the house as I point out the pedestal sinks, the English garden, the custom draperies with the fleur-de-lis print that I just know will floor them (being in the clothing biz, we're all fabric junkies). They nod their heads and walk through each room silently. I can't take the silence any longer. Flustered, I turn to them, "Oh come on, guys! I thought you would love this place!"

"You're rushing in to this," Scott says sternly. Sarah stands behind him, arms crossed, furrowed brow.

"Look, you don't know what it's like. The four of us have been living in a bedroom together for almost three months, on top of each other constantly. I just can't live at my mother's anymore."

"You should get a one-bedroom apartment and keep saving," he says.

Troy interjects, "The kids need a home, and a yard to play in. Eventually they'll want a dog again."

I add, "This place just feels right to us. I mean, look at it! Look at that garden. This is a place we can heal."

Scott scoffs at us. "It's a bad decision."

I feel the hairs rising on my neck, heat flushing my face.

He continues, "We helped you raise this money. We didn't do it so you could waste it on a bad decision like this."

I cross my arms and take a step back, "I didn't realize the money came with conditions."

He shakes his head and stiffens. "If you do this, you'll never make it," he says.

That's about the worst thing you could ever say to me. My jaw clenches.

"Watch me," I say.

AFTER THAT DAY, Scott changes. The hand of support is quickly withdrawn. I can barely get a return phone call. Neither of us yelled or attacked, it is nothing more than a simple clash of wills. Scott isn't used to being challenged or disagreed with. I bristle at the thought of anyone trying to make decisions for me. How dare he infer that he knows better than us, when it comes to our own family? Yes, it is a leap of faith, but isn't everything? We're working our way back to normal. We have money in savings. Troy is working. I'm singing at corporate gigs with him on weekends. Deirdre and I shipped most of our spring orders. We'll pay off our business debts with the money that's surely arrived at Deirdre's house by now, and after the kids are settled, I'll get a part-time job. Everything is going to be fine. It hurts that Sarah and Scott don't believe in us. But it doesn't matter. Since the fire, I've learned to trust my own intuition. I know deep in my soul this is the right place, and the right time. And so does Troy. We sign the paperwork, and start packing.

January 24, 1995

Tonight we took the kids to see Little Women, *just the four of us. It was a beautiful version. Cissy was so taken with it, she came home dancing and singing. Then I presented her with a new copy of* Little Women, *to replace the book I had handed down to her from my childhood, the one that was destroyed in the fire. She cried when I gave it to her. We started reading it again, from the beginning.*

We are just days away from moving into our new home. I am so antsy to get in there and make it ours, and then to get myself set up to start creating. Although I am afraid of the unstable uncertain future, I am also excited to set out onto a new path.

Maybe I was waiting for this experience to alter my life, my priorities, my way of thinking. Suddenly I am coming across articles and books about women who have followed their callings (including Louisa May Alcott who wrote Little Women*). I'm discovering how intentional life is. The signs, signals, clues are all there if you pay attention. Here is a Johann Goethe quote I just read, "Whatever you can do, or dream you can, begin it."*

And so I begin.

I CRANK THE VOLUME on our donated boom box, blasting my favorite Shawn Colvin album as we unpack the last boxes. I set new photos on the mantel in our home. We moved into the Happy House on February 1, and got everything in order quickly to have this housewarming party. In just a few hours, these rooms will be filled with family, friends, music, children, and love. Surely that will chase away the evil spirits that defeated us. This is a new day, a new life. Our new life. New memories are about to be made in our home.

Home. I love that word.

It seems impossible but we have everything we need, and almost all of it is donated. All we bought was a bunk bed and mattresses for the kids, since they're sharing a room. The house came with a washer and dryer, and it seemed everyone we knew had something "extra" just sitting in their garage: refrigerator, microwave, TV, bedframe, Aunt Edna's sofa. They were glad to let go of old stuff, and we were grateful to receive.

We rented a truck and drove all over town picking up donations. One family who read about us in the newspaper had just lost their elderly mother. They took what was important to them, and said we could walk through the house and take anything that was left. At the risk of sounding morbid, I loved walking through that house. I felt a connection to this woman. She had been an artist, and left behind art supplies, art books, beautiful antique chairs and end tables. I said a silent prayer, letting her know I would care for and cherish these possessions of hers.

You'd think with all these random donations that our house would look like a terrible mishmash, but actually, it works. Our last home was filled with modern furniture we had acquired in the eighties. Our home now reflects a warm, Victorian, shabby-chic feel that matches the style of the house.

I smile, a tingly feeling overtaking me as I stand in the center of the light-filled living room. Through the picture window, I watch my husband raking leaves on the front lawn. Our lawn. The owner, Deanna, left a bottle of champagne and note that read: *Welcome to your new home.* I tap on the window, holding up the chilled champagne.

Troy walks through the front door smiling. "Don't mind if I do."

"Let's toast to our new beginning, just you and me, before everyone gets here. You know . . . kinda like christening a ship."

"I like your thinking." He pops the cork while I hold up two champagne flutes.

Shawn Colvin softly sings in the background, "There will always be something to believe in," as we clink our glasses together.

"To our new beginning," I say.

Troy wraps his arms around me and we sway to the music. I lay my head on his shoulder, closing my eyes.

"Everything's going to be okay now," he says.

"I'm starting to believe you."

"Look at the evidence," he says, "you're standing in your home."

I put my hand on his heart, "This is my home."

TROY LEANS BACK IN his chair and puts his feet up as we sit in our English garden, sharing a bottle of wine. This is our new nightly ritual. I love the way the light falls in our new yard at this time of day. He is quiet, lost in thought. As am I. Our new phone line is beginning to ring with calls from bill collectors: the hospital, the ambulance company, my credit cards. Chaos swirls around us like a daily dust cloud as we work to get ourselves back on solid ground. But at dusk each day, we surrender, share a glass of wine, and talk about our day. Or not. Some days it's too much.

After settling into the Happy House, Troy and I have sunk into the worst depression of our lives. Here we are with our bright new beginning, but I'm still up vomiting at night, my body shaking uncontrollably every time I hear a siren. I pace the house in the middle of the night, checking the walls, checking electrical outlets, checking the kids breathing, and then wander around all day like a sleep-deprived zombie. Troy is feeling inadequate and depressed because he can't fix me, can't fix life, can't get enough work to cover the slew of medical bills. I guess this is the time Frank from the Red Cross warned us about. He said that after all the well-wishers had gone home and the excitement of the tragedy was over, the loss and trauma would begin to hit us.

I try not to burden Troy with my worries. I know he's got enough of his own, so often at dusk, we don't talk about the hard things. We talk about the easy things.

"Cissy said she'd like to have a sleepover for her birthday," I say.

"Great. Sounds doable," he says, adding, "I think we could hang a hammock on that hillside, right between those two pines up there."

"Perfect," I say, but what I don't say is what's really rattling around in my head. I feel betrayed by God. Up until now, I had a deep faith. Troy and I shared a general philosophy that life was what you made it—and always, always, the Golden Rule applied. I guess you could have called us optimists. We prayed. We believed in love and the goodness of people. But now, I am filled with doubt. Why did this happen? Why us?

Fear begins to occupy the space where my faith once resided. I no longer live under the illusion that tragedies happen to *other people*. Anything can happen to us, at any time, and I don't know how to live with that. I lie awake at night, wondering if there really is a God? If there is, why would He do this to us? If not, what is the purpose of life? Who will watch over my children? Is God a fable or a myth, like the Easter Bunny? If there is no God, and everything in the world is some accident of DNA, then I'm really not supposed to be here. After all, I too was an accident, a terrible mistake two wayward teenagers made. Maybe He is the God I heard preachers rail about when I was a child—trying to wipe me out, as I was a bastard, an error—not conceived in marriage, nor love. God is a jealous God, the preacher said. God is a vengeful God. If that's true, that's not the God I want as my "Father." Hell, I wouldn't even have a beer with that God. Maybe there is more truth in the teachings of Paramahansa Yogananda, who said that we are all one, that God is in each and every one of us and in every tree and bird and drop of rain. But if that's true, someone please explain Hitler to me.

Troy refills my wine glass.

"Thanks, honey," I smile at him.

"Pretty sunset tonight," he says, nodding to the hillside.

"Yeah."

Maybe it's like the Hindus say, that I'm now living out karma for something bad I did in a former life. But that doesn't feel true to me. Or maybe there is no God, only chaos, luck of the draw. How do I live with that? I am lost, untethered, a cork bobbing in the middle of the ocean. And faith is only one of the things I worry about in the middle of the night.

I don't know who I am anymore. Before the fire, I was a clothing designer. I was an entrepreneur. I was sparkly and fun —the life of the party. I was a person of deep faith and clarity who friends relied on for advice. I was the girl Troy fell in love with. Now, I am none of those things. So who am I? And am I still lovable?

Troy shifts forward in his chair, squinting into the distance. "There it goes, just about to disappear over the mountain," he says, "5, 4, 3, 2 . . . ."

"It's getting dark," I say, "I need to start dinner."

"Yep."

I gather up the glasses and wine bottle.

I'm worried about my friendships. The housewarming

party was a great day. Warm, hopeful, and yet . . . though Deirdre came, things feel tense between us since we talked about dissolving the partnership. Scott and Sarah came, but I felt an emotional distance that made me uneasy. Am I imagining this? The last few months have been an emotional ride for everyone. Surely things will come back into balance now that the storm is behind us. We just need a little time. And mostly we need a little faith, which none of us have in large measure.

Troy opens the patio door for me, and gives me a peck on the cheek.

"That was nice, watching that beautiful sunset with you," he says.

Did the sun set? I didn't even notice.

MEANING IN THE RUBBISH HEAP

❦ ❦ ❦

Driving Cissy and Taylor to school in the morning, I pass home after home with piles of rubbish out front —the aftermath of the earthquake last year. Homeowners are finally coming into insurance and FEMA money, and construction is booming. Mountains of discarded wood and cement chunks line the curbs as houses are gutted, foundations rebuilt. I slow my car and stare at these piles, marveling at the remnants of someone else's life. The cornflower-blue tiles that someone had once painstakingly selected, doors that had been slammed shut in anger and reopened with love, the wood frame from a family home, all of it tossed into the trash.

I pull over and sit motionless behind the steering wheel, staring into the rubble. This is a reflection of my own gutted life. All of this garbage will be hauled away to the dump soon and I can't bear it.

I slink out of my car and dig through the piles. Hundreds of roof shingles lie scattered about the heap. I pick one up and study it with the concentration of an archeologist. In this piece of trash there is a story. Like the inner rings of a mighty sequoia, I see years passed, the damage of raging hot summers, the pounding of countless storms. I grab as many as I can carry. I know I look crazy but I don't care. I salvage old windows and throw them in my backseat. I load stacks of tiles, even broken ones, into my trunk. I pay no attention to the Gladys Kravitz peering through her curtains, thinking I'm a crazy bag lady. Maybe I am.

At home I unload my finds in the carport and drag out boxes of donated art supplies from the deceased woman's home. I feel her spirit with me. (Yes, maybe I am a crazy bag lady.) Eying my materials, I pace until I become inspired. I put on a ratty old T-shirt, throw my hair up in a ponytail, and get to work. I paint snowy scenes on the roof shingles and attach old rope for hanging. I paint glass bottles, adorning the tops with crystals or little feathered birds. I decoupage the discarded kitchen tiles with angels and messages of hope, then attach black felt to the bottom, turning them into sets of coasters. I am beyond inspired—I am compelled. Obsessed, maybe. I have found the power to transform something. I have no control over the devastation in my life, but I can turn this trash into something of value, and maybe on a deeper level, that's what I hope for myself. I, too, was a throw away—the daughter of a convict who wasn't supposed to be born. God tried to burn me down and get rid of me. But maybe I can be transformed. Maybe this rubbish heap of a life is salvageable.

THE NEXT DAY I cut up the boxes we used for moving, and cover the cardboard pieces with fabric scraps. These become the covers of books I will make. I write each book by hand in calligraphy, conveying messages of hope. The covers are adorned with gems and pearls, and tied with satin ribbon salvaged from the cutting room floor of friends' clothing warehouses.

Eventually I have a cache of trash art. Months later, after I over-gift my friends and family and have nowhere to store my obsessions, I take them to a local boutique called Our Favorite Things. The owner, Patty, loves my creations and places a sizable order on the spot. I put my sunglasses on to hide the fact that my eyes have welled up. I feel so worthless and broken down, and yet here she is, reacting as though things I make actually have value. Within a week Patty has sold out of my pieces and reorders. She begins to call with special orders. June is coming. She asks if I can create handmade inspirational books for graduates, brides, and for Mother's Day. And what about wish boxes for bridesmaids and birthday girls? I'm on it. I take a ridiculous amount of time on every piece, as I want each to be unique and "One of a Kind," which is what I name my new gift line. But what else do I have if not time? From then on, every day while my kids are at school, their crazy mom is out rummaging through the rubbish heaps.

I don't make a lot of money on this venture—it's grocery money for the month, at best. But I work like a maniac. I work like my life depends on it, determined to turn out new pieces every day. It's important to make money, but more important to make the art—to salvage broken pieces of a life that has been thrown away, redeeming myself in every piece I create.

IT'S A WARM SUMMER night as Cissy and I stand at the front door of my weekly art class. I knock on the door, "Hello? Phyllis?"

"Let yourself in," Phyllis shouts from the art room.

Phyllis was an art teacher in public school, but now at seventy, she's retired and teaching private classes in her home. After I left home at eighteen years old, I began spending every

Monday night painting with her. Art gave me a place to be when I didn't know where I was going. I want Cissy to have this now.

In Phyllis's art studio, florescent lights buzz overhead and the sound of a solo saxophone floats in the background. This room was originally a backyard patio, but her husband Bernie had it enclosed to create space for her art. The windows look out onto a swimming pool and a hillside of ivy. The walls and carpet reek of turpentine, oil paints, and cigarettes, a combination I've learned to love. Phyllis is leaning over the shoulder of another student, a cigarette in one hand, paintbrush in the other. "Use lighter brushstrokes—we're painting grass, not tree trunks!"

Cissy stands beside me, quiet and wide-eyed, not her usual outgoing self. I think she senses the serious *coming of age* ceremony this is. At nine years old, she will now sit with us each Monday night, the only child in a group of grown women who paint, smoke, and talk about real life.

"Hello!" I announce our arrival cheerfully, "I've brought your new student."

Phyllis turns, slightly stooped as she has come to be these days. "Ah! Sit here, young lady." She points to an empty chair in front of an easel. Cissy obediently swoops in to occupy her appointed space, and opens her tackle box full of paintbrushes.

Phyllis is tall and formidable, a tough broad. There's no doubt in your mind who the boss is when Phyllis walks in the room. But she carries no pretense. She'll be the first to tell you she suffered a nervous breakdown in her thirties. And although she can be hard-edged, she'll lavish you with hugs and kisses when you experience a win in life. I tease her that she's like a candy bar—crunchy on the outside, a little nutty, with a soft, mushy center.

Through Phyllis I've learned that there are undertones and overtones in painting, and everything in life, including our relationships. She and I have had a long and complicated, multihued friendship. She's not easy, by any means. She is intense, demanding, short-tempered, and, at times, immature. She is also talented, creative, compassionate, deeply loving, interesting, a great listener, and my biggest cheerleader. She is a die-hard democrat, and expects me to be involved in my community and take a stand for what I believe in. We've butted heads, and had periods of time that we didn't talk, but I always come back. She is family to me, and I to her.

I lamented to Philly, as I called her, over all my paintings that had been lost in the flames. People said I could just paint them again, but I couldn't. "Art is an expression of who you are at that time," I complained. "It can never be replicated because the artist is always evolving."

"Wrong," Phyllis said in her gruff manner. "Art can never be lost because it is in you."

That deeply imprinted on me. Life can take a lot from you, but it can never take your ability to dream, imagine, and create. My art still lives in me, as does the memory of my animals, and the songs I recorded.

Phyllis pulls up a chair alongside Cissy. "Now. Have you ever painted before?" She takes a drag off her cigarette.

"Not really. Only watercolors and stuff," Cissy shrugs.

Phyllis cuts her off, "You see the sky out there?"

"Yes," she nods. "Those are cirrus clouds, but actually, cumulous are my favorite," she replies in her chatty, precocious manner. I smile to myself. *That's my girl.*

This catches Phyllis off guard for a split second. "No, I'm not talking about the clouds. What *color* is the sky?"

"Ummm . . . sky blue?"

"Wrong!" Phyllis says triumphantly, and I smirk because I know Cissy is about to get the same speech I'd gotten thirteen years earlier. "Learning to paint is learning to see," Phyllis says, as she has said to every new student. "A sky is not blue. It is indigo and violet with Naples yellow undertones. Now look there," she points out the window, "that cloud is Payne's grey with Mattison pink edges, and a little cerulean blue breaking through in places."

Cissy nods her head enthusiastically.

"Soon you'll begin to see the world through different eyes."

Now is a good time for Cissy to see the world through different eyes. For months, our world has been dark and grey, but it's time for us to paint a new picture for ourselves, to train our eyes to see the highlight behind the cloud that reassures us the sun is still there. I learned this lesson from Phyllis when I was young, and am still learning it.

Phyllis demonstrates the elements of painting to Cissy while a sax rendition of "Starlight Melody" wafts in the background. Phyllis's husband Bernie always practices his sax while we paint. "Starlight Melody" is his personal favorite—we hear it most every Monday. When it's your birthday, you get a personal serenade while you blow out the candles. I remember one night when the girls and I arrived and it was quiet in the house.

"Where's Bernie?" I asked.

"Oh, he's probably in the back room polishing his horn. Or maybe fiddling with his flute." The other girls and I tried to suppress our giggles at the sexual double entendre, which Phyllis seemed oblivious to. Or was she? You never know with Phyllis.

Bernie was the lead sax player in the Ricky Ricardo band. Cissy and I love finding him in old *I Love Lucy* episodes, marching across the Alps in an oom-pah-pah band, dressed in drag, or of course up front playing alongside Ricky at the Tropicana Nightclub. *I Love Lucy* is Cissy's favorite show, so Bernie is a rock star to her.

What Phyllis has created in her home is more than an art class. It is a community of women, tightly bound together, and now my daughter has been accepted into the clan. While we sit those three hours painting each week, stories pour out of us. We share our deepest fears, our joy, our worries. We comfort one another, commiserate, and advise. I am grateful for Cissy to be part of this village of women. Troy and I want nothing more than to paint a brighter picture for Cissy and Taylor. We want them to see that darkness is temporary. Although our vision is obscured by pervasive sadness and loss, we are all *learning to see,* or trying to at least.

THE MEMORY OF RAIN

❦ ❦ ❦

April 27, 1995

A ray of sun cut through the dark, forboding cloud
If only for a moment
it warmed my soul

Light spilled down
Tumbling over the corpses of my dreams
Giving them cause to rise and sway
But this was not my time to dance

I resolved myself to fate
As thick blankets of grey
Came rolling back
And tucked me in

I SIT WITH MY children at our donated kitchen table, a blond-wood butcher block from my friend Keri. Keri can always make me laugh. I miss laughing. I miss Keri. I wish she weren't so far away in Nevada. I wish everyone weren't so far away. So strange how all my close friends—Keri, Tara, Diane, and Kelly—moved away right before this awful time in my life. Who could have known? Outside, the rain continues to pound, as it has for days. Cissy concentrates on her homework and Taylor is drawing strange little monsters, as he always does. Thankfully, he's drawing less pictures of houses on fire.

It is spring, and here we are in this new home with a Jacuzzi and a beautiful yard and we've been stuck inside as it rains for months on end. It pours from the sky and inside my head. Ironic that it didn't rain that cold night in November as our house succumbed to the inferno and our animals lay trapped inside gasping for their last breath.

The sun hasn't shone in so long that I can't conjure the feeling of its rays against my skin. We are cold down to our bones, and we are sad. A pretense of cheeriness is all I have, and my children try to thrive and grow under the circumstances.

Spring has always been my favorite time of year. A time of new beginnings. A hopeful crocus pokes its head above the snow. Fields of grass appear overnight saying, *Look at me—I begin again! I am alive!* As flowers blossom and new life unfurls all around me, I pray that hearts will begin to thaw, but Scott and Sarah distance themselves from us, the chasm growing wider by the day. I am drowning in despair and faithlessness. I crave their steady and calm energy, but my phone does not ring.

After not hearing from them for a while, I write Sarah a letter, telling her that I love them both so much, and though there is some tension in the friendship, I know we will get through it. I write a poem for Sarah, "The Strawberry Girl," because she has that wide smile and those strawberry-blond curls, and because I first met her at a roadside strawberry stand. I send it along with another letter apologizing for the fact that Troy and I have been depressed and not much fun to hang around with. I miss them. My kids miss their kids. We are so alone in this little cottage, under a deluge of rain.

Cissy swipes a marker out of Taylor's hand, "You can't use those! They're my markers for school!" she barks at him.

"Hey! Give it back!" Taylor whines.

I intervene, "What's the big deal? Just let him use the marker for Christ's sakes."

"But Mom! He'll ruin it!"

"He won't ruin it."

"Yes he will. He always leaves the caps off and then I . . ."

I jump up from the table, my chair screeching and then falling over, "Oh for the LOVE of GOD—WHO CARES?" I shout, leaving both of them silent and stunned.

I am instantly remorseful. I've been short-tempered for days now, and that isn't fair to them. It's just that I haven't slept in so damn long. I pace the house for hours like the night watchman, my anxiety never letting me rest. I lie awake thinking about our dogs and cats—trying to remember how their fur felt the last time they slept with me in my bed. I wonder if I made the right decision in letting my business go. I pray that if I dare fall asleep, God will protect my children. But I don't trust God.

I am more tired than I've ever been in my life. Tired of the heartache, the loss, the donations, and the endless thanking of everyone. Tired of my weakness and vulnerability. Tired of the cold and damp and grey. I am tired of bill collectors, abandonment by my friends, and pretending to be strong in the face of it all. I am thirty-one years old and my body aches with how tired and used up I am.

I obsess constantly over the one question that applies to everything but will never be answered. Why? Why is this our life now? We worked hard. We had our proverbial ducks lined up in a row. We weren't drunk and smoking in bed when our house burned down. We were sleeping while the electrical wiring went on a rampage of its own making. Even if I had filled out those damned papers, there is no real insurance policy for the loss that affects us now.

We lived a neat and orderly life. We followed the rules. We volunteered in our community, paid our taxes, we even recycled for fuck sake. And for what? Living by the rules didn't save me from having to toss my four-year-old son from a window. Living by the rules didn't save our animals, or our careers. My heart begins to pound wildly. This is a different feeling, something I'm not used to. For the first time, instead of sadness, I feel anger. Anger!

The kids are restless. They bicker and whine, their energy becoming too big for the tiny house. I get up abruptly and pace the room like a caged tiger. I've had enough. We've all had enough. My heart is screaming: *Fuck the rules! Fuck this rain! We will defy you!*

"You guys wanna go outside and play?"

"What?" Cissy squints, dropping her pencil.

"Yeah!" Taylor jumps up and down.

"Go for it." I storm through the living room and swing open the front door. A gust of cold air blows through the house. The sound of rain pounding cement is almost deafening.

Cissy hesitates at the table, "But . . . we'll ruin our school clothes, and our shoes."

"Who cares. We're not following rules today. We're doing what we want." I declare, my breath still hanging in the frosty air.

Cissy looks at me with worry. I can almost see the thought bubble above her head, *Has Mommy gone nuts?*

"Do you guys want to go out there and jump in puddles and splash in that mud? Well?"

Cissy and Taylor look at each other wide-eyed. "YES!" they shout in unison, jumping up from the table.

"Go!"

They run for the door, giggling. I know this freaks them out to see me acting like this. I'm pretty structured, strict with them about homework, bedtimes, sugar intake. But now my heart cheers as they tear outside in their good clothes and shoes, splashing in mud, drenching themselves from head to toe. I stand in the doorway watching them dance in that rain. They slosh and slide across muddy patches in the lawn. They stomp in every puddle with both feet, making sure not to miss a single one. They are drenched and filthy and I don't care. Their joy replaces the sun that's been missing for so long. I now know, better than anyone, spirit must be preserved at all costs, because at this point it's all we've got. I venture out on the front porch, where sheets of water pour down from the overhang. The mossy smell of earth and new life fills my senses, my own spirit renewed by the sight of my children laughing and dancing in the rain. *Fly, little ones. Defy, little ones. Let your spirits shine blindingly bright.* Taylor slips and falls on his butt and I laugh, wiping tears from my cheeks, astounded by the perfection of this moment. My children are my hope. They illustrate for me that no matter what comes, joy is always possible. I step out onto the front lawn, turn my face toward the sky and let the rain soak me.

AFTER DROPPING THE KIDS at school, I grab my journal and a cup of coffee, nestling into the armchair in front of our picture window. Troy is at a recording session, and I have the house to myself this morning—a perfect time to write. I put my pen to paper, but nothing comes. Nothing but pestering thoughts. The only thing I can be sure of right now is the steady rain that continues to fall outside.

Something is stirred up inside me, in my circle of friends. I feel everyone pulling away, even as I'm sitting here. If it were the mere fact that everyone was just busy with their own routines and lives, I'd be fine with that. But that's not the way it feels.

Last night, Cissy dragged all our pillows and blankets to the living room where the four of us cozied up to watch the *Star Wars* trilogy. Troy had never seen them before, and I'm determined to make a *Star Wars* geek out of him, like Taylor and me. But since facing death, I now walk through my life wide-awake, hyperalert, hypersensitive. Everything is a revelation. Even *Star Wars,* which has always been my fun escape *from* reality, now *mirrors* my reality. Like Luke Sky-walker, I, too, faced my nemesis in a dark cave. I, too, sense a disturbance in the force. Something is up, something negative, but nobody's telling the truth about it.

Steam rises from my coffee cup, as I remember an odd encounter I had with Sarah a few weeks before the fire. I'd just stopped by her house to pick up some paperwork for the New York show. While there, we caught up for a moment, but she seemed edgy. Somehow, every time we were together, our husbands, kids, Deirdre, and other friends were there too. It was kind of nice to talk to Sarah alone for a minute. But she was distracted, bustling about the kitchen. I felt I was intruding.

"I'm sorry, did I stop by at a bad time?"

"No, no . . . just got a few calls to make and you know, pick up the girls and . . . gotta run to the market," she said, in constant motion, her back to me.

"Well, I'll get out of your way, love." I picked up my keys and purse, walked over to give her a hug good-bye. She was stiff. I moved back.

"Let's have lunch this week," I suggested, as I started to walk toward the door.

She went back to her bustling, "I'll check with Scott's schedule. He's got a busy week."

I stopped, turning around, "No, I mean, just us girls."

"I'll have to check with Scott," she repeated.

"Why? Can't you and I just go to lunch?"

She stopped what she was doing and stepped behind one of her kitchen chairs, clutching the outer rungs like a lion tamer. "I don't know . . . I'll have to see." Her knuckles were white from gripping the chair so hard, as it nudged slightly toward me.

Apparently, I was the lion.

"WAKE UP, WAKE UP! It's Easter!" The kids jump into our bed at the first sliver of light, like every holiday. Their faith in childhood magic never waivers. I nestle into Troy's shoulder. He kisses my head, our feet intertwined under the covers.

"Happy Easter, my little Easter chick," he says, groggy.

"Yes. *Happy*. I've already made my mind up that this day is going to be happy." Nothing will pierce our bubble. No bill collectors, no nightmares, no sirens. Today is ours.

"You know, it would be just as happy two hours from now," he gripes, rubbing his eyes. "What is it . . . like . . . zero dark thirty?"

"Well, one day they'll be teenagers and we won't be able to get them up. Imagine that."

"Imagine it? It's what I live for!"

Troy gets up to start the coffee while I lay out the kids' Easter outfits. My Mom and Eric soon arrive to have breakfast and watch the kids gather their eggs. Eric walks in bearing a honey-baked ham, and Mom holds two beautifully wrapped Easter baskets from See's Candies. My mother wears heels, an Ann Taylor blouse, and slacks. I am wearing ill-fitting hand-me-downs that hang even looser with all the weight I've lost from stress. As Cissy and Taylor swarm around them, chat-tering and clamoring for their attention, I sneak out back to survey the yard, making sure no raccoons or squirrels got to the eggs we hid so carefully at midnight. A light rain has fallen. The grey clouds still hang above us, but all that rain has made our yard beautiful and lush. Even the rain serves a purpose, I remind myself. This time in our lives is a season. It will pass.

This year, we can't afford the toys or See's Candies. Every dime we eke out goes to hospital bills, my business loans, and to pay the seamstresses who worked for me, the ones who made the clothing that burned up in the fire. In lieu of store-bought Easter baskets, I gathered twigs and assembled tiny chairs and benches held together with glue. I fashioned tables three inches high. I made twig fairy wands wrapped in ribbon and coated them in glitter. I assembled a fairy village in our garden under a fern, then sprinkled glitter over it, and pressed tiny footprints into the dirt, as though fairies had just scattered.

Troy follows the kids with the video camera while they make their way through the foliage. Cissy leads, Taylor trails behind. Trudging through the soggy soil, her white patent leather Mary Janes are coated in mud, and she starts to fuss about it, but I just wave it off. I don't worry about things like that anymore. Cissy pushes aside the fern's branches and gasps,

"Mommy! It's a tiny little table and chairs and . . . look!"

Taylor anxiously peers over her shoulder. He picks up one of the fairy wands to examine it.

"Be careful," Cissy warns, "it's very delicate!"

He looks it over, shrugs, puts it down.

"Look! Footprints! Mommy there's footprints!" Cissy says excitedly, her cheeks rosy, eyes brimming with tears as they always do when she's happy or excited. It's as if the beauty of the world is too much for her little self to hold.

Taylor inspects the miniature scene, quiet and thoughtful.

Cissy throws her arms around me, "Oh Mommy, this is the best Easter ever!" I hold her tight, grateful that in spite of the sadness I'm carrying, I can still bring happiness to her. She looks up at me with a huge, bright smile, then runs off to find more eggs. And because life is messy and perfect moments are fleeting, she slips and falls in the mud. Her new lace dress and white shoes are covered and she starts to cry. My mom and I help her up. "Sweetheart, it's only a dress," I say. "We'll get you all cleaned up and you can change into something else."

"No! It's not only a dress, Mommy!" she wails, "I barely have anything! I lost all my nicest dresses in the stupid fire and now this one is ruined! Everything's ruined!" She gets herself worked up, and soon she's inconsolable.

I try to downplay the drama. "It's no big deal," I say. The more I downplay, the more hysterical she becomes, and I am at a loss. My mom steps in.

My mom—the woman who forgot me at after school pickup and left me sitting in a parking lot until nightfall.

My mom—the one who missed my high school graduation.

My mom—the one who sent me to live at her sister's when I was Cissy's age.

No, not my mom, I remind myself. Cissy's grammy.

When I had kids of my own, I saw this as a second chance for my mom—and I wanted her to get it right. I invited her into the room when both Cissy and Taylor were born, and she held them when they were only minutes old. She rose to the occasion, and has been a loving and devoted grandmother to both my kids. Unlike my childhood, she never misses an important moment in their lives. She is at every recital and birthday party. All holidays are spent with Grammy Sandra and Grampy Eric. Sleepovers and vacations, too. My children know a different woman than the one who raised me. Because of this, I let the past rest. Or so I thought. I chose not to dwell on it, but it still dwells in me.

My mother, Grammy, puts an arm around Cissy, "Honey, this will all come out in the wash. I promise. Let's get this dress off you and we'll soak it, and it will be as good as new." She walks Cissy inside.

Troy and Eric hang outside, talking about music and guitars. This is always the safe place to go when things get too deep, although I'm sure they don't think anything deep is going on, other than that a little girl slipped in the mud. But I get it now. I know what's happening with Cissy. It isn't about the dress. This is about the loss that she, at nine years old, hasn't even begun to process. It's the fear that anything she loves will be taken from her; a dress, her pets, her home, her best friend Lauren. I want to say to her, *Don't worry. You can trust in life. Everything will be okay.* But I can't, because I don't believe it. So I play up the Easter bunny and faeries and Santa Claus stuff and hope she doesn't ask any questions about God.

The rain begins to fall again. I usher Taylor inside and start setting up brunch in the kitchen. Taylor runs his matchbox cars along the windowsill, humming. I wonder what he's feeling. I remember how he didn't speak for three days after the fire. Was that the end of his processing? Taylor is such a quiet, easygoing kid, it's hard to know. He is funny, and intensely creative, but in a quieter way than most little boys his age. Our nickname for him is little Buddha, because he is mostly unflappable. Even during the fire, as I was screaming and dangling him out the window, he was quiet and calm, although it was most likely the carbon monoxide poisoning. Little Buddha announces his bedtime at night, "It's 8:30, I need to go to bed." He'll turn down treats I offer him, saying he's had enough sugar for the day, whereas Cissy at his age was mischievous and dramatic, would hide from us in department stores, and once ate candy until she puked. These are my kids —night and day. And I have to find a way to help each of them navigate this time in their own ways. My God, but where is the manual for this?

Cissy and my mom return to the kitchen table. Cissy is calmer now, wearing sweat pants and a sweatshirt, wiping her little nose with a tissue. I hug her, and kiss the top of her head, wishing I had the perfect words, but I don't. The six of us sit down for sausage and eggs and coffee cake, and as my family recovers from the moment, laughing and talking around the kitchen table, I feel the stirring of hope. Just then I feel warmth on my shoulder. I look behind me out the window, and see that the sun has come out. But I don't trust it.

I MEET DEIRDRE FOR lunch at Stanley's restaurant on a warm, spring day. I'm aiming for a peaceful resolution but we're coming to the table with entirely different agendas. Deirdre wants to rebuild the business. I want to pay off the debt and get out.

This was originally my business before Deirdre joined me in partnership, and all of the debt and credit are in my name. Deirdre's credit score was bad so we had to leave her off all the loan paperwork. Before the fire I took $20,000 in cash advances on my personal credit cards to finance this season. We owe another $20,000 to the government for the FEMA disaster loan we had to get after last year's earthquake, and $10,000 to Deirdre's father. Not to mention all the money we still owe our contractors.

All I can see is a mountain of debt looming over me. I must get out from under it before it crushes me, just like the dream I had before the fire.

The café is bustling and cheerful. Our opening chitchat is light and pleasant, and I'm feeling optimistic that we can talk this difficult situation through and resolve things.

After we place our orders, I begin, "Deirdre, I think you know, we're bailing water out of a sinking ship."

Her face is rigid, her eyes unblinking.

I continue, "I'm carrying all this debt on my personal credit cards right now, and obviously, I'm in no position to do that."

"What are you trying to say?" Her jaw clenches, unclenches, clenches, and unclenches.

"I'm saying that when the money comes in for this season, we have to pay off our debt."

She interrupts, "We can't afford to pay it back now—I'll have no money to produce the next season!"

"The next season? When a ship is sinking, you're not charting your next course."

She stares at me unblinking, her mouth a grim straight line. Her leg bounces anxiously under the table.

"Deirdre, be realistic. We are a small business hit with two natural disasters in one year. It's over."

"I knew you were going to say that!"

"Look at the situation here. We're drowning. We lost half our sales in January from the earthquake, and now the fire . . . we have no computers or customer files, and we lost all our patterns. How are we going to replace all of that with no money?"

"I'm not quitting!" she shouts. Diners at nearby tables look over their shoulders at us.

I feel my face and neck flush with heat, "You can't finance another season with money from my credit cards. I am broke, Deirdre! I have astronomical hospital bills to pay."

"Just because you're *quitting* doesn't mean I have to."

"You're not taking another step on my credit," I say, firmly.

The waitress swoops in with our salads, "Here ya go ladies," she says cheerfully, "enjoy!"

Deirdre stares down at her plate, her jaw still clenching, unclenching.

I flash on a conversation I had with her one night about what we valued most in life. I said love. Deirdre said money. People are undependable, she said, but money gives you security. Troy always says, *People tell you who they are.* Sometimes they tell you who they are, and you just don't want to believe it.

"Look," I soften my voice, "after the debt is paid, you can have everything. We settle up, then dissolve the partnership. If there is any profit at the end of this season, which I doubt there will be, you can buy me out. Even if there's no profit, you can have the business name, the designs, all the clients. It's yours, okay?"

"I can't pay off all the debt and still produce another season. You know that."

"The business is failing, Deirdre! And I'm not going down with a sinking ship."

"I knew it. You're ditching me! You're only thinking of yourself."

And here is where it goes off the rails. She flips out, accuses me of trying to destroy her, says I'm ripping her off. I'm walking a fine line anyway, and after thirteen years of dealing with her, I snap. "I am not carrying you anymore! I'm done!"

"Carrying me? What's that supposed to mean?"

In a disastrous move, I blurt out the baby and bridal shower incidents, my wedding day, all the times she's hijacked my big life moments, "and now you're the victim of my fire? Really?"

She stands up, "Well, it's nice to see how you really feel about me." She throws her linen napkin down and storms out, leaving the lunch bill for me to pay.

Driving home, I'm in a state of shock. How is there a question as to what needs to be done here? Even in the midst of grief I'm still clear-eyed about the business. But I remember times in the past when she bounced checks, and called her Dad screaming, telling him to fix it with the bank. It's foolish of me to expect her to behave differently now. I'm kicking myself for choosing her as a business partner. I have to face the fact that I have made an idiotic mistake.

Soon after our disastrous lunch, I begin getting calls and notices from my credit card company and FEMA. No payments have been made for months. I call the bank and check our business account balance. It is down to $50. Numerous checks have been written out to "CASH," as well as checks written out illegally by Deirdre's sister. She has wiped us out. I call in a fury. She won't pick up her phone.

An attorney friend advises me to close the business account immediately, which I do. If any other checks come in from our clients, Deirdre can't cash them without coming through me. A week later I get a certified letter from a lawyer friend of Deirdre's, threatening a lawsuit against me if I ever try to interfere in "Deirdre's" business again. Deirdre's business? I walk circles through the house, my hands on my head. Am I living in an alternate universe?

Deirdre and I booked $100,000 in sales that season, and I never saw a penny of it. I thought I had already been ruined by the fire, wiped off the map. But now, I am beyond ruined. I am in serious debt, with little recourse to do anything about it.

While our business funds were disappearing, I find out that Deirdre covertly started a new clothing line of her own, and took it to the New York trade show to sell. I contact attorneys, but they say there's really nothing I can do. The police won't get involved in a white-collar crime like this. Had she broken into my home and stolen a ten dollar watch, she could have been prosecuted. But I have no way to recover $100,000 that has gone missing. I could sue her, which would cost me thousands, but the attorneys advise me it would be a waste of my time. Deirdre has no credit and owns nothing. She rents a house with her dad's money, and leases a car, also with his money. Now she has financed a new business—presumably with my money and credit—and left me the debt.

And my crime? Stupidity. I trusted her. I trusted her because she was my friend for thirteen years. I trusted her to have my back while I was getting my life back together. I left the fox (the fearful girl who valued money above people) in charge of the henhouse. I was foolish. I was blind. And my family will now suffer for it.

And as if this weren't bad enough, Deirdre turns to Scott and Sarah playing the victim. Hollye abandoned me, she's trying to take the business from me, poor me. And Scott and

Sarah take her under their protective wing. Soon, the three of them are inseparable, and Troy and I are on the outside wondering why. I call Sarah but she says she doesn't want to be in the middle of the conflict between me and Deirdre, and abruptly hangs up.

It seems the fire inflamed all Deirdre's childhood fears, erasing the loving side of the girl who rescues strays on the side of the freeway, who loves her sisters, who loves Cissy and Taylor. I guess I thought she loved me, too. But fear is bigger than love in Deirdre's life, and that is a dangerous situation.

Unraveling

※ ※ ※

After the fire, these are the things people say to us. They say, "Lightning doesn't strike twice." But when Troy and I were in the Social Security waiting room bandaged and on crutches, a woman sitting next to us said her house had burned down, too. Twice. So there went that theory.

They say that nothing bad will happen to us again because, "What are the odds?" But what were the odds of my seven-year-old brother being shot in the head? What were the odds of our house burning down in the middle of the night for no apparent reason? Screw the odds. I am not a gambler. Don't take me to Vegas.

They say, "It can only go up from here." I had lived under the delusional belief that karma was a real thing, and since I was a decent person who had already lived through more than my fair share of trauma, nothing bad was going to happen to me—not anymore. According to what "they" say, the rest of my life should be up, up, up. And that certainly is not playing out.

I no longer trust what "they" say. I no longer trust God. And now that I have destroyed my family financially because of my poor choices, I no longer trust myself.

卯 卯 卯

I STORM INTO OUR bedroom and slam the door, my arms crossed tight against my chest. Troy bursts through the door, "Don't walk away from me!" he shouts.

"What's the fucking point? You're not even in the room anyway," I snap.

"What's that supposed to mean?"

"I've been on the phone all day with these bill-collector piranhas and you're Mr. Magoo, walking around with your head in the clouds."

"I am working my ass off so we can get out from under this. Do you not see that?"

I shout at him, my voice breaking, "What I see is that you are numb. I'm up every night worried while you sleep like a baby. Where are your feelings? You know, I never even saw you shed one tear for our animals."

With this he turns on his heels toward me, his voice ferocious, "Don't you tell *me* how to grieve, Hollye. You don't know . . . I dug their bodies out of the ashes. You don't fucking know how I feel."

He storms out of the room and I collapse into a heap. He's right. I don't know how he feels. I don't have any idea. But I fear he is falling out of love with me. He told me in the middle of one fight that maybe I'd be better off if he left. I know it's only a matter of time before he'll disappear, just like every other man in my life.

Not knowing what else to do, I get on my knees and I pray.

HELL IS THE PLACE *where God can't hear you.* That's all Troy remembers from his brief experience in the Catholic Church, the one thing he deems to be true. These days, we spend a lot of time on our knees, pleading and begging for some omniscient deity to swoop down and rescue us. But it seems we are in the place where God can't hear us.

I sit alone in the middle of this oppressive stillness, with nothing but memories and feelings about myself I had long pushed away.

Some days I have the energy to put on a happy face and be supermom, and those are usually the days I throw myself headlong into mothering my kids, whether leading a field trip or helping them with a school project. Other days I put on my armor and get on the phone, fending off creditors. But most days I feel like an insignificant bug, with God in the role of bully, pulling my wings off, watching me writhe on the ground under his laser focus. These are the days I wrestle with obsessive suicidal thoughts, and I can't blame it on a lousy year and losing our home. The roots of my brokenness run deeper than that. I managed to outrun my past for a good, long time. But now, just like the firebeast that almost killed me, the truth of my past is gaining on me and threatening the same. It sucks all the oxygen out of the room, choking me, burning me, searing into my psyche. But unlike the fire, there is no escape, no window to jump out of. So, one day, I jump out of the car.

May 3, 1995

I tried to throw myself from the car today. I didn't care anymore what happened to me. I wanted to hurt myself. Troy grabbed me by the hair and yanked me back. I lost a lot of hair, but now I see how drastic a situation this is. I called the psychologist who helped me after the fire. I am going to see him tomorrow.

WE ARE DRIVING. Troy is distant, and I am desperate to find the place where we once connected. I needle him for a reaction until he explodes. He is yelling at me, and it all feels so hopeless. I can't hear him. I feel fuzzy, numb, like I am leaving my body, and then . . .

"Jesus Christ!" Troy slams on the brakes. My upper body collides with the dashboard, one leg hanging out the open car door. He yanks me up hard by an elbow, his eyes wild with fear. A clump of my long, blond hair hangs from his tightly closed fist. "What is WRONG with you?" he screams.

I don't know how to answer that. I whimper like a child, as he drives me home.

Deeply ashamed, I lie in bed and cry big, huge, ugly sobs until there is nothing left in me. I am unraveling.

This is not the first time I've tried to throw myself into traffic. At another place (Arizona), at another time (1973). I was nine years old—the age Cissy is now. My mother, Kyle, and I had just fled Walt, her insane, drug-addicted boyfriend. My mother's plan was to run across state borders to Kyle's father, Gene, hoping to win him back. Gene was the only one who had ever been good to us, until he ran away. We were homeless, and school was about to start. So we drove, twelve hours straight. I had a hopeful, optimistic heart, because during those few years we lived with Gene, everything was okay. He didn't hit us. He wasn't a drug addict. He read me books and held me on his shoulders. If he and Mom would make things right now, I knew everything would be okay again. We'd have a place to live. I'd go back to school. Driving through the Arizona desert I'd said the Lord's Prayer at least fifty times while holding tight to the lucky rabbit's foot in my pocket.

When we got there, Gene rejected us. He said he was happy now, and he didn't want to come back. My young heart couldn't take anymore. My dog Rusty had just died, my Grandma had just died, and everyone told me they had "gone home." Home sounded like a good place. So I set off toward the main boulevard, and stood at the curb surveying the traffic, waiting for a car that was going just fast enough. And then, the screeching of brakes, the horns honking, my mother dragging me into the house.

"What is WRONG with you?"

"Did you want to kill yourself?" Gene shouted, fear in his voice.

I nodded yes.

Gene angrily handed me a pair of scissors and said, "Here, go ahead." And then my mother tried to explain it to me, something about reverse psychology, blah, blah, blah, but I couldn't hear her. To me he was saying, *It really won't matter anyway*, which justified how I felt.

My mother could barely handle her own problems, let alone a suicidal kid. The next thing I knew, I was living with my Aunt Laura, and that's when I became the master at tap dancing. I decided I wouldn't disappoint anyone again. I would be perfect—a saint, in fact. And in private, sleeping in my aunt's sewing room, I would hyperventilate until I made myself faint. Those were my little moments of peace—my minideaths.

Because I buried it and never dealt with that incident in my nine-year-old psyche, it was bound to play out again. Here she was today, that nine-year-old girl trapped inside a thirty-one-year-old life, pushing me out of a moving car.

I haul myself out of bed and stand at my bedroom window, watching the traffic go by. I feel like I've added 100 pounds to my 110-pound frame. My knees ache, my back aches, my head aches from the full weight of revelation: the woman who convinced everyone she had it together is falling apart. I am deeply ashamed for what I put Troy through, and that I risked harm or death to myself, which would have hurt my children. But it wasn't premeditated. I did it suddenly, without thought. I am losing my fucking mind. It's just one more thing to lose.

IN MY HEAD, I struggle daily with suicidal thoughts. Although I don't act on them, and made a vow to myself that I never would, the thoughts persist. I don't know that "intrusive thoughts" are a common symptom of post-traumatic stress disorder. I just think I am defective. I push the ugly thoughts away, and try to busy myself with creative projects, gardening, cooking. I try, I mean I really, really try, to shield my kids from this darkness in my soul. But children are intuitive. They are natural empaths who feel the energy in the house no matter if you are the Meryl Streep of feigning cheeriness. Cissy is with her dad part of the time, so she gets some reprieve from my inner turmoil. But Taylor is with me night and day, my constant companion—my emotional Siamese twin.

One day I was bustling around the house searching for something, lost in my own thoughts, and Taylor, five years old, said, "Your book is in the car and your keys are on the mantel." I froze. I hadn't said anything about what I was looking for—how did he know? Taylor is quiet, seems like he's in his own world not really paying attention to our adult concerns, but he doesn't miss a thing. Years later he will recount with accuracy adult conversations that have taken place, things we thought were over his head. He absorbs everything, including my camoflaged depression. It is in a small ordinary moment as I'm applying a rub-on tattoo to his arm that I come face to face with this. I pat his arm and start to walk away, but he screams, "Nooooooo!"

I turn to find him crying. Taylor only cries when he's hurt physically.

"What's wrong?"

"That's not how I wanted it!" He's never screamed at me before. I am stunned.

"Well . . . why? What did you want?"

"I hate this. I hate this! Just go away and leave me alone!" His face is red, his arms thrashing wildly at the air. He is completely unhinged. My heart pounds, my mouth dry. This is not my little Buddha, not my Taylor. What is happening?

I stand up straight, pretending to be in control, "I see you're wanting to have a tantrum," I say, my voice shaking, "but you may not scream at me. You can have your feelings by yourself, and talk to me when you're calm." I walk out and shut his bedroom door behind me, my heart thrumming through my chest. And then, my four-year-old child, who still wears Pull-Ups at night, screams this behind his closed door, *"I hate myself! I hate my life! I want to die!"*

My knees crumple beneath me as I clutch the doorjamb for support. I can't breathe. He is too young to know what these words mean. No, these aren't his words. My son is screaming what has been inside my head every day for months. He screams out everything I have been suppressing. I can no longer hide what is happening inside myself, inside the walls of this "Happy House," inside the confines of my marriage. The jig is up.

I hesitate at his door, compose myself, then push it open. He sits on the floor, his face red and sweaty, his eyes wild and confused. I pick him up and rock him.

"We never say ugly things like that about anyone, *especially* not ourselves. Okay?"

He nods.

"Your mommy and daddy love you so much. We prayed for you to come into our lives. You are an answered prayer—our precious gift," I say, "and the fact that we are all even here on this Earth is a miracle. Our lives are a gift." I hold him close against me, wiping his tears and my own with the sleeve of my shirt, unable to say any more. With every word, I am learning a hard lesson. Am I going to live my life as a hypocrite, expecting my children to believe in the value of their lives, when inside I believe mine is worthless? No. I cannot live this way any longer. I am not going to let another generation of children grow up as damaged as I am. Doing my best is no longer good enough. I have to do better than my best. I have to find a way to heal myself, for only in doing that can I heal my family.

Facing death has awakened me to the truth of my own life. I have to unravel completely to find out who I am, what I'm made of. Everything I once felt certain of is shaken loose like soil from the roots of an upturned tree, leaving me raw, exposed. I have to find a way of taking root within my self.

May 6, 1995

Troy and I are sitting side by side in the garden, writing. It's Saturday morning, a beautiful day. I am stronger today. I went to therapy yesterday with Dr. A. I felt comforted knowing that there is hope on the other side of this. I trust Dr. A. He has bright, clear eyes, a steady, confident gaze, and he seems to understand me even when I don't. I'll be seeing him every Wednesday, and he has commissioned a piece of my art to cover the costs. I am so grateful to be getting help. Maybe God was listening to my prayers after all?

VERMEER SKIES

✦ ✦ ✦

No one knows I tried to throw myself from the car, but everyone knows we need a break. One sunny afternoon in May, my friend Steve calls and invites us to come to Northern California for a few days. Steve and his wife, Amy, have plenty of room in their home and give us an open-ended invitation. I want to drive away from this sadness and breathe air that isn't tainted by tragedy. I want to give our children a memory that does not include disaster and loss. We throw some clothes in a bag and hit the scenic 101 the next day, driving through the golden plains of Paso Robles wine country, over the rocky cliffs of Carmel and Big Sur, the cerulean blue ocean stretched out to the horizon line.

Steve is a buddy of mine from back in my teen years when we worked together at a restaurant. He's about five years older, and sort of mentored me when I was floundering in college, and floundering in life. Steve grew up with a mom who was constantly sticking her head in an oven and threatening suicide, which made him hyper-responsible. His ticket out of crazy town was his brilliance. He focused all his energy on learning and bettering himself, so it's no surprise that he's a software guy in Silicon Valley, living in a gorgeous home in the redwood forest, driving a convertible BMW. We laugh about the old days, when we competed for who could carry the most plates on a tray, and he drove a lime-green Ford Fiesta with a sunroof he'd cut out himself—with a saw.

On Thanksgiving, Steve and Amy were visiting in Los Angeles and had driven up to our house to surprise us. When they reached our home, they saw only charred ruins, the caved-in roof. No doubt the place was still smoldering. Steve said they drove the twenty minutes down the hill in complete silence. Neither of them dared say aloud what they feared. Later, by calling around, they were able to get my mother's number and track us down, tearfully relieved to hear our voices on the phone.

On our first day in Monterey, Steve and Amy play tour guide, taking us to all their favorite places. First we take the kids to the aquarium. We walk along the shore, study tide pools bursting with exotic anemones and starfish. We watch otters play in the surf. We collect sand dollars. It is a relief to slow down and connect to the natural world. I can feel my soul regenerate as I expand my myopic view and take it all in.

The next day we hit the The Mystery Spot where we walk through crooked houses that defy gravity, then walk along the Santa Cruz boardwalk where we play arcade games and eat hand-pulled saltwater taffy. Amy and Steve take the kids by the hand, leading them on to the beach where they look for treasures in caves and tide pools, allowing me and Troy a moment together to breathe. We walk along the beach and immerse ourselves in the small, simple details of nature. We stop to look at each beach house, imagining the lives that inhabit each place, and the stories behind them.

On our last day in Aptos, we take a hike through the redwood forest. Heavy fog hangs over the treetops, giving it a

King Arthur mystical feeling. We weave our way through a thick tangle of trees that existed long before us, coming to stillness in the center of it. I feel a deep respect standing beneath these trees, to feel the protection of their outstretched limbs above me. Cissy—a child who never liked to get dirty and as a baby hated the feel of sand or grass against her feet— becomes energized in the forest. Suddenly she is charging ahead, our fearless leader. "Follow me!" she says, as though she's trudged this path a thousand times before. She and Taylor run ahead, hiding from us inside a thousand-year-old tree, ogling the enormous banana slugs and iridescent green moss that creeps along its trunk. On this day, we witness a change in our daughter, as she leaves behind her cautious, anxious younger self, and Cissy the Adventurer emerges.

Troy and I stay up late that night, drinking a Napa cabernet and watching Jeanine Garafolo do a stand-up routine on TV where she impersonates a very suave, very young Alec Baldwin. She says that when Alec hosted *Saturday Night Live,* aside from being devastatingly handsome, he was the consummate gentleman. Every time you'd reach for a door, he'd shoot ahead of you and open it. You put a cigarette to your lips, he appeared out of nowhere with a lighter. You coughed, he'd be at your side with a Ricola. "Lozenge?" he'd offer. With our defenses down, Troy and I are free to laugh again, so we laugh our weary asses off. We laugh away all the ugly fights and the tension that has built between us as Troy reaches across the couch for my hand. Steve comes into the living room at one point and, with groggy voice and sleepy eyes, asks us if we can please keep it down. But ours is an uncontrollable laughter that wells up from deep inside—a merciful, lifesaving laughter that can't be contained. The release is so sweet that Steve, standing there mildly peeved in his flannel PJ bottoms, is powerless to stop it. Still laughing, we apologize and thank him for giving us this space to feel alive again. He doesn't know how close I've come to not wanting to be alive. After all he went through with his suicidal mother, I'll never tell him this.

Driving home on the 101 Highway the next morning, I see a cemetery on a hillside, overlooking the Pacific Ocean, and ask Troy to stop. The cemeteries in Southern California are sterile miles of generic rolling hills with flat indistinguishable grave markers. They could almost pass for a golf course. But here is a real graveyard with enormous headstones that tell sad stories. Dead Christmas trees with sparse, weathered ornaments lie toppled over on their sides. Multicolored pinwheels spin in the wind atop the smallest graves. I need to confront death to see what life means to me. I walk through and read the headstones. I sit on gravesites. I lie down upon them, trying to absorb the meaning of life. Troy waits by the car, arms folded tight against his chest. He reluctantly tolerates my strange behavior while I meander and ponder. Did I really want to die? Or do I really want to live? Is there a God? Was there a soul once connected to this body now decomposing in the ground, or are we all just a freak accident of nature? What's the point of building a life if God can stomp through like a cranky toddler having a tantrum, knocking all your building blocks down?

I step carefully between headstones, taking photos. Cissy sits quietly in the car reading *Nancy Drew*, but Taylor's high-pitched plaintive voice calls through the crack in the car window, "Can I get out? Daddy, can I get out?" As Troy stalls for an answer, the wide-open grass and multicolored pinwheels are too tempting. Taylor bursts out of the car and tears across the graveyard giggling. *Look, I'm an airplane!* He runs, arms outstretched, leaping over the graves of other children. I am breathless as my joyful, alive, rosy-cheeked four-year-old boy runs toward me. Five months before, he lay listless in his bed as death hovered over him, the carbon monoxide seeping into his veins. My throat constricts, my ribs caving in on themselves. It's time to stop contemplating all this death bullshit.

"Let's go," I say. Troy is happy to oblige.

The long ride home is quiet. Cissy reads. Taylor sleeps. I take in the sights along the road. Cows graze in soft ocher meadows. Hawks overhead make slow, lazy circles. The sky is dramatic with its moody clouds and piercing rays of light, rebelling against nightfall with a final flush of blood-orange fire. My heart aches from the wonder of it all. The world is a stunningly ordered place. I can't deny there is an intelligence that set this all in play, something larger than I can comprehend. I remember walking with Phyllis through the Getty Museum in LA, stopping in front of a Vermeer painting. I was awed at the feeling he'd captured in just a sky, how light and shadow brought the landscape alive. His paintings filled me with emotion. I wondered if the sun was feebler now, if light filtered through such different clouds, because I'd never seen a sky like that. But here it is today: a Vermeer sky. A highway has since been built, but we are driving through such a painting, and this time, God is the artist. Maybe. I can't believe a sky this perfect is an accident, a random stroke of chaos. And if it isn't, that means that even my puny life must carry some significance, because I am created by that same intelligence.

I turn to look at the faces of my two happily exhausted children, now sleeping in the backseat. I know that they belong in this world, that we hoped for them before they ever existed. I am certain their lives have purpose. If they came into this world through me, how could my own life be meaningless? I watch the sun until it vanishes beneath the mountain range. As Venus and the others take their place on the celestial stage, I lay my worries down, at least for now, nestling back into my seat and closing my eyes. The hum of wheels on pavement lulls me into a calm state. I have a feeling that maybe all is as it should be, as I surrender to sleep.

Hope Is a Thing with Feathers

🐦 🐦 🐦

May 10, 1995

*C*linical depression. That is what I have. Yet there is a certain calm in it that I like. It's become familiar, almost comforting because it's reliable. I don't want to deal with people. I don't answer the phone. I rarely leave the house. Sometimes I can sit and stare at the wall for a half hour or more. I'm content this way. I don't want to have to "be happy" or charming or funny. I just want to be. And I want to be left alone. We're supposed to go out to lunch with Carrie and Jack, and Scott and Sarah tomorrow. I don't know if I can do it. What can I possibly talk about? When they ask me what I've been up to, what will I say? "Well, let's see, I'm suffering from debilitating depression, I tried to throw myself from the car, my kids are falling apart, and I'm in therapy."

Carrie and Jack are going to Cancun next week. Scott and Sarah are going on a Carribean cruise. Me? I'm going insane, that's about the only trip I'm taking.

IN EARLY JUNE, I'm driving Cissy to her dad's house, where he is hosting a barbeque for her birthday. The day before, Troy and I threw a party for her in the park. We had zero budget to work with but we figured it out. Cissy and I made the invitations. Troy and I built homemade carnival games where her friends won silly little prizes—an eraser, pencil, candy—things I got for pennies. I made her cake, decorating the top with M&M'S and lollipops. The kids loved it so much I wonder why I ever wasted money on store-bought cakes.

We'd been at Lauren's birthday party the month before, a fancy princess party Sarah had thrown her at a teahouse. I made Lauren a planter basket with her own fairy village inside (at Cissy's request). But when it came time for Cissy's birthday party, Sarah didn't RSVP, and Lauren never showed up. Their absence was crushing.

As I round the corner and pull into Gary's driveway, I'm shocked to see Sarah standing on his front porch. Sarah has been my confidante through my custody woes with Gary. She knows the conflicts we've had. Yet here she is, showing up for his party for Cissy, rather than mine. I feel this like a direct slap in my face. What have I done to deserve this meanness? After months of tears and sadness over her, I feel anger move through me like a firestorm. I give Cissy a kiss good-bye, and after she's in the house, I march across Gary's lawn toward Sarah.

"Why are you doing this?"

She crosses her arms defensively, "What are you talking about?"

"Really, Sarah? Are we going to bullshit each other at this point? What's going on? You don't answer my calls or letters, and now this? What's wrong with you?"

"What's wrong with *you?*" she shouts, "Why did you even bother coming to lunch with us that day? You've been acting . . . *weird.* You're moody, distant. I don't even know you anymore."

I shake my head in disbelief. "You'll have to excuse me for acting *weird*, Sarah. My life is falling apart, okay? I've lost everything. Everything I believed in has been shattered. I'm in a lot of pain right now."

Sarah rolls her eyes, muttering, "Yeah, so you've mentioned." I see in her expression, *Get over it, already.* Seconds before I felt pleading, almost apologetic, but now I see a different side of her, and something shifts inside me.

"I needed you to be my friend . . . is that too much to ask?"

"Well, I'm sorry. I can't be there for you in the way that you need," she says, her voice flat, unemotional.

I pause for a few seconds, absorbing that sentence. Troy's voice plays like a tape in my head, *People tell you who they are.*

"Good-bye, Sarah," I say. I get in my car and drive away. I don't look back.

I'm shaking with anger as I drive down Ventura Freeway. The solstice sun beats down with a relentless fury, making it hard to see, and reminding me that this awful day will indeed be the longest of the year. I pull to the side of the road and take a few slow deep breaths to calm myself. As anger subsides, the tears come. I just said good-bye forever to my best friend, and I have no idea why. I loved her so much, and yet we ended up like this, for no reason I can see.

I cry on and off for days, inconsolable. I recount all the scenarios in my head, over and over, trying to figure it out. Why? How could they be so cold to us? I'm not perfect, but I'm a good person. Aren't I?

I struggle with that question, always have, knowing my father is a "bad person" who was in prison, and I am the result of a terrible mistake my mother made. I spent thirty-one years trying to prove myself but still I can't measure up. If only I could be perfect, the perfect wife, the perfect mom, the perfect friend, then surely God would find favor with me, and I would deserve good things. And I would be loved. But as much as I try, excelling in school, dancing, singing, painting, smiling for everyone, I'm not perfect. Of course I'm not. I'm a deeply flawed human being just like the rest of the human race. I've been the Wizard of Oz, trying desperately to dazzle the world with my brilliance, praying they wouldn't look behind that curtain and find out that fear was the operator that ran this machinery.

The reality is that I am a walking dichotomy. I'm gregarious and outgoing, friendly, and genuinely interested in others. And I also want to be left alone, don't want to answer the phone, or be bothered by people. I'm positive, encouraging and strong, and can just as easily fall into depression, hopelessness, faithlessness, and negativity. Part of me is free of my past, and part of me is trapped there. I'm loving and supportive, a do-gooder, a thoughtful friend who always remembers birthdays. I'm also irreverent and sarcastic, can be judgmental, even critical sometimes. And for as much as I go out of my way to make others feel special, I'm sometimes a shitty friend who runs late and forgets to return phone calls. So maybe I deserve this.

Night after night I lie awake, torturing myself with these thoughts. The sleeplessness makes my daytime depression worse. I am weepy and hopeless. Troy, the one who said everything would be okay, the one who said we'd come back stronger after the fire, the one who always wants to fix things, tells me to just let them go. *Hurry up and get over it.* He is suffering the loss too, but he won't admit it. He goes into that "we don't talk about things" mode: his eyes glassed over, a frozen smile plastered on his face, joking about everything. But that isn't strength. That's bullshit, and I tell him so. No matter who's showing it and who isn't, we're both living on a razor's edge. We're short-tempered, emotionally tender to the touch.

One night, when my crying has jangled his nerves, he snaps. He grabs me by my arms and shakes me, shouting in my face, "Just let them go, Hollye! They're dead!" His face is flushed, the veins on his neck strained. He shakes me harder, screaming, *"Do you hear me? Dead!"* In his sweaty, red face I see my stepfather Bullet beating my mother. Like a trapped animal, without even knowing what I'm doing, I break his grip and punch my husband in the face.

He steps back and stares at me like I am an alien.

"Get away from me!" I scream.

He turns and walks away. I hear the front door slam.

EVERY CRACK IN OUR foundation has widened until we wake one morning to find the Grand Canyon running through our living room. I can't reach him anymore. We've spun off into different galaxies. Without him, I am lost. I turn away, creeping inside my own silent spaces to grieve. I start smoking again. I drink a lot of cheap wine. I sit outside in the carport, hiding from my children with my glass of chardonnay and cigarettes. I am so broken down, I can't even find the will to paint or create. I still pray, just in case, but I am empty inside. Maybe I thought the nicotine and alcohol would fill that emptiness, but it only makes it ring more hollow.

I never felt grief over the loss of things. Not one tear was shed over our bath towels or refrigerator or side-by-side washing machine and dryer. My deepest grief is over the loss of our belief system, because that is where Troy and I lost each other. Life no longer measures up to our philosophy. Life is not fair. Bad things do happen to good people. Deep down, people aren't all good at heart. Even your best friends can't be trusted. So what now? I continue to pray every day. I pray not for money or things, but for healing, for a sense of peace, for a glimpse that God is there in my life. I feel nothing but a cold empty silence in return. *Hell is the place where God can't hear you.* I begin to believe that God is just something I made up in my head during my fucked up childhood, like an imaginary friend. "Jesus loves me," I sang to myself. "Who's Jesus?" you might have asked. "Oh he's my invisible friend. He's always nice to me, always helps me, he wears a white robe and sandals, and he lives on a cloud." It worked for me, then. As an adult, the more I think about it, the more ludicrous it seems. But then, there was that voice in my head the night of the fire. That voice that said, *Check the baby.* That voice that woke me three times. Maybe that was God. Or maybe it was maternal instinct. But where is the voice now, when everything is falling apart and I am more afraid than ever? I beg on my knees for just a glimpse, a simple feeling of calm, a sign, or even the ability to sleep through the night.

In frustration, I sit down with my guitar and bang out an angry rock anthem, challenging God to show His face. I come up with the ugliest chords I can muster. Troy later informs me that one of the chords is so dissonant, it isn't even a chord. It is now, I say. I called it the H chord, because it sums up who I am.

Tell me God
Do you hear
Or are my words just tumbling through the atmosphere?
'Cause I keep praying
But I fear there's no one listening
But I keep praying
'Cause the Bible tells me so
So tell me God, do you hear?

If there is an all-powerful God, he should be big enough to handle my rant and the H chords that accompany it. Or maybe I'll piss him off just enough to show up and defend his mighty self. But still, nothing. My grief is pervasive, a long, sad shadow I drag behind me.

One day, as I'm sneaking a cigarette on the side of the house, I hear Taylor's voice, "Mommy? Mommy, where are you?"

I duck beneath the window, hiding from him. I down the rest of my wine and stomp out my cigarette. And then I become disgusted with myself. I have a Ghandi quote taped above my desk. "Happiness is when what you say, what you think, and what you do are in harmony." I am so far from harmony—I am dissonance. Here I am lurking around, ducking beneath windows so my kids won't see how broken I am, knowing a life without integrity is hardly worth living. I remember something Dr. A said, "You don't have any control of what happens to you in life, but you can control how you choose to react to it." So I have a choice. I can lurk in the shadows with my cigarettes and wine—which is not effective at all—or get up off my sad, sorry ass and take my power back. I have a marriage that means the world to me, and two children who need a strong, loving mom to guide them. I can't afford to wallow in my sadness another moment. If I don't clean up my act, my children will absorb my bullshit.

So this is when I start reading positive, uplifting books about healing my spirit, even though I am cynical. I get videos on yoga, and start to practice it every day, even though I suck at it. I write and write even though I believe no one will ever want to read it. I go to therapy every Wednesday where I do nothing but cry, but still, at least I'm doing it there, and not at home. I keep at my trash-to-treasure business, and write songs like crazy, venting my pain and anger.

My faith has become anemic, at best. There is nothing in my outer world to make me believe. No signs or proof of God. But children cannot thrive in a hopeless world. If I am going to raise mine to have a better life, I must find my way out of faithlessness. I dig deep in my memory, remembering all that I survived in childhood. Surely there is a reason I was not struck down in traffic that bleak day in my nine-year-old life, and because of that, Cissy and Taylor were born. Because of that, I got to experience spinning in place with Cissy in my arms, falling in love with Troy, Taylor's peaceful birth, sitting under a Jamaican sky with my husband, watching electric storms dance over the ocean. Emily Dickenson wrote, "Hope is a thing with feathers that perches in the soul." It's up to me now, to find that thing with feathers, and to make sure my children inherit it.

COLUMBUS'S SHIPS

❦ ❦ ❦

July 31, 1995

I t started out a wonderful birthday for Troy—just us and the kids. It ended up being the weekend from hell, and yet, incredible revelations were made. There were moments when I thought my marriage was in serious ruins, and then I realized that I took my vows "for better or worse"—and this is definitely the "for worse" part.

I am worried about my marriage. It's weak right now, and yet we love each other so much. I don't know if love is enough, but for now it's keeping us both here.

LATE IN JULY, just after Troy's birthday, his Grandma calls. I'm cheered to hear her voice on the phone.

"Hi Gram! How are you?" I say as I bustle through the house, a laundry basket on my hip.

"Well, I'm okay," she says, hesitantly.

"Is anything wrong?" Gram never complains about anything—not her health, not the state of the world—maybe occasionally about the Dodgers playing lousy. That's about it.

"I don't understand," she says, "Why won't you let Troy see his family?"

I drop the laundry basket to my feet. What is she talking about? I pause a beat to center myself, "Gram, Troy is a grown man. I don't make decisions for him, especially regarding his family," I say, keeping my voice calm and steady. I am so hurt. So shocked that someone is feeding her this lie, so devastated that she believes it, as if my husband is a mindless idiot who can't make his own decisions.

"Well, he needs to come and see us. *We* are his family. *This* is his home."

There's that familiar kick in the gut: *you are the unwanted outsider.*

"Yes. And we are also his family, Gram. And this is his home. Whatever this is about, you should talk to Troy about it," I say.

Yeah, that's what I say.

But what I don't say is this: that I invite you, his family, to every moment in our kids' lives, every birthday, holiday, even Taylor's birth. But Dennis and Shelby said, "We have a lot going on in our lives, we don't want to be obligated to show up to all these events." What I don't say is that when they don't show up for my children, it exacerbates my own feeling of being an unwanted child. What I don't say is that I am the one pushing Troy to call. That I send flowers on his mother's birthday, buy cards and sign his name when it slips his mind. That I nag him to see his Grandma, and to call his sisters. That I do this because I want Troy to work it out with his family, and I want my kids to have what I never did—that big happy family. But I don't say any of that. I just get off the phone.

When Troy comes home that evening, I tell him what had happened. He waves it off, casually.

I once heard a story about how the Native Americans, having no reference nor understanding of what a tall ship was, couldn't see Columbus's ships coming. Because of their inability to process the image, the ships were virtually invisible to them. That's my husband with conflict. He can't see the storm clouds gathering because he doesn't understand the emotions that formed them. I, on the other hand, am hyperaware, trained from birth to scan the horizon for trouble. Which is also why Troy sleeps like a baby every night while I get up and pace the house, sweeping under beds for monsters (checking electrical outlets, carbon monoxide detectors, holding my hands under the kids noses to check for regular breathing patterns). I am also the only one to detect the trouble brewing in his family relationships.

Tonight he has that deer-in-headlights face that I know too well, which tells me he is never going to call her back, and this misconception will grow. The more he denies the problem, the more worked up I become.

"They blame me for your distance! I'm tired of it!"

His response, "What are you talking about? My family loves you!" *What tall ships?*

I want to set my hair on fire and run screaming down the street. I practically do.

"You're not going to call her, are you? You're not going to call her, and the lie is going to grow, and I'm going to be blamed for everything."

He sits on the edge of the bed, frozen. "I don't know how," he says, almost under his breath.

"What do you mean you don't know how? Just pick up the phone and call her for Christ's sake!"

He shakes his head. "I. Don't. Know. How."

How can this be the same man who saved us from the fire? The man who stoically watched his life burn down and said we'd come back stronger? The man who dug through the rubble to find our pets' bodies? I have to leave the room before I turn into a freekin' nut job. Lord knows I'm already well on my way.

For years, Troy sold me the script of the idyllic life he led as a child, leaving me confused as to how his relationship with his family, or lack thereof, is now such a mess. How can a fracture this deep be *my* fault? I've asked. No one in his family will answer. "We don't talk about those things." Now and then, when his grandfather has a few drinks in him, he'll talk about things. But no one will ever come straight out and say what the issue is, or why it seems to be directed at me. Instead, there will be underlying tension at every family get-together, or the occasional out-of-the-blue explosion.

Once, during a family vacation, a close friend of Troy's parents said to us, "You know, I've gotta tell you. There's been a lot of crap said about you over the years. I think its horseshit. You're a great girl. You both are great people." On the one hand, the truth was put in my husband's face by someone other than me, and he could no longer deny it. But on the other, it verified my fear that I was unlovable.

The thing is, his family doesn't even know me. No one knows anything about who I am, my background, where I come from, or why I didn't have a father to walk me down the aisle. They don't know that my brother had been shot. Instead of asking, they make assumptions about who I am, and as they share those assumptions with others, misconceptions harden into a false truth.

People see what they want to see. Troy only wants to believe in the fairy tale of what he wants his family to be. His family wants Troy to stay trapped in a bell jar of happy memories from the past—and I don't figure into that picture. I am only an outsider who changed the Troy they knew, and by change, I mean he grew up and became his own man. Did they not realize this was going to happen, with or without me?

Troy was the peacemaker in his family. He never individuated in the way most of us did as teens. No drugs, no screaming hateful things at his parents, no dramatic rebellions. He could only recall one time he had been rebellious in his whole life. When he was about twelve, his mother had him walk to the doctor after school every week to receive allergy shots. They were painful and he hated them, so one day he simply slipped away and didn't show up. That was it. And that's exactly how he individuates as an adult. He slips away, and doesn't show up. His quiet, suppressed rebellion takes place over the course of our marriage, and subsequently, I take the fall for it.

Whatever their reasons, our marriage is suffocating under the intense scrutiny we feel from his parents. I feel like we (especially me) are under a microscope, our every move being judged, misinterpreted, talked about to others. What we need is their love and guidance. We need their mentoring. We need them to be the rock we can lean on. Instead, our relationship with them becomes another rock in the avalanche, a rock that forms a wedge in our marriage.

THE GHOST OF CHRISTMAS PAST

The trouble began on Christmas in 1988. Troy and I had recently moved in together. It was our first time setting new traditions and bonding as a new family. Cissy was three years old. With my new job in sales, I bought Cissy the elusive Barbie Dreamhouse I had longed for throughout my childhood. This was the first of many things I would "fix" by making sure my daughter's life was better than mine.

It was also Cissy's first Christmas as the child of divorced parents. I did all I could to make it special, so maybe she wouldn't notice her daddy didn't live with us anymore. Cissy was excited, discovering all the rooms in her Barbie Dreamhouse.

"Look Mommy! Here's her bed—it's pink!"

"Isn't that a fancy bed, baby?" I sat with my arm around her, enjoying the moment.

Troy pushed a pile of gifts in front of Cissy.

"Here, have her open these," he said, looking at his watch.

"Stop rushing her!" I scowled at him.

"We have to go."

"Christmas is for children, *Scrooge*. Let her enjoy her gifts."

He looked at his watch again, "I'm worried about time. There's always a lot of traffic going to Orange County."

"It's eight-thirty in the morning, for God's sake!"

He squirmed and heaved a big sigh.

"Oh my god! Just call and tell your mom Cissy is opening her presents. What's the big deal? She's a mom, she'll understand."

He didn't call.

When we got on the freeway, as Troy predicted, there was terrible traffic. Bumper to bumper all the way. Cissy had to stop to use the bathroom at least once, and then she was hungry. Troy was stressed out. This was the first time I had seen him so grouchy. It was a miserable three-hour trip, and not at all the way I had planned to spend our Christmas morning. We got there at about 11:30 a.m., which I thought was early, since we were planning to stay the whole day and through dinner.

We got out of the car, shook off the stress from the long ride in traffic, straightened our clothes. I lifted Cissy out of her car seat, and picked up the basket I had made for the Dexter family. It was filled with my homemade cookies and candies, plus Christmas coffee mugs and ornaments I'd hand painted for each of them. I had wrapped the basket in cellophane and tied a velvet ribbon around the top. I felt unsure of my offering, and hoped it would be enough.

The Dexters were opening their stocking gifts when we walked in. Troy's parents hugged him and gave Cissy and me a curt but polite hello while his sisters remained seated. Everyone had a place at the table. I was still standing like an idiot, my arms full with the gift basket. I set it down in the entry. There was palpable tension in the air, but we all carried on as though everything was fine.

After Christmas dinner, I took a stack of dirty dishes into the kitchen, where I walked in to the middle of a maelstrom.

Shelby was crying, shouting at Troy, *"How could you do this to me on Christmas?"*

Troy stood in the middle of the kitchen, looking crushed. With tears in his eyes, he said, "Mom, I'm so sorry. I didn't mean to hurt you."

I hesitated in the doorway, my arms full with dirty plates, wondering what was going on. Shelby's back was to me. Troy looked at the floor, his hand gripping his forehead.

His sister stormed out of the kitchen, screaming at her mother. She ran down the hall to her bedroom, slamming the door so hard the walls reverberated with the force. Moments later she was crying in the hallway. Her cat had tried to run out of the room and got hit when she slammed the door. We all set out searching for the injured cat. All over the house were plaintive cries of "here, kitty, kitty." I searched under beds and sofas, walking in and out of the Dexter closets, wondering what kind of surreal world I'd just entered. Moments later, the cat was found bleeding from his nose. His sister scooped the cat up, took him into her bedroom, and shut the door. Everyone retreated to different corners of the house.

This was Christmas with the Brady Bunch?

SOON AFTER, Gram called everyone to the table for her homemade pie and coffee. We took our seats around the dining table. Everyone was visibly shaken. I was quiet, keeping to myself. Cissy was sitting in my lap. But for the sound of forks clinking and scraping on pie plates, there was a terse silence.

Troy spoke up, "Mom, I don't understand. What's the problem here?"

Shelby basically went on to say that *I* was, in fact, the

problem, that I had an attitude, and that our lateness was nothing more than manipulative and controlling behavior. I had no idea we were late. Late to what? Shelby's voice got louder as her emotions took over. Troy's grandparents got up abruptly and left the room. My brain was swimming. I couldn't even hear what she was saying anymore. I sat there like a scorned child. I wasn't going to get into a screaming fight with Carol Brady. No way. I clutched Cissy tighter against my chest. I was twenty-three years old and didn't know how to stand up for myself. I sat there like a cornered rabbit, all of that anger like a harpoon aiming for me, but going right through my child. I know that scene imprinted deeply on Cissy.

As we got our coats and gathered our things, my brain kept circling what had just happened, trying to make sense of it. None of this matched the stories Troy had told me. Did I really cause all this?

I approached Shelby to say good-bye. "What did I do to make you so mad?" I asked. Even as I said it I could hear the smallness in my voice, the wounded little child.

"Nothing. I'm not mad," she said.

That untrue statement, delivered with such conviction, gave me nowhere to go. Because it is my nature, I kept digging for truth, "Is it because you don't think I'm right for Troy or something? Because I'm divorced, or have a child?"

"We don't make those choices for Troy," she shot back defensively.

Tears of frustration welled up in my eyes and in a pathetic, vulnerable moment I cried, "I just want you to like me." I reached out and hugged her, laying my head against her shoulder, which felt bony and sharp against my cheek, not soft like Gram.

"Everything's fine," she said.

❦ ❦ ❦

AS WE LEFT THROUGH the front entry, I saw my basket of handmade goods toppled on its side, unopened, as I was sure it would remain. I felt embarrassed by it. Stupid, handmade things from someone they despised. I wanted to snatch it and throw it in the trash.

Driving home afterward, I stared out the window, my back toward Troy as I stewed in my humiliation. All the neighborhood lights twinkled. Christmas trees sparkled on top of buildings. The cathedrals were softly lit, the church bells chiming, reminding me it was the time of love, faith, hope, belief. But this was not Christmas.

Troy broke the silence. "I was glad to see you and my Mom worked it out at the end there," he said in a chipper voice.

"Are you kidding me?" I snapped. "What universe are you living in?"

He shut down.

I stewed.

The 405 Freeway was a sea of red taillights. We sat in miserable silence for three excruciating hours. I couldn't believe I had allowed myself to be so vulnerable in front of her. How could I be so stupid and weak? I decided in that moment I would never, ever allow that to happen again.

TWO MONTHS LATER, Troy and I were engaged, and immediately got into counseling. We asked Dennis and Shelby to go with us. They came once, but it ended disastrously.

Troy asked Shelby to join us in therapy before our wedding so we could clear the air. Two weeks before the wedding, Dennis called our house to tell me that Shelby would not be attending therapy with us.

"I just got the pictures back from my shower. I don't want my wedding to be like that," I said.

"Like *what*?" he asked, a sharp edge to his voice.

"They looked so unhappy."

"So what!"

This completely knocked me off center. I never knew it was an option to respond with *so what*.

"I want our wedding to be happy. I want to be surrounded by friends, and people who actually like me."

"*We don't have to like you!*" Dennis said, his voice tight with frustration. "We have to accept you because Troy's going to marry you, but we don't have to be your friends."

Finally someone was telling the truth. No longer could Troy play ostrich and pretend that everything was hunky-dory with his family. It had now been said out loud, just weeks before our wedding.

August 1989

I am a bride again, but this time, I'm going to do it right. It will be a fairy tale, not a failure. My dress and headpiece are snowy white, sparkling with crystals. I will carry white calla lilies. Cissy will walk down the white aisle, sprinkling white rose petals in the white princess gown I had specially made for her. Cissy and I take this journey together, enveloped in this noncolor of all possibility. This is our fresh start and the slate must be clean. My promise to this man must be new and pure.

ON WHAT SHOULD HAVE been the happiest day of my life, I was buckled over with nerves, sick in the bathroom in my wedding dress. I was marrying the love of my life, and with him came a family who rejected me and I had no idea why. I wasn't sure if I was strong enough to withstand it. I had already failed at one marriage. I had a child now. I couldn't afford to fail again.

I took my first few steps toward the aisle and saw my Cissy at the altar, her cheeks rosy, a little basket in her hand. The aisle was strewn with the petals she had scattered. I saw the smiling faces of the people who loved me; Aunt Laura, Aunt Diane, Kelly, Tara, Keri, Lori, Phyllis, and Bernie. And then I saw Troy's sister Valerie standing in a black dress, black hat, black demi-veil over her face, his parents beside her, all in black, their faces drawn and sad as though a casket were being carted down the aisle, not a young bride. It was too late to back out now. *What had I done to myself, to my child?*

I first felt it in my face as my forehead became numb. Then came the wave of nausea, and ringing in my ears that drowned out the distant sound of violins. My legs collapsed under me as my vision began to fade. My mother and Eric were on either side of me. They caught me by the elbows and propped me up. "Just breathe . . . breathe," my mom whispered. "There's your husband, honey. Just keep looking at him. Only him."

Three days before, I had panicked and called off the wedding. My mom and Eric took me to lunch and talked me back into it. "You'll never find a better man than Troy," they said.

A string quartet played "Pachelbel's Canon." I breathed until I regained sensation in my body, letting the nausea pass. *Come on . . . pull it together.* I focused on Troy's eyes. Even from a distance I could see the love they held for me. I kept my focus on him and Cissy, letting everyone else fade away. I paused before the bridge that led to the aisle. *Once I step over that bridge, this wedding is happening.* I flashed him the big, bright smile he had fallen in love with, and let his love pull me like a magnet, floating down the aisle, no feeling in my extremities. At the altar, I took both Troy and Cissy's hands. We stood together at the altar, a family.

Doug, who owned the recording studio where Troy worked and was also a cantor and good friend, officiated for us. "Now you will know no storms," he said, "for you will be a shelter to one another." Troy and I read the vows we had written for each other. I cried. He cried. Our friends cried. Troy held both my hands through the entire ceremony.

At the reception, our friends Matt and Kevin played the Letterman theme as we were announced not as Mr. and Mrs. Troy Dexter, but as *The Dexter Family.* Troy, Cissy, and I walked in together holding hands, while our friends cheered. Later, Valerie pulled Troy off the dance floor, crying. They disappeared into the crowd. When the wedding coordinator said it was time for the first toast, I searched the room for my husband, eventually finding him in the darkened front entry of the wedding hall, his sister beside him in tears.

"It's time for the first toast," I said, looking at Troy with questions in my eyes.

Valerie turned away from me.

He touched her shoulder, "I have to go."

She nodded but didn't look at him.

"What's going on?" I asked him.

"I don't know. She's upset, she said she had some things she wanted to get off her chest."

"Like what?"

"I don't know. She never got around to telling me."

"At our wedding?"

He shrugged it off as though this was a perfectly normal

moment, and I reminded myself that I just signed up for this—
all of it. In the background I could hear them calling us over
the PA as everyone gathered. We moved through the toasts
and speeches. My beautiful girlfriend Tara got up and sang our
wedding song, "You Bring Me Joy." A hundred people
gathered around us, but I didn't see them as we moved across
the floor. Troy held me tight and we looked into each other's
eyes through the whole song. When we made eye contact, my
fear and anxiety fell away. And then the band (our good
friends and some of the finest studio musicians in town)
kicked into "Signed, Sealed, Delivered I'm Yours" packing the
dance floor. The room vibrated with warmth and electric
energy. I let it lift me. I floated above it all in a happiness
bubble, dancing carefully around the underlying conflict.

When we returned from our honeymoon and watched
our wedding video, we smiled and laughed as we relived every
moment, until we saw his sisters on screen. "What's your wish
for Hollye and Troy?" the videographer asked.

His sister Valerie waved him away. "I don't want to talk."

He kept on, "You don't have to make a speech, you can just
wish them good luck."

She put her hand up, "I have nothing to say."

He then turned to Troy's younger sister Dawn, "How
about you? Any wishes for the happy couple?"

She shrugged, "Good luck . . . I guess."

His parents did not appear on the video.

Troy would never again watch our wedding video.

WHEN GOOD PEOPLE
WRITE BAD CHECKS

❦ ❦ ❦

September 26, 1995, 5:30 a.m.

I woke up from a nightmare involving Deirdre and Sarah. It's eating me alive. I can't even sleep in peace. I don't know who I am, or more importantly WHY I am.

I love my husband so much, but why does he love me? Why?

I wish I could change my name and move far, far away. Start completely over where no one knows me. I'd get in my car and drive until I came to a place that felt right. And maybe I'd not make any friends. I'd get a job and an apartment, and when I wasn't working, I'd be alone. I might like to paint. I could paint my life story all over the walls. I would depend on no one. No one would know me, or have any expectations of me. No one would have the opportunity to rip my heart out again.

FALL HAS NEVER BEEN a good time of year for me. In Southern California, fall is fire season. Flu season. I envy those who love the turning colors and the chill wind and the smell of freshly sharpened pencils on the first day of school. But for me, as the days get shorter and the sun becomes elusive, I slide into melancholy. This fall also marks the one-year anniversary of our house burning down, and our animals' death. I don't want to mark the day; I can't let myself feel it. I have kids starting school, business to tend to. I keep busy to let the season pass unnoticed.

In September, Cissy enters the fourth grade and Taylor starts kindergarten. I sign up as kindergarten-room mom, just like I had for Cissy. Every Tuesday, I volunteer in Taylor's class. After school I help the kids with homework, and coach Cissy on her science-fair project. I force a positive attitude, read my inspirational books, fumble through yoga, struggle to meditate. We decorate our front yard with pumpkins, and make our own scarecrow. Troy's Gram comes over and shows us how to make her famous fried chicken and pumpkin pie while Troy videotapes. We don't discuss the unpleasant call we'd had earlier. We "don't talk about those things."

One night that October, as Cissy and I are just about to leave for Phyllis' art class, the lights go out.

"What happened?" Taylor asks.

"Looks like we're having a black out," I say, but I know we've been cut off. Our debt is capsizing us. Our first priorities in bill paying are the ones that have the greatest impact on our credit rating, which puts utilities at the bottom of the list. We have no electricity but we still have our credit, by God.

I stand in the dusky light from the front window, my purse on my arm. I'm not sure what to do. Troy waves me off. "Go ahead, honey. Take Cissy to class. I'll deal with this." I feel bad about leaving but realize normalcy is the best thing for the kids.

While we paint, have tea and cookies and enjoy the benefits of Phyllis' electricity for the evening, Bernie plays a plaintive "Misty" in another room. Phyllis pulls her chair beside me, "How ya doin', kiddo?" she asks, playing with my long hair. She loves to do that while I paint.

"I'm fine, Philly. Just a bad day today," I answer quietly.

She thinks for a minute, pulling my hair up into a chignon then letting it fall down my back. "You know . . . fire isn't always a bad thing," she says. "Did I ever tell you about my trip to British Columbia?"

Phyllis loves to tell us about her travels when she was younger. We often hear about her trip to London, the museums, the food. She continues, "We went on a group hike through the forest. Our guide told us the most amazing thing about forest fires. He said that fire is a blessing in nature, because it strengthens the forest. Most of the wildlife will escape—they have good instincts to run. But some trees, like oak and pine, can't regenerate without fire. Only that intense heat can crack open their seeds. And then, the ash enriches the soil so new things can take root. So actually, the forest needs the fire to grow."

"Wow," I say, "I would have never thought about it like that."

"Well, think about it, kid," she says.

I'm quiet on the drive home, thinking about it. God isn't punishing the forest by striking it with lightning and setting it ablaze. It happens because it needs to. Maybe we don't have bad karma after all, don't have bad luck, and aren't being punished by God. Even Phyllis's life burned down when she had a nervous breakdown at my age. She, too, had to find a way to take root again. Maybe my life needed to burn down so that something new could regenerate.

When Cissy and I return home late that night, there is a dim light in the front window. Inside, the living room is lit by the glow of our camping lantern. The house is quiet.

"Hello? Anybody home?" I call.

Cissy peers out the back window. "Mommy! Look!"

Troy and Taylor sit in camping chairs on our back lawn, our tent behind them, sleeping bags rolled out on the grass. Taylor is roasting marshmallows over the hibachi. Troy plucks at his acoustic guitar. Peering through that window, I marvel at how Troy is able to turn this disaster into a tiny miracle, and my heart swells with love for him. Moments like this make me sure that no matter how bad things are, I can never leave this man.

Cissy and I change into our pajamas and run outside to join the party. We spend that night making s'mores and looking at the stars as we try to remember the names of the constellations. We trace the big dipper with our fingers until we become sleepy, the four of us in sleeping bags, side by side.

In the morning, I wake to the sound of birds. I lie still, listening to the rhythm of my family breathing. Somehow, everything seems possible again. We'll find a way to pay the power company—everything will work out. I unzip the tent, and quietly sneak out. Sitting on my back porch under the misty haze of morning, I remember Dr. A's words. We can choose how to react to life's difficulties. When we resist what is, we suffer. I can choose to be happy in the face of adversity. And while our kids have seen us stressed, fighting, depressed, and broken, what I hope they'll remember from this time is our family, reciting the names of constellations on a starry night.

That afternoon, like an answered prayer, a check for $3,000 comes in the mail. Troy had been waiting three months for that check from a flaky client. He rushes over first to the bank, then to the power company to get our lights turned back on. I stock the fridge with groceries, and spend the afternoon writing checks to pay off the loudest, angriest creditors.

Three days later, our minivan won't start. I don't panic because it's under warranty. We have it towed to the dealer for repair. That same day we receive notice in the mail that the $3,000 check we just paid all our bills against has bounced on us, meaning all the checks we wrote against it will bounce. Meaning our payment to the power company is no good and they will once again cut us off. And then, in a surreal moment that only happens in bad sitcoms, the dealer calls to tell us the warranty was for the first 50,000 miles. The van now has 52,000 miles on it, and the van's engine is blown. A new engine will be $7,000. A ball bearing came loose—that's all it took to destroy a two-year-old car. Boulders, perched dangerously on the ledge, begin to teeter . . .

IT TAKES FIVE DAYS for Troy's client to cover the bad check, and during those five days we don't have one dime to our names. The only food we have is whatever's left in our cupboards. But I grew up with a single mom who worked nights as a waitress. We bought our groceries with food stamps. I know how to do poor. I find a bag of potatoes in the crisper, and make potato tacos and potato salad. One night we have pancakes for dinner. We tell the kids it's "Crazy-Mixed-Up-Backwards Day." The kids love Crazy-Mixed-Up-Back-wards Day and can't wait for the next one.

Though Cissy and Taylor go to different schools, they both have picture day that week. I knowingly write bad checks to their schools, so they can have their pictures taken just like every other kid.

We're down to one car and Troy needs it to work, so I can't get to therapy—when I need it most of all. Troy stops at the store and writes another bad check for food for the kids' lunches, and while he's at it, he throws some vodka into the cart. He figures Mommy needs a martini.

AS FALL PROGRESSES, we spiral deeper into money hell. Every time we think we can dig ourselves out, another unbelievably shitty thing smacks us upside the head. Like this, for instance: on the way to a weekend gig, the axel on our Honda, our one remaining car, snaps in half on the freeway. I mean, it just snaps in half, and it's only a five-year-old car. We miss the gig and the entertainment company threatens to fire us, but we beg for mercy. Standing on the shoulder of the freeway, not knowing what to do, I go to the call box and call my good friend Stephen (or La-dee-dah—as my friend Kelly and I call him, because we can't pronounce his Dutch last name and also because he's crazy smart). Stephen La-dee-dah is that friend you call at 3 a.m. if you're in jail. Not that I've ever been in jail, but I'm in hell, and that's close enough. Stephen arrives twenty minutes later. He rescues us from the side of the freeway and loans us the money to have the car towed. I don't even have to tell you what this does for my husband's pride. I watch Troy retreat further into a dark, remote place. We are beyond "down" on our luck—we are underground, buried, submerged. Luck is something in another stratosphere.

While we wait for the Honda to get a new axel, I stay home depressed, and Troy takes the city bus to get to his gigs. We do our best to focus on our kids, trying to keep our spirits up, because really, what other choice do we have? If it weren't so damned tragic it would be funny. They say tragedy plus time equals comedy. That's what they say.

A few days later, the water is cut off, so the kids take baths in the Jacuzzi, and we use bottled water to wash and brush our teeth and cook. We pour buckets of Jacuzzi water into the toilet tank to flush it. I have my Scarlett O'Hara moments, my eyes to the sky, fist raised in the air, *"As God is mah witness, Ah will nevah bail watah from the Jacuzzi agayan!"*

After the kids are in bed, I read my Deepak Chopra book. Chopra says that every upsetting situation is an opportunity to create something new and beautiful. He says to accept each moment as it occurs because everything is as it should be. If you struggle against what is, you are struggling against the order of the entire universe. I try to put this into practice, accepting that we are being melted down, stripped bare. Yes, we are busted flat. So now what?

We can't afford to go to dinner and the movies anymore. But when it's warm, we eat outdoors in our garden, and then hop in the Jacuzzi under the stars. When it rains, we lay a blanket on the living room floor and have an indoor picnic. The kids bring pillows and blankets into the living room. I make popcorn and we cuddle up on the floor to watch movies together.

One night, after a particularly grim day of fending off creditors, I go to Blockbuster to rent a video for us, desperate for escapism.

"Your card is expired," says a blasé, pimply-faced teenage boy.

"Can I just renew it?"

"You have to reapply." He pushes a form toward me, looking over my head. "Next person in line."

I move to the side of the line and fill out the new application. I give him a credit card to secure the membership, then wait for the apathetic teenager to run my credit.

"Sorry. Your membership is declined," he says, loud enough for everyone to hear. He shrugs, pushes the form back to me. "Next person in line."

After all our efforts to pay those damn credit cards, our credit is ruined anyway. I sheepishly put my wallet back in my purse. People in line stare as I return the videos to the rack. I feel like such a lowlife, being turned away from Blockbuster video, knowing I have to go home to the kids empty handed. This small simple thing levels me. Outside, I crumple on the curb and just lose it. People pass by and stare. I don't care anymore. I've lost everything. What more can I lose, my dignity? So what.

At home I walk in, defeated. Troy looks up, "What did you rent?" he says in a chipper voice.

"Nothing."

One look at my face and he knows. We don't even talk about it. There is too much grief, too much bad news. If I even utter one more word about it, I will fall over the edge of hopelessness. He doesn't ask any questions. Instead he falls into his own quiet desperation. And that's how the wall between us builds, with each of us running dangerously low on self-worth and faith, boiling under the surface, quick to snap at each other.

Since we can no longer rent movies, I spend a lot of time with Taylor at the library, sitting in a rocking chair, reading him stories. Cissy still enjoys sleepovers and dress-up parties with friends. While we scramble to keep food in the fridge, Cissy and Taylor are busy being kids. They put on plays and make funny videos to entertain us. They play tag and hide-and-seek in the backyard, and set up lemonade stands in the front yard. Our lives are no different from anyone else's, except that we are destitute. But you make do with what you have, and nothing is what we have. Nothing, and the Happy House.

❧ ❧ ❧

I SIT UP IN BED, sleepy-eyed. It's a gorgeous Sunday morning, brisk but sunny fall weather. Although we Californians miss out on the fall colors, we get to hold on to spring weather most of the year. For that I am grateful. The kids are in the living room watching cartoons. Troy sleeps soundly beside me, our feet touching—a good sign. When we're fighting, if he reaches his foot out to mine under the covers, I quickly jerk away. But when in a place of forgiveness, we touch toes—it's a reassurance that we'll be okay by morning.

I'm such an ass when we're fighting. I revert to the feral, self-protective loner—the girl who was raised by wolves. I won't make eye contact with him, because if I do, I'll see the goodness in him, and wonder how someone so good can hurt me so badly.

He always says to me, with sincerity, "My arms are open to you, whenever you're ready." Before the fire, the worse thing he ever said to me during a fight was this, "You're being really fucked, sweetie." And I had to turn my back in mock anger because I didn't want him to see me laugh.

But these days, we say things like this.

I say, "Fuck you." A lot.

He calls me a bitch.

I say, "I fucking hate you."

He says, "I'll divorce you."

I say, "Go for it."

Though fast asleep, he looks exhausted. Too exhausted for a thirty-four-year-old man. I love this man more than anything in the world. He is the last person I'd ever want to hurt, and yet I do. I kiss his creased brow and quietly slip out from under his arm, careful not to wake him.

Cissy and Taylor are playing quietly in the living room. The light through the picture window casts a soft, warm glow around them.

"Hey, whatcha up to, monkeys?"

"Nothin'" Taylor says with a mopey face. Troy and I joke sometimes that he's a grumpy old man in a five-year-old body. We threaten to buy him a cardigan and slippers.

Cissy jumps up, super charged, "Mommy! Can we make chocolate chip pancakes?"

"Sure!"

I turn off the TV and put on my favorite Winans gospel CD. Soft streams of morning light filter through the trees outside my kitchen window. This is my church: the drip and hiss of coffee brewing, the good aroma that fills the house, my babies in the kitchen with me. I make the batter while Cissy and Taylor take turns stirring, then I show them how to make a smiley face in the pan before pouring the circle over it, like my mom did when I was little. We experiment with making silly faces out of chocolate chips, making snake-shaped and letter pancakes.

After we gorge on fluffy stacks of pancakes, we settle in the living room in front of the picture window. I nestle into my favorite armchair with a book, while the kids play on the floor below me, building roads and cities with wooden blocks. We are happy. We are calm. We are bankrupt.

A few weeks earlier, I handed over all our financial records to Cheryl, a woman from Consumer Credit Counseling. After a day of poring over them, she said, "You have no choice but to declare bankruptcy." Although we were making payments, our debt was increasing due to interest and penalties. At the rate we were going, it would have taken us the rest of our lives to pay it off. Our credit was already ruined, simply from the debt-to-income ratio (which was why I'd been turned away from Blockbuster video).

She explained, "If you go bankrupt now, you can start with a clean slate and rebuild your credit. If you don't, you'll never be able to qualify when it comes time to buy this house. No bank will take you on with all that debt hanging over you."

We couldn't lose the house. No way. I sat, nervously wringing my hands, "I feel like such a loser. Do I have to go bankrupt against everyone? Can I go bankrupt against just my business debt?"

"That's not how it works. Bankruptcy is across the board. You can't pick and choose."

Troy and I looked at each other. *How did we end up like this?*

"No one in my family has ever declared bankruptcy. I don't know if I can do it," Troy said, looking defeated.

"Look," Cheryl assured us, "this is what bankruptcy is designed for. It's to protect people like you from having their lives destroyed due to circumstances beyond their control—disasters, medical bills . . . things like that. It's not like you guys were out partying and buying designer clothes and cars on your credit cards. You have nothing to feel guilty about."

So we declared bankruptcy. And we did feel guilty. But for as depressed as it made Troy, in a way, I feel free. So we've lost our credit. What is credit anyway? Will I be worried about credit on the last day of my life? I am free. FREE! No more fighting with those awful collection hounds on the phone—those inhumane robots who didn't give a shit about what happened to us. It's like I've been drowning, dog paddling for so long, and now, I simply stepped out of the water.

It's not as if I ever imagined myself going bankrupt. This isn't the promise I held in my heart walking across the stage to receive my high school diploma. But here we are. The good news is I never have to talk to Deirdre again. I never even have to think about her. The storm is over. Maybe now is finally our new beginning.

Troy shuffles into the living room, squinting against the light, hair sticking up. I look up from my book and smile. The furrow between his brow has softened. I can tell he feels the peace in the room. He smiles back.

"Daddy!" Cissy jumps up. "We made smiley-face pancakes! Want some?"

"Are you kiddin' me? I can't think of anything better than smiley-face pancakes!" He puts his arm around her shoulder, "Thank you sweetheart." He kisses the top of her head.

"I made the pancakes, too, Daddy," Taylor grumbles.

"You did? I'm gonna put a block of ice on your head to stop you from growing up so fast!" Troy puts his hand on top of Taylor's blond head.

We are smiling, really smiling, for the first time in so long.

That afternoon, I take a cup of coffee and sit outside in the garden, surveying the damage from the recent windstorm we had. The wind was ferocious the week we had to declare bankruptcy, as it always seems to kick up at the same time life does. Several large branches lie on the hillside, snapped like twigs. I wonder how we'll get rid of them. Maybe chop them up for firewood? Then I get an idea. I call out to the kids, asking them to help me drag the branches down the hill.

"Why do we have to do this? This sucks." Taylor complains with his slight lisp, or shall I say, lithp.

"Because Mommy has an idea," I say, "And don't say *sucks*, please. It's not nice."

"What's the idea, Mom?" Cissy looks ready to take it on.

"Well, I thought we could build our own teepee."

"A real one?" Cissy asks, bouncing on her toes.

"Cool!" Taylor says.

We build the frame of the teepee out of fallen branches and tie it together with vines we scavenge from the hillside. We cover the frame with a large blanket someone donated to us that actually has a sort of wigwam design on it. Inside, we build a hearth of sticks and twigs.

Cissy insists we eat lunch in the teepee, so we prepare an authentic Native American meal of peanut butter and jelly sandwiches and invite Troy to join us for our powwow. Inside, we sit cross-legged around our fireless hearth as I work on Cissy's wild mane of blond hair, wrestling it down into two Indian braids. "One of the things the Native Americans used to do was to tell stories around the hearth." I say, my fingers weaving through her hair.

Troy adds, "That's right, and the chief would pass around the talking stick. Only the person who held the talking stick could speak—everyone else had to be quiet until it was their turn."

"That could be very useful in this family," I add.

The kids become enthralled with the idea of this all-powerful stick and scramble out of the teepee to find one. They bring back a broken branch they've wrapped in long grasses, and the storytelling begins.

They ask how the Indians cooked their food without a microwave? How they called each other without a phone (smoke signals and drum beats, we explained) and how they could tell time without a clock.

"That's a great question. They used something called a sundial. According to where the shadow was cast, that's how you knew what time it was." I answer.

"I wanna make a sundial!" Taylor says.

So we fashion our own sundial in the side yard using sticks

and rocks, and are able to see from our long shadows that the sun will soon set.

"Let's watch a movie and have a picnic in the living room," Cissy suggests. *Dances with Wolves* happens to be on TV, which falls perfectly in line with the theme of our day. Cissy drags all the pillows and blankets in the house into the living room, while I make popcorn. Over the *pop, pop, pop,* I hear Troy being silly, my kids giggling in the living room. I feel a lump rise in my throat, hot tears in my eyes. As the four of us snuggle together to watch the movie, I know this is a gift. We must cling to days like this, because we'll need to remember it the next time we feel like giving up, the next time I want to jump out of a moving car, the next time Troy can't get out of bed because he feels broken and worthless. This moment is everything.

BROKE-ASS AND HAPPY

✤ ✤ ✤

Jamaican people sing, all the time. The cabbies, the porters, the chefs, and the busboys. It doesn't matter if they have terrible voices and no pitch. They aren't concerned with anyone's judgment. They sing mightily because it's in them.

When Troy and I were on our honeymoon in Jamaica, we fell in love with the people and their capacity for joy. We made fast friends with the locals and spent much of our time hanging out with them. One day we were on a rickety, old bus traveling to Dunn's River Falls. All the windows were open, the damp tropical heat upon us. As we drove through a thick, tangled jungle in Ocho Rios, I was touched by the sight of women with dewy, cocoa-colored skin, washing their laundry, bathing their babies in the river, and of course, singing. The scene became a permanent snapshot in my mind, reminding me how beautiful the world can be. A tourist sitting behind us on the bus blurted out, "How can they be happy when they're so poor?"—as though happiness was an extravagance reserved for the rich.

Happiness can be found in the oddest of places; hospitals, homeless shelters, third-world countries. We catch glimpses of it while our lives are falling apart. Money and things come and go. You have them one day, and then you don't. But we are learning that happiness is always attainable—even to the man with empty pockets. And we learn that we can still sing, just because.

Tonight is Christmas Eve, one year after the fire, and we are poor. We put aside fifty dollars for each of the kids and twenty-five dollars for each other. We could only afford a small tree, but I put it up on a table so it looks bigger, and swathed the pedestal in fabric and twinkle lights.

Because we couldn't afford to shop this year, I made gifts for everyone; a doll for Cissy's collection, a hand-painted checkers set for Taylor, and my trash-to-treasure creations for everyone in the family. I wrapped the gifts in butcher paper, tied with twine, topped with eucalyptus sprigs from the tree in our front yard. As I set the last of our meager presents under the tree, I feel content. The upside of being broke is we didn't spend our days hustling around the mall, trying to find parking spaces, railing at the crazy traffic. Instead, we watched classic holiday films together. We baked cookies. We made ornaments out of salt dough and pinecones. We read *The Night Before Christmas*, *Little Women*, and *The Littlest Angel*. We caroled with friends, and sang like Jamaicans.

Troy's parents dropped by yesterday for a couple hours, and we had a lovely visit. Everyone is trying their best to make things better, though I'm still at a loss as to what went wrong. I made them gifts from my One of a Kind trash-to-treasure business, and they seemed to really appreciate it. Anyway, it was a far cry from our first Christmas with them. Every small step toward progress gives me hope.

On Christmas morning, we make the kids wait in their room until Andy Williams sings "It's the Most Wonderful Time of the Year." Two brightly colored nutcrackers stand at attention on the coffee table, hard candies and tinsel scattered around them. The Polly Pocket Mansion Cissy's been pining for is set up under the tree, as is Taylor's shiny red scooter. Troy starts the music and the kids burst through the door like they've been shot from a cannon. They stop short at the threshold of the living room, gasping. Cissy's eyes are wide and misty. Taylor can barely take it all in. You'd think Daddy Warbucks brought Christmas.

Later that night, we lounge with the kids on the couch, watching *A Christmas Carol*. Ebenezer Scrooge takes inventory of his life, and I begin to think of my own. Not since I was very young have I felt the spirit of Christmas the way I do now. Year after year, I realize we've insulated ourselves. We numbed out with the mindless shopping, pushing ourselves to exhaustion, trying to make others happy with what we buy, all the while anesthetized to what we should be feeling. If I wasn't broke, I may have never known this. In a way, I feel richer now. I think about forest fires, bursting open seed pods, and how we are beginning to experience our lives in a new and profound way.

Just as I'm nodding off on the couch with Cissy and Taylor curled up on either side of me, Cissy looks up at me with sleepy eyes and says, "Today was the best Christmas *ever*." She closes her eyes, and as her breathing becomes slow and even, I hear Tiny Tim's famous words on the TV, "God bless us, everyone."

IN FEBRUARY, Troy gets a gig scoring a film called *The Road to Flin Flon*, a comedy starring up-and-coming actor Jamie Kennedy. The producers want a soundtrack with acoustic guitars and a bluegrass feel. Right up Troy's alley.

After tucking the kids in bed, I nestle in my favorite armchair to work on some lyrics, close enough to see Troy in my peripheral vision. He's completely in his element. Comedy and music are his greatest joys in life. This is an indie film, which means the pay is low, but that's usually the way it works in our business. The more enjoyable the gig, the lower the pay. Troy sets up a small TV and VCR in the corner of our dining room where he runs the scenes day and night, composing the soundtrack.

I watch him work for hours without eating or getting tired. He is on fire, impassioned. He's in his own world, far away from me. I long to understand his language, but I can't read a note of music. I made my way through the music business entirely by feel. But Troy is a wunderkind, from a young age he's been a kind of musical genius. He taught himself how to play the guitar by dropping the needle on Eagles records, listening to the solos over and over until his dad thought he'd lose his mind. But that annoying hobby of his became his life. Music is a language all his own, a language he understands. Music was also his refuge, a place to hide when things got tense in his childhood home. A place to hide now.

After high school, which he hated, Troy went to a four-year music school where he would eat, sleep, and breathe music. He was a prodigy. Everyone, even his music professors, said he would be a star. Bankrupt and struggling at thirty-four is not what anyone envisioned for him. I wonder, had he not married me, if he would have fulfilled that dream and been a star. I wonder if marrying me held him back, if I was an anchor around his neck. I wonder if he thinks about that. I wonder if one day he'll get sick of all this stress and bullshit, pack up, and disappear just like my stepdad Gene did. And then I tell myself to trust him. Trust him.

For months I've been telling him I want us to be a band, like Fleetwood Mac. We're already writing and recording new songs to replace the album we lost in the fire. I want this album to be a mixture of both our songs, and suggest we call our band the Brave Souls. He says he doesn't want to be in a band with me—it's too risky.

"Come on," I say. "You're my Lindsey Buckingham, I'll be your Stevie Nicks."

"Bands always fight and break up," he says.

In his early twenties, he was engaged to the lead singer in his band. Their future was all set—the wedding plans, the joint bank account, the furniture in storage ready for their new home. It ended badly. That's an understatement. It ended Disastrously, with a capital D. She was a nice Catholic girl who didn't believe in premarital sex. In order to marry her, Troy had to be baptized in the Catholic Church. He has terrible memories of that day, the holy water dripping from his hair, his mother sobbing in the pews. Soon after, Troy would find out that his sweet little Catholic girl was fucking the drummer in their band. It would take him a year to crawl out from under the emotional wreckage, and a lifetime to forgive himself for not knowing.

"But I'm not Catholic," I say. And I promise him I'd never fuck the drummer. He still says no to the band idea. He says he will play *in* the band, and produce the songs, and co-write with me, but we won't *be* a band.

"Then you should make your own album," I say. "You are too great a songwriter—you can't leave that part of you behind."

"I will," he says, "one day."

But "one day" seems far off, completely unreachable.

Troy talks a lot these days about quitting music. He thinks

our money problems are his fault. If only he made more money, he says, none of this would have happened. He wants to be the one to save us, just like he did the night of the fire. He thinks maybe getting a "real" job will set things right.

"So what are you going to do? Throw your talent away and be a bank teller? A door-to-door salesman? What?"

I tell him there is no way I'm going to stand by and let that happen. And anyway, he's making a good living as a musician, there isn't any job that he could start at this point that would bring him a higher wage.

"Music has nothing to do with our financial problems," I say. "If anything, music has saved our asses, both financially and emotionally. Music keeps us alive and hopeful."

I'm smart enough to know Troy is the one with promise in that arena. I have music in me, but he has genius. If anything, I'll go get a corporate job, while he builds his career. I am willing to put my time in. The way I see it, it's like supporting him through medical school. I know one day his career will carry us.

THE NEXT MORNING, I start working on a new resume and scouring the want ads. Something will come through for us. It has to. Every day I remind myself: *This too shall pass.* I know that to be true, even if it's taking a long, damn time. In the meantime, my children are sleeping in their beds, healthy, whole. My husband is working, an array of guitars and banjos and various stringed instruments surrounding him. And who knows? Maybe something good will come from this film. I'll find a job. We'll pull ourselves out of this mess, and he'll get his big break. Better days are surely ahead of us.

THE AVALANCHE

❧ ❧ ❧

As we sit at the Mexican restaurant, a fundraiser for our kids' school, we know there is a good chance we'll see Scott and Sarah today. It's a year since I said good-bye to Sarah in Gary's front yard, and I'm finally feeling stronger. We still see them from a distance at every school function, and though it's like a kick in the gut, the kick gets duller as time passes. But Cissy and Lauren now ignore each other at school. It breaks my heart to see what we've done to our kids. I am cutting Taylor's quesadilla for him when Troy gets a worried look on his face. "Don't look now, but Scott and Sarah are coming our way," he says.

"Hmm," I shrug, trying to seem disinterested.

"And Deirdre is with them."

"What? Why would they bring her here?" They know Deirdre threatened to sue us. And they knew we would be at this luncheon. There is no reason for Deirdre, who has no children and no association with the school, to be at our children's school fundraiser. They breeze past our table, looking past us, laughing loudly. It feels like a cruel intentional slap in our faces. But why? Why kick a family who is already down?

Cissy is ten years old, but too old for her age. She drops

her fork, watches them walk by, narrowing her eyes. She knows what's going on. I look around the table at my family. Troy looks away, shaking his head in disbelief. Taylor watches them pass us without saying hello, a confused look on his face. This needs to stop.

"I'm going over there," I say, fuming.

"Don't do it," Troy warns.

"Why? Should I just sit here like a victim? I'm done!" I throw my napkin down.

Troy shakes his head as I get up and march across the restaurant.

I lean across the table, eye to eye with Deirdre, and ask what's been on my mind all year. "How do you sleep at night, knowing you've bankrupted my family?"

Sarah immediately jumps to her defense, "How do *you* sleep at night?"

"Fine, thanks," I lie.

Deirdre broods in silence, her jaw clenching, unclenching, letting everyone handle her problems for her.

Scott jumps in, "Just get out of here, Hollye. No one wants you." He waves his hand dismissively. Scott knows this is my Achilles' heel. I had confessed to him my deep insecurity about being unwanted. He goes straight for the kill. He shoos me, "Leave, so we can enjoy our dinner. Stop playing the victim."

Just a year before, as my house burned, Scott sat on his knees in front of me and Taylor, holding our hands, crying, "Thank God you're alive. Thank God."

And now this.

I straighten my back. "Yeah, Scott. I have been a victim. But I will never let you hurt me or my family again. I *will* overcome this, and come back stronger." I turn and walk back to our table, shaking.

Troy told me not to go over there. He told me not to do it. But I couldn't sit there like a sad, frightened rabbit in front of my kids. More than anything, I had to do it for myself, to convince myself that yes, I *would* get through it. But at this moment, that doesn't seem possible. Troy hurriedly pays the check and we leave the restaurant. He puts his arm around me, guiding me through the parking lot. I can't even see straight. He helps me into the car, handling me like a china doll, and as he gingerly shuts the car door, I lose it. I cry with all the pain and fury I've been carrying for a year. Cissy and Taylor witness this from the backseat. Cissy makes grand attempts to cheer me up. "Who cares what they think, Mommy! They stink!" Cissy and Taylor call Deirdre "Diarrhea Blockhead"—which is the worst thing a five- and ten-year-old can think of to call a person. Shame wells up in me when I feel their little hands on my shoulders. "Please don't cry, Mommy."

At home, I take to my bed and let it all go until there is barely anything left of me. The kids make me cards and draw pictures of rainbows and happy faces. I still have these beautiful acts of mercy. If not for my kids, I don't know how I would believe in anything again.

OUR MUTUAL FRIENDS CARRIE and Jack can't understand it. Even Sarah's parents call and ask us what on earth happened? They say they ask Scott and Sarah why our friendship ended, but their questions go unanswered.

I have to understand, have to know why they stopped loving me. If it's something I've done, or said, or something in the way I am, maybe I can fix it. I can fix me, I can change and be someone who is lovable, but just like the situation with Troy's family, no one gives me any answers.

May 13, 1996

My heart has been racing, all day and night, for a week now. At times it is so intense I feel like I'm dying. I feel so frightened and alone. Troy has been thrashing in his sleep with nightmares. I imagine he is still dreaming about the fire. I miss my marriage. Things have been so difficult for so long, there's no time or space for us. I know he misses me, too. We've definitely had our problems in the last year, but we love each other so much. How can we get back to that? How do you embrace each other when you're both trying desperately not to drown?

WHILE MY KIDS ARE at school, I go through the want ads with my red pen. Having fallen from my perch in the fashion industry, I quickly realize how supremely unqualified I am for everything else. I have no degree and no computer skills to speak of. No one wants to hire an entrepreneur. I feel truly desperate. I join a temp agency, but they are not able to place me at a single job. Not even for one day. Two years earlier, I was in New York selling my spring clothing line. Buyers from Macy's, Barneys, and Fred Segal lined up to place orders. I was so busy I couldn't even take a lunch break for the four days of the spring show. Now I am someone who can't get hired as a temp.

I'm kicking myself for not taking a normal, safe job in the first place. It was such a huge gamble to own a business, and on top of that, I entered into a business relationship with Deirdre? What an idiot. My family is suffering and it's all my fault. Every bit of it. I have to find a way to bail us out. I keep at those want ads, sending résumé after résumé. I call, leave messages. I will prove to the world that I am worth something. But the world instead proves something to me. My phone does not ring.

꙰ ꙰ ꙰

AT MY LOWEST POINT, I take a telemarketing job. I dress in my best, donated clothes, and arrive hopeful and willing. The office has a stale and musty smell, the overhead fluorescent lights flickering, the desks in ramshackle order with drawers that don't quite shut. It's everything you'd expect from a telemarketing operation selling printer cartridges. Well, let's call it what it is. In training, they instruct us to "fool" people into believing they've already ordered the cartridges, and have forgotten to give us the credit card number. Some office managers fall for the scam. The upside, they tell us, is that the hours, 6 a.m. to 2 p.m., are great. Quick cash and you're out of there, with the rest of the day free to take care of your kids, or go on auditions (the top sellers are actresses). Two hours into the training, I walk out.

A few weeks later, my friend Martina and I are doing a recording session together, singing backgrounds on a Disney album. In between takes, I tell animated stories about my desperate job search, making everyone laugh. My wisecracking and sarcasm have carried me a long way through grief.

"You know, I just quit my job. It's in the beauty industry," Martina says, "I'll bet they still have my position open over there—you want me to put in a good word?"

"Are you kidding? Please, put in many, many good words! I implore you!"

"Done," she says.

Martina worked at a company that manufactured skincare and haircare lines for high-end salons and celebrities. She tells me they use natural ingredients, don't test on animals, have good health benefits, and a 401(k) plan. Sounds good to me.

Several days later, I walk through the doors at Aware Products, scrubbed shiny as a new penny, praying in my head as I wait to be interviewed. The receptionist leads me down a long, weirdly lit hall, reminiscent of *The Shining*. My eyes dart back and forth looking for a kid on a big wheel. At the very end of this hall, in a corner office, I meet Kevin, the sales manager. He rises and gives me a firm handshake and I can't help but notice he actually kind of looks like Jack Nicholson. *Heeere's Johnny!* We seem to hit it off. I interview well, I think. I feel confident as I tell him about my history both as a national business owner and a corporate salesperson. As we wrap up our conversation, Kevin says he really likes me, but they just hired a new guy to fill Martina's position and he doesn't have a position open right now. But he says he'll keep me in mind for the future.

Discouraged, I pick up the paper on my way home, and keep circling ads with my red pen. I interview at one crap job after the next. In a moment of financial panic, I accept a job as a telemarketer for a phone company. Never mind that I had owned a national company. Forget about the fact that my designs were featured in magazines and in the windows of Barneys in Manhattan. I am about to become one of those vultures that call while you're eating dinner. There are only so many times I can play the "camping" charade with my kids.

Before my first day of telemarketing, I call Aware Products one more time, and give the sales manager, Kevin, my last pitch.

"If you can find a place for me, I will be your top seller. Selling is what I know. If you can't, I've got another offer and I'm going to take it." It's a bluff for sure, but I've got nothing to lose.

He pauses, "Let me see what I can do. I'll call you back."

I hang up the phone, and pace the floor, wringing my hands. Oh please, oh please, I pray for this job. I literally get down on my knees.

The next day, Kevin calls me. "We are going to create a position for you," he says. Redemption. I feel the burden being lifted. "Can you start on Monday?"

"Absolutely!" I thank him for the opportunity and assure him I'll rise to the challenge. "You won't regret this," I tell him.

A lump rises in my throat as I contemplate my new life. Yes, I wanted this job because we are starving. And yes, this also means that I have failed at pursuing my dreams. No more creativity, brainstorming, or trips to New York. No more trash-to-treasure creations. Instead I will now be punching a time clock, and toeing the line. Though I want to feel grateful, hot tears are spilling out and before I know it I am lying face down on my bed in a sea of wadded Kleenex.

ON MY FIRST DAY at work, Kevin sets me up at a cubicle. Grey partitions separate me from the other sales reps. There is a grey desk, a beige phone, and a blank wall with no window. I am handed boxes of files with leads I am to follow up on. This is my new world.

I sit next to another sales rep named Richard, a six-foot-four, handsome gentleman. He steps around my partition and seems surprised to see me.

"Well, hello! Who are you?"

"I'm the new kid in cubicle town," I joke, pretending to put a gun in my invisible holster.

He falls into character with me, "What's your name, little filly?" He's understated, but registering on my gay-dar.

"They call me Hollye. And how about you? You're one tall drink of water."

"They call me Big Gulp," he smirks as he walks away.

Excellent. I think I just met my new best friend. This is a

relief after my less-than-successful encounter with Kevin's assistant, Erin. When I met her, I couldn't read her mind, but her face said, *Who's the blond bimbo?*

Boxes of files sit before me, mountains of paperwork I must climb. I told Kevin I'd be his top seller. I told him he wouldn't regret hiring me. I take a deep breath, thank God for the opportunity to work, and start dialing that phone.

CLIMBING THE MOUNTAIN AFTER THE AVALANCHE

❧ ❧ ❧

I sit cross-legged on the prickly half-dead grass, unwrapping my sandwich. I have a half hour for lunch each day, and always spend it outside on a narrow strip of lawn that stretches along the employee parking lot. I feel like I'm living my life in a fog. The huge company sign AWARE looms above me, and I am well "aware" of the irony. I lean my back against a telephone pole, eating my peanut butter sandwich and writing in my journal.

I am grateful to be working at Aware. It's a good company. My whole family has bouncy, shiny hair, and my bills are getting paid. I can finally exhale for the first time in two years. Even still, punching a time clock and sitting in a grey cubicle all day with no window makes me nuts. I feel the walls of my tiny grey space closing in on me, and wonder how I drifted so far away from my old life. And as Troy drops me off for work in the mornings in our one car, he is quiet and distant. I know he feels badly that I have to work, but in a way, I feel like he resents me for it.

I put down my pen and watch the birds that linger a few feet away, waiting to swoop in for my crumbs. I'm not surprised by the pigeons, but I am dumbfounded by the flock of seagulls that hang out in this industrial area of Chatsworth. They are a good thirty miles away from any seashore. Don't they know that? Are they some sorry-ass generation of gulls hatched in a parking lot that never knew they were seabirds? They could be living in Malibu, feasting on clams and sand dabs. Right over the next mountain range stretches the glorious shoreline of the blue Pacific, but they can't see it from where they're perched, on the edge of an industrial dumpster. I am just like them. I know there is somewhere else I'm supposed to be. This is not my destiny, yet here I am, and I can't see my way out either.

Kevin's assistant Erin, the one who didn't seem to like me, steps outside. She looks back and forth, then asks, "What are you doing out here?"

"Just relaxing, eating lunch." I smile.

"Don't be by yourself! That's ridiculous. Come inside!" She waves me in, holding the factory door open with her foot.

"I'm not by myself, I have all these birds."

She looks at me like I'm nuts. "It's gross out here. Come on!" It seems she's not going to take no for an answer. I toss my bread crusts to the sorry-ass lost seagulls of Chatsworth, and head inside with Erin.

The lunchroom is filled with mostly women from the office, and Richard (Big Gulp) chatting and laughing. There is good camaraderie here. They have their office traditions: birthdays, baby showers, and special office days they've invented like "purple day" or "bring baby pictures to work day." It's a fun crowd and I like everyone. I'm still not too sure about Erin though. She was definitely irritated on my first day of work—frustrated that her boss Kevin never told her he hired a new employee whose training and paperwork she would now be responsible for. That irritation got projected on to me, but now she seems to be softening.

Everyone at the lunch table is talking about *Saturday Night Live,* a show I've watched religiously since my teens.

I join in the conversation, "Did anyone see the one Alec Baldwin just hosted?"

"I love him!" Erin shouts.

"Me, too," I say. "*Prelude to a Kiss* is my favorite movie. But when I saw him on *SNL,* I mean . . . wow. He's one of the funniest actors I've ever seen host that show."

"I know! Did you see that skit with Jan Hooks in the café, where he's a cowboy?"

"Yes! That's my favorite skit ever!"

All other conversation fades away as Erin and I recount the entire scene, laughing as we recite the line simultaneously, "You shouldn't give away your pie with breakfast—makes you look cheap." There is an instant click. We find out we have so much in common; music, pop culture, comedy, movies. Our Alec Baldwin obsession has sparked a connection. Before we even realize it, everyone has left the lunchroom and it's just the two of us.

"Wow, I guess we cleared the room," I laugh.

We get up and dump our lunch sacks, grabbing a cup of coffee on our way back, still gabbing nonstop.

"You know, I knew about you before you ever came to work here," Erin says.

"What do you mean?"

"You're the girl whose house burned down, right?"

"Yeah."

"When Martina worked here last year, she told us about

you. She asked us all to donate clothes and blankets and stuff. I donated some stuff to you."

I'm floored. I wonder if I've worn her clothing or wrapped my kids in her blankets. "Thanks," I say.

From that day forward, Erin grabs me from my desk at every lunch hour, probably for fear that this poor little fire-victim waif will end up alone on a pitiful stretch of dead grass with a bunch of misfit seagulls.

Erin and I share the same sense of humor. I admit, mine has become edgier. More than a chip on my shoulder, I guess you could say these last few years took a chunk out of me, and I don't much give a rat's ass if I piss someone off. What can they do, abandon me? Ha! Just an average Tuesday in my life. As our friendship progresses, I find that Erin likes that about me. She gets my sardonic wit, and it seems that all we ever do together is laugh. When a terrible tragedy hits our world, Erin will wait a few months and then say, "Let's start joking about it now, okay?" Laughter is a healing balm for us, a reminder not to take life so seriously. We are terribly irreverent at times, but it works for us.

Erin is the real deal. Comfortable in her own skin, she looks you straight in the eye when she talks to you, her eyes a pale, piercing green. If she thinks you're full of shit, one eyebrow might be slightly raised. She doesn't try to impress anyone, and doesn't care much if you don't like her. Subsequently, everyone loves her. She is beautiful and funny and passionate about life. Always game to go anywhere, try something new, be spontaneous, just like Troy and I are.

Erin comes from a close family; she's the the youngest of three sisters. Her father died in his sleep just a few years ago. He was only fifty years old. She's the one who pumped his cold chest, giving him mouth to mouth, trying to bring her father back to life. After the loss, her mother and sisters clung to one another, and mostly, to Erin. Although she's the youngest, there is a strength and dependability about her. In her family, at work, in friendships, everyone knows they can count on Erin. She is the rock—devoted and loyal, trustworthy, smart, competent—the opposite of everything I grew up with. I feel safe in my friendship with her. Safety is a feeling I long for.

Erin and I go out for happy hour after work. She comes to the house to watch *Friends* and *Ellen* with our family on Thursday nights. She adores Troy and the kids, and the feeling is mutual. Cissy develops an instant bond with Erin.

Troy and I were exhausted, run down. Our wells were dry. But Erin brings life back into our home. And so I decide to take a big risk and let someone back into my heart.

RIGHT AFTER I GOT my job, Troy got a gig producing an album for the actress and singer, Gloria Loring, a good friend of ours who he'd toured with over the years. Gloria called a few weeks ago to tell us she got a gig on a luxury cruise ship through Alaska's inland passage, and wanted to know if Troy could do the gig and bring me along. It happened to fall during the week of our seventh wedding anniversary. I had no vacation time accrued yet, but I promised my new boss Kevin I would work twice as hard when I got back, and he accepted. Erin offered to house sit and watch our new puppy, a black Lab we named Sky.

So here we are on the ship's deck, gliding through Glacier Bay on the day of our "Lucky Seven" anniversary. I can't believe the magnificence of the scene before me. Blue cathedrals of ice tower over us, tall as Manhattan skyscrapers. Chunks the size of Volkswagens calve off from ice walls and slosh around the cobalt-blue water, filling the air with a constant crackling sound, like a God-sized bowl of Rice Krispies. The Alaskan air is so cold it stings my face and fingers, the only exposed parts of my body. The first inhale is a shock to my system. I pull the hood of my parka close around my face and snuggle into Troy's side, giggling. We stand at the railing, alongside hundreds of other passengers huddled together, *oohing* and *aahing*. The massive ship drifts through narrow inland passages, around jagged edges with shades of blue I never knew existed. Gloria and the rest of the band join us on the deck, and we chat excitedly, taking pictures. After a few minutes, they've had enough of the cold and head back indoors. Troy and I stay outside as long as we can stand it, not wanting to miss a minute of the experience, but eventually our teeth are chattering so badly, we can't speak.

"Th-th-this isss s-s-so mu-mu-much f-f-fun," I say to Troy, a smile frozen on my face.

He looks at me with concern, "Honey, you're freezing! Let's get you back inside." He wraps his arms around me.

The automatic glass doors *swoosh* open. A gust of toasty warm air engulfs us as a waiter steps forward bearing a tray. "Hot chocolate, ma'am?"

"Yes, thank you!" I look up at Troy, beaming.

He touches my face. "You look so beautiful right now. Even with your little red nose. "

"It's because I'm happy." It's been so long since I've said those words, and so long since my husband has looked at me like this.

"I like you happy," he says.

"Me, too."

❦ ❦ ❦

INSIDE, WE CHANGE INTO bathing suits and robes, and saunter over to the glass encased top deck where fountains spray over the top of the pool, creating water tunnels you can swim through. We ease ourselves into one of the hot tubs on the Glacier Bay side of the ship, and before we are even half submerged, another waiter appears with flutes of champagne. Troy and I thank him, laughing under our breath at the absurdity of this dichotomy—this break from our real life.

I shrug and raise my glass, "When in Rome . . ."

We toast to our marriage, and to our endurance. I sidle up against him, slipping into the crook of his arm. I am awestruck by our sudden good fortune. We were drowning and life threw us a lifeline. Music brought us here, like an oxygen mask dropping down from the sky. The very same music that at times leaves us scrambling, has now given us this. We sip our champagne in silence while gliding past panoramic views of magnificent blue glaciers.

Troy juts his chin out and says in a mock British accent, "I wonder what the poor people are doing today."

"They're drinking champagne in a Jacuzzi in Glacier Bay."

We laugh and do our secret fist bump, clicking our wedding rings together, "Shazam," we say in unison.

We have nine days on the ship with full passenger status, and Troy only has to play shows on two of the nights. Since I'm along for the ride, Gloria asks me to sing backgrounds on a couple songs, which I gladly oblige. We have a room with a window—an extravagance on a cruise ship. Every day through that window, we see eagles soaring, blue whales gliding past, orcas breaching. We dine in elegant restaurants where Alaskan king crab, lobster tails, soufflés, and fine wines are our nightly fare. A ridiculous contrast from pancakes for dinner on Crazy-Mixed-Up-Backwards Day.

After dinner one evening, Gloria, who has carte blanche on the ship, hosts us at one of the exclusive bars. "What would you like to drink? The finest wine? The finest scotch? You choose!"

I order a glass of champagne. Troy chooses a fifty-year-old scotch that is seventy bucks a shot. No sooner have they served it to him then the glass is empty. When Gloria spies the empty glass, she shrieks, "What happened to your *seventy-dollar scotch?*"

Troy shrugs, "I was thirsty."

That sends everyone into an uproar of laughter, and becomes the story Gloria will tell again and again that week.

Gloria's opening act is a comedian named Wayne Cotter, who has brought his very pregnant wife Lucy, a no-nonsense New Yorker who unwittingly plays the perfect straight man to Wayne's offhand schtick. We hit it off with Wayne and Lucy right away. Wayne keeps us all howling at dinner each night. At one point, after catching my breath, I turn to Lucy and say, "It must be so much fun being married to a comedian!"

Lucy responds in her deadpan New York manner, "Yeah. It's a nonstop laugh riot."

Troy and Wayne are partners in comedy crime, riffing off one another, breaking into spontaneous juggling contests, or fashioning various elements of our dinners (napkins, crab legs) into party hats. Troy is alive and vibrant again. This is the guy I used to hang out with at Denny's until 4 a.m.—the one who could make me laugh for hours. How I missed him, as I'm sure he missed the girl who sparkled with joy and laughter.

ON THE EIGHTH DAY we pull into port at Skagway. Our group piles into the local saloon (a refurbished brothel) to

drink, play piano, and sing. Troy and I stop by for a bowl of
the famous salmon chowder, but we want to get out into the
wild to really experience the majesty of this place. We ask the
locals where we can see some "real" Alaska. They point us
toward a hiking trail on the outskirts of town.

Troy and I set out on the trail, which winds up a steep
mountain. The path is about eighteen inches wide and skirts
the edge of the mountainside. There are no guardrails if we
lose our footing. This requires Zen focus. The trail leads us
into a lush, dark forest, where the ground is thickly blanketed
in orange pine needles, so soft and untouched by human feet
it's like stepping on a spongy mattress. At times we have to
bend back branches or scramble over fallen logs covered in
mysterious vines, hoping we don't return home with equally
mysterious rashes. The forest is so dense we can see nothing
behind or ahead of us, and I begin to think of this journey as
metaphor for our lives. It is full of twists and turns; we have
no idea what to expect or where we're going. We are
submerged in darkness one moment, then suddenly we find
ourselves in a clearing, silent and peaceful. Minutes later, we're
climbing over a boulder, or clinging to a ledge with a fifty-foot
drop below. And still we keep marching forward, not knowing
if we're even on the right path. I don't know if Troy is
thinking the same thing, but he seems to be in deep
contemplation. We've been climbing for almost an hour. I can
feel the elevation in my lungs. Finally, breathless and red-
faced, we reach the top of the mountain. Stepping out of the
forest into the clearing, we stop.

"Wow," Troy whispers. Before us is a vast meadow
surrounding a cobalt-blue lake. We are so high the sky seems
close enough to touch. Grey-blue clouds hang above us,
grazing the edges of the lake. A soft mist falls, giving a

sparkling effect to the air. But for a few birds, it is absolutely still. We have just stumbled into nature's most sacred cathedral. I slip my hand into Troy's, leaning my head on his shoulder. It seems bad form to talk in a place like this. Hand in hand, we walk to the edge of the water and sit together on a log where, without speaking a word, we fall into an instant, deep meditation. We sit side by side, wordless, for I don't know how long. A subtle vibration moves through me like a wave. I feel like I'm floating inside myself. I am completely at peace, and for just these few moments, for no reason that I can explain, I have a deep knowing that everything is exactly as it should be and I have nothing to fear. Ever.

As time passes, the feeling gradually subsides, and my city-slicker fears begin to emerge. We are all alone at the top of a mountain in Alaska. No one knows where we are. We don't even know where we are. That's typical of us. When we travel, we always involve ourselves in some crazy shenanigan we would never consider at home. Like boarding the bullet train in Japan with no idea where we were going, or climbing up a wet, mossy rock three stories tall, and then cliff diving into the Jamaican ocean, or traveling deep into Mexico to get a taste of "authentic" Mexican food, and finding ourselves in the middle of a revolution, angry mobs protesting in the streets. We squeeze every experience for all it's worth. But sometimes we have to stop and remind ourselves, we have kids at home who need us to return in one piece.

"Ummm," I punctuate the silence, "remember that grizzly we saw from the deck yesterday?"

"Mmm hmm," Troy says, his voice calm. "That was amazing."

"Yeah, it really was. But umm . . . I was just thinking . . . maybe we should head back?"

Troy rises slowly and stretches. We stand together in the stillness, breathing in that air, that peace.

"I don't want to leave this place. This was . . ." I take a sweeping look around me, but words fail. I close my eyes and lay my head on Troy's shoulder. It feels so good to be close to my husband again.

Troy pulls me tight against him, lightly stepping on both my feet. He squeezes me tight, and lets out a long, heavy sigh, one he'd been holding in for a year.

"We're going to be okay, baby. Everything's going to be okay."

This time, I believe him.

We take one last look, absorbing every detail of that sacred place before heading back down the long mountain trail.

AS WE PULL INTO the driveway at the Happy House a day later, we are shocked to find the mountain behind our home scorched. There had been a brush fire while we were gone. It burned all the way to our fence, but the house remained unscathed. This time, we got lucky.

DREAMING IS FREE

❦ ❦ ❦

I peruse the aisles of our neighborhood bookstore, running my fingers along the spines of books both old and new, breathing them in. Bookstores have always been my place of worship, my refuge. In my college days, when I felt like a fraud that didn't belong among the best and brightest, I'd have panic attacks (eventually causing me to drop out). When the symptoms would start—heart beating erratically, rib cage tightening, mouth dry, hands trembling—I'd run for the campus bookstore, sit on the floor and literally stick my nose in a book. The smell of fresh print on the pages soothed me. I would breathe. Breathe in. Out. Beautiful, hopeful words. I would breathe them. And then when I was calm, I would read them.

Books have always been my compass. When I didn't know how to be in the world, I found my answers in books. When I needed parental role models, I found them in authors. In college, Hugh Prather was my imaginary father, Maya Angelou my mother. And music! Todd Rundgren was my life guide. His lyrics lit my path. "You can't stop love in action . . ." I'd sing it over and over to myself.

Bookstores suspend reality for me. I lose myself in them,

literally. I tell no one where I am, sit in a corner with a stack of books, and read for hours, with no concept of time.

On this particular day, I am scrunched up on the floor, knees against my chest, in a narrow aisle of the store, poring over *The Artist's Way* by Julia Cameron. Donna recommended it to me, saying I must read it to rescue my creative spirit. I read until it grows dark outside. I'm shocked to discover I've been here three hours.

When I notice the sun waning, I go ahead and purchase the book. The store's owner, a slight balding man with reading glasses perched halfway down the bridge of nose, appears to be relieved, either that I'm finally making a purchase or that I got up off the floor after three hours. At home, I stick a frozen pizza in the oven for the kids, then curl up in my armchair and read it to the end. Something kicks on, like a switch has been flipped. Something has ignited inside me. Is it . . . hope?

Cameron's book requires weekly exercises, in which she asks you to take on a practice of "extreme self-care" and nurturing your dreams. Sounds frivolous, I think. My unconscious belief is that I can't afford to have dreams. Dreams are for people who live easy lives. But the more I think about it, I know that concept is wrong. Even people in prison have dreams. Dreaming is actually the one thing I can afford. The real problem is: I've forgotten how to do it. Instead, I've perfected the art of worrying and waiting for the other shoe to drop.

I need to build a supportive community to give me the courage to dream. I ask Troy to join me, but he says he can't spare the time. Late that night, I call Joy and Bob, my musician buddies that Troy and I have been doing gigs with on weekends. I'm fired up, just having read the entire book, and I'm preaching the word. They see the light and jump on board. Hallelujah!

Joy is a powerhouse singer and songwriter, hoping to record an album with her band. She just turned forty, and is worried about her relevance in the music industry. Bob is a keyboardist who lost two fingers in a high school metal shop accident. With only eight fingers, he manages to outplay every keyboardist I've ever worked with. He is also the part-time father to a three-year-old daughter and going through a divorce. Each of us is lost and fumbling in our own ways. The timing is perfect, so we join forces, make a pact, and I feel the slightest twinges of renewed faith. Maybe *this* is my new beginning, I think.

Joy, Bob, and I meet Saturday mornings for pancakes and coffee and inspiration. We keep each other accountable to the exercises, which require us to write three pages every morning upon waking, take daily walks as a meditation, make goals for ourselves, and take a baby step toward them each week. Once a week we have to go somewhere alone, and immerse ourselves in inspiration, whether that's walking through a forest, a museum, a bookstore . . . whatever it is that lights us up inside. This is what Cameron calls "filling the well." As she explains it, you can't pump water (creativity) from a dry well, and Lord knows—my well had run dry on so many levels.

My goal is to do another album. The songs we lost in the fire no longer fit me. I want to do an album with new songs that reflect who Troy and I are now. My grief already squeezed a few good songs out of me. Love, loss, and betrayal make for prolific songwriting.

Troy works most days producing independent artists at Doug Cotler's studio, and Doug lets us use the studio anytime it's not booked. We spend so many nights there recording, Taylor lying on the floor coloring, or riding his matchbox cars along the windowsills, humming to himself. There's one song on that album where we can hear Taylor's little voice whispering in the background. Only Troy and I know it's there. I love that. Joy sings the background vocals on the album, and Bob plays keyboards, time-stamping this chapter of our friendship and all that we've shared: carpooling to gigs together on weekends, the long car rides home, our artists' breakfasts, the camping trips we take in between.

At night, after we read them stories and tuck the kids into bed, Troy and I sit in the living room with acoustic guitars and work on our songs. Sometimes they pour out of us, sometimes not. The process of writing together is not different from living together, from loving each other. Sometimes it's fraught with tension, sometimes it flows easily, and sometimes it seems impossible. But always, it is good for us. Always music lifts us out of our heads, and our worries about money, and our questions about God. Somehow, in music, we find a path, much like the one in Alaska. We don't know where we're going, but we believe it will lead us to a good place. And my newfound book is teaching me how to map out my own course.

FIGHT CLUB

❦ ❦ ❦

My brother Kyle no-shows my mother's annual Christmas Eve party again. He never calls. Of course we worry, but we pretend that we don't, because we want to be happy on Christmas. This is just business as usual with Kyle.

Early Christmas morning, I know my mom is worried sick. I call her at the crack of dawn and say, "Hey, why don't you and Eric jump in the car right now and come watch the kids open their presents from Santa?" And within twenty minutes, they are at our front door. I know she needs this distraction. No mention is made of Kyle, whether he's lying dead in an alley somewhere, whether he's ODed or in jail again. Later that night, we go to Mom's for Christmas dinner. After dinner, as the kids are opening their gifts from Mom and Eric, Kyle walks in. He is bloody and disheveled from a fight with a drug dealer. There is a gash in the back of his head, and he tells my mother that just hours before, a drug dealer pinned him to the ground and put a gun in his mouth. My mother ushers him into another room to protect my kids from hearing this, but it's too late. A pall has been cast over us. Kyle comes back into the living room, and spies the big boxes by the tree with his name on them.

"This is for me?" he asks with mock surprise, because I know this is the only reason he's showed up tonight. He opens his gifts. My mother, hoping against hope, has bought him an electric guitar and an amp.

"I know you lost your last guitar," she says. "Now you can start again."

My stomach turns with anger. He didn't "lose" his last guitar, and he won't start again. It's obvious from his condition that he won't start again. Within the hour, he is screaming at my mother in front of the Christmas tree, in front of our kids. "Fuck you! I don't need your fucking judgment! I don't need you!"

He turns around to the rest of us, "Fuck all of you!"

He takes the guitar and amp, slams the door. We don't say anything, but we all know he's headed straight for the pawn shop.

LIFE GOES ON

✿ ✿ ✿

Last night I dreamt I was watching my dad walk out of my life forever. I was standing there with my guitar, calling his name softly. He wasn't listening. I only wanted to say good-bye. The title track of my album is about him:

> "Life goes on without you
> And the seasons still change
> I don't talk much anymore about you
> It's easier that way . . . ."

MARCH 3, 1997 IS the big night—our CD release concert at Luna Park in Hollywood. The stage is set, instruments in place. While checking my microphone, I'm shocked to see my brother, Kyle, walk into the club. He sang backgrounds on my album, on a song I'd written about domestic violence, a charge Kyle will later be jailed for. After Christmas, I hadn't heard a word from him until a few days before the show. He called, expecting to show up and perform with me. I wasn't having it. This was not an "anything goes" kind of night where Kyle could show up late, high or drunk. We fought about it on the phone and he hung up on me, but not before blaming me for his addictions. Tonight, he walks in like nothing ever happened. At least he appears to be sober and humble.

The room fills and soon is buzzing with excitement. This is not your average CD release party. Everyone knows what we overcame to make this happen. Right before I take the stage, I run to a payphone to call Cissy. She has come down with the flu, and is so disappointed to miss the show. I tell her I'll be singing the songs we wrote for both her and Taylor tonight, so in a way, they'll be here. "Break a leg, Mommy," she says with her scratchy, sore throat. That's all I needed to hear. I'm ready now.

I take the stage. A black, velvet curtain is draped behind me. Silver strands flutter, reflecting light that dances around the darkened room. As my eyes adjust through the fog of cigarette smoke I see the faces of people who love me: Kelly and Tara (who flew in from Arizona), Stephen La-dee-dah (who stepped up to be the record's executive producer), my mom and Eric, neighbors, childhood friends, lifetime friends, relatives. My mom and Aunt Laura sit by the door selling CDs. A brief wave of sadness passes through me that Deirdre, Sarah, and Scott aren't here, sitting right up front like they used to before everything changed, but then I have a moment of clarity: Erin, Joy, and Bob *are* here. The universe is taking care of me, and always has been. I was so lost in my sadness I couldn't see what was right in front of me. These friends came into my life when I was my weakest, my most broken down, and they loved me. They fill the sad, empty spaces that the others left behind.

The stage lights come up, the music begins, and I sing. I sing from my soul—telling our stories, pouring out all the emotion behind every song. Troy supports me with his solid guitar playing, bursting out in wailing, inspired solos. We are riding a wave together—he and I, and the audience. I feel it. No more dissonance. Now there is harmony.

After I perform the title track "Life Goes On," Kyle walks up to the stage and hands me a rose, which I assume my mother arranged. People who are using don't think ahead, go out, and buy roses for someone. It's hard for me to even know how to feel. Mostly around my brother, I feel profound sadness, for everything he's been through, for the lack of love and attention he had growing up. He is still a wounded little boy acting out. A boy who never grew up.

After the show, we pack the car. Our box of CDs is empty, which means people all over Los Angeles are listening to our songs tonight. Maybe they are driving down Sunset Boulevard right this moment, hearing my words. We are connected now. This is the beauty of art. Troy starts the car, and before we pull away from the venue, I lean over and kiss him, "You're amazing. Thank you. For everything."

"You did it, baby."

"*We* did it. And you are my Lindsey Buckingham whether you like it or not."

"Okay," he smiles. "I like it."

He looks so handsome, slightly weathered, a little rougher around the edges. Inside the unsteady, young guy I married, the man I'd caught glimpses of is beginning to emerge. I brush the side of his face with the back of my hand, feeling a surge of love for him, so powerful. It isn't about the show, or the CD. It's about getting knocked down and getting back up, crying ourselves to sleep and starting again the next day, it's about bankruptcy and injuries and laughter—everything that led us to this night.

Driving home, Sunset Boulevard is alive with music and

people and rockers and freaks and crazies at well past midnight. I still hold the rose my brother gave me. I run my fingers along the stem, feeling its sharp thorns.

"I remember how excited I was when I found out my mother was pregnant," I say. Troy puts a gentle hand on my thigh. "I counted the days until his birth. I filled a treasure box with gifts I'd gathered for him. Things like feathers, smooth stones, orange-and-red fall leaves. He was born in the fall. I got to hold him when he was born. I was seven years old. I remember thinking he weighed less than my pillow. He had these tiny dimpled hands, and he'd reach out to grab my finger," I trail off, tears in my eyes.

"You loved him the best you could. It's up to him now to make things right," Troy says.

There was hope back then, when Kyle was small and new, before his parents failed him, before the bullet entered his brain. It could have turned out a million different ways. But this is the way it panned out, with me shining on stage, and him standing in the shadow.

The Santa Ana Wind

✿ ✿ ✿

"I'm concerned about Taylor's eyes," his kindergarten teacher says one Tuesday when I show up for my usual volunteer time. She says that although he's in the highest reading group, he's missing out on a lot of class information because she's pretty certain he can't see the board. I hoped this day wouldn't come. I hoped his issues were something minor, that we could just slip under the radar. But now I've been confronted with it. I have to face it.

Because it's in line with his shy nature, no one thinks it odd that Taylor turns his head slightly away, looking at you out of the corner of his sleepy blue-green eyes, kind of like the shy skunk character in the movie *Bambi*. It appears to be one of his mannerisms—a cute affectation. But he looks at you like that because it's the only way he can focus. He also watches TV that way, and reads books that way and tries to read the board at school that way, but it isn't working anymore.

Taylor is bright, headed for the gifted program just like his sister. I taught them both to read at four years old, and they began kindergarten reading at a second-grade level. I'm not about to let anything set my son back from learning. I remember years before, when his optometrist said surgery might eventually be an option for him. I'd known it since he was born. The time has come for us to start exploring unpleasant but necessary options.

WHAT WAS DIFFERENT ABOUT my pregnancy with Taylor was that I knew at the moment of conception. I knew. I lay wide-awake in Troy's arms as his breathing became deep and even, very aware that something was about to change.

Taylor was born by cesarean section on a Friday the 13th, just a few days shy of his due date. He was so breathtakingly beautiful. Unscathed by the brutal passage through the birth canal, his tiny face and body were perfect. His little nose upturned, his lips full and rosy. Just after he was born, as Troy tried to snap a picture, Taylor held his hands up to his face, his long slender fingers shielding his eyes like a rock star ditching paparazzi. We marveled at those long slender fingers, and said then he'd be a musician.

In the days before and just after his birth, I worried. I was young, and it was my habit to worry about everything, as if worry could prevent anything bad from happening, like a reverse good-luck charm. But once I was home with him, I was completely calm. It was the first time in my life I had felt such peace. I'd had happy moments in my life, of course, but always shadowed by instability, a dark cloud looming overhead.

When Cissy was born, I was happy, but I wasn't at peace. I was in a stormy marriage, home alone with a sick baby girl every day. Cissy had begun projectile vomiting a few days after she was born. She was diagnosed with pyloric stenosis, a muscular blockage in the stomach, and had to have emergency surgery at two weeks old. She had terrible gastric pain and screamed and howled for the first six months of her life. There was nothing I could do to soothe her, though I tried. I paced, bouncing her on my shoulder, walking her up and down the street, putting her in the car seat, driving her around for hours, setting her on top of the washing machine, but nothing worked. Gary was absent for most of her infancy, working long hours. Instead of the joyful experience all the mothering books promised, I lived on a desert island of grief, doctor's visits, and worry.

In contrast, the first two months at home with Taylor were easy. He ate well, slept well, didn't suffer from colic the way my poor Cissy did. He gained weight rapidly, becoming a fat, little Buddha baby, and for that I practically fell to the floor and kissed the ground every day.

After Taylor's birth, my world consisted of only my baby boy, my little girl, and the husband I loved so much. Nothing else was real. I would dress Cissy for kindergarten in the mornings, taming her blond dandelion mane with barrettes and bows, then Troy would drive her to kindergarten while I nestled with Taylor, singing to him, promising him a beautiful life as the Gulf War blazed on TV in the background, the sound muted. I couldn't be bothered with the Gulf War and it's night vision cameras and flashpot bombings and eerie green glow. I was in an oxytocin-induced love-fest with my newborn. The Gulf War was just a TV show I could turn off. So I did.

Two months was the cut-off point. Two months was the end of my maternity leave, meaning I'd have to leave my nirvana state and return to my corporate sales job. Two months was when the reality of the war hit me. Two months was when Taylor had his well-baby checkup, and when my unflappable, easygoing pediatrician told me, "I'm concerned about Taylor's eyes."

Taylor's eyes shifted back and forth involuntarily, and he seemed unable to make eye contact with us, but I assured myself that this was normal for his stage of development.

"But all new babies have wiggly eyes," I argued with Dr. Calig, as if I could make what he'd just said untrue.

Dr. Calig nodded, "Yes, but it should be under control by two months. Taylor's gotten worse."

Since Cissy's medical-emergency-filled first month of life, I'd rushed her into Dr. Calig's office with every small sniffle and fever—and he always smiled, shrugged, and assured me, "She's perfect. Nothing to worry about, Mom."

This was the first time I had ever seen Dr. Calig register concern. I felt like I was going to throw up. I immediately called the pediatric ophthalmologist, Dr. Carter, and was told they had no appointments for three weeks. Troy and I showed up at his office the next day and said we'd wait there all day long until he could see us. This was our newborn baby—if something was wrong there was no time to dillydally.

Dr. Carter took pity on us and did examine him that day. He told us, with compassion but straightforward candidness, "There are three things that could be happening with your son. He could have a brain tumor. He could be going blind. Or he could have congenital nystagmus, which is basically a short in the neurological wiring between the brain and the eye. If he has nystagmus, he'll be affected for the rest of his life, but with luck, he'll still be able to drive and read with special glasses."

I left the office praying for my son to have congenital nystagmus.

My immediate, illogical response was to bring Cissy and Taylor to have their photos taken together. I had to have an image of Taylor when he was perfect and new, when he was nothing but a fat, happy baby, untouched by any diagnosis.

Our first step was to rule out the possibility of a brain tumor. We took Taylor for a brain scan. He had to be anesthetized so he would lie still inside the machine. Seeing him drugged and unresponsive set off all my maternal alarms. He fell over my arms like a sack of flour. I wanted to run, scream, beg someone to assure me that two-month-old babies do not get brain tumors. Tell me God simply wouldn't allow it. Instead Troy and I quietly submitted to the tests, terrified, a wheel of prayer spinning inside our heads.

The technician who took the scan came out of the room. "All done," he said.

"And?" I asked, a panicked edge to my voice.

"I can't tell you that. I'm just a technician. You'll have to speak to the neurologist. She's in surgery now."

"When will she be back?" Troy demanded, putting a protective arm around me.

"Not sure, but you can go in and get your baby now," he pointed over his shoulder.

I burst through the door and swooped Taylor up, holding him tight against me.

We sat in the aptly entitled waiting room, waiting, waiting, waiting for the doctor to return. We read every *Good Housekeeping* in print. I tried to wake Taylor up enough to nurse but he was still too groggy.

"How much longer?" Troy would ask the receptionist about every half hour, and she would shrug.

By almost 5 p.m. (and this was a Friday) the receptionist said, "She probably won't come back to the office at this point. But she'll be in Monday morning."

I felt like I got kicked in the chest. At the same time, through the front window I saw the technician leaving, walking across the parking lot. I gave Troy the baby and ran after him, catching up with him just as he was getting into his car.

"You're leaving?"

He looked up, startled. "I told you, ma'am. I'm not allowed to read the scans."

"But you saw it! You saw the image of my son's brain, right?"

"Yes."

"And you're going to go home and have a nice weekend, and I'm going to be pacing, nauseous all weekend, not knowing if my baby has a brain tumor," I said, my voice breaking, "Please, just tell me if you saw anything bad in that scan. Don't leave us like this."

He sighed, then groaned, "Aw come on lady, I could get fired for this."

"Please," I implored, on the verge of hysteria.

He looked down, hesitated, "There's nothing wrong with your baby's brain."

"Oh god," I put both my hands over my face, tears of relief flooding me.

"But when the doctor tells you that on Monday, act surprised. Okay?"

I nodded, barely able to speak, "Thank you."

He got in his car and sped away. I ran to Troy in the waiting room, my face a red, sweaty mess of tears.

"What happened?" He looked scared, clutching Taylor against his chest.

I picked up the diaper bag and told him to follow me outside, where I delivered the greatest news of our lives. Our baby was not going to be taken from us. God was not a monster. Blindness or nystagmus I could handle.

The next week we took Taylor to the world renowned Jules Stein Eye Institute at UCLA, where he would be tested for various conditions that could lead to blindness. I won't say it was worse than the other scare, but it came in a close second.

Taylor was strapped to a board, his head fastened with Velcro straps so he couldn't move. Contact lenses with multicolored spaghetti wires sticking out of them were attached to his corneas. His eyelids were taped open so he couldn't blink, like some horrible scene out of *A Clockwork Orange*. Then they ran strobe lights and colored lightbulb flashes in his face. He was wailing and so was I. I felt like I was reliving the nightmare from Cissy's first week of life: helplessly watching her through an observation window, my tiny, less than seven-pound baby, strapped to a board in only a diaper, while they pumped her body full of barium dye, and prepped her for surgery. And now this.

At the Jules Stein clinic, by the end of the testing, they were able to tell us that our baby boy was not going blind. They diagnosed him with congenital nystagmus, and we left there feeling like we had just won the lottery.

April 21, 1997

The Santa Anas are blowing hard today, but I'm not afraid. Sometimes the wind has to blow things away, make a clean sweep. It feels like it's bringing an exciting new change—good change. Not the destructive change the chill fall winds bring. I trust this wind.

SPRING ARRIVES, and with it strange mail begins arriving at our house—all addressed to the house owners, Mark and Deanna. Some of it is certified mail from the bank. A lot of it appears to be junk mail, but with a central theme: foreclosure. I stack the mail in a pile, one that grows larger by the day. I call

Mark to ask what's going on, but get no answer. I leave messages but don't hear back. Then Troy calls Mark again. And again.

In January, we'd renegotiated our lease with Mark and Deanna. Because we'd gone bankrupt, we needed extra time before the actual "purchase" part of the lease-purchase. It felt like a warm and fuzzy meeting. They agreed to extend the time to two years from the bankruptcy, and we wrote up a new contract. We thought everything was hunky-dory but now, all this mail and no word from him.

On the first of April, Troy leaves Mark a different kind of message: "Hey Mark. It's Troy and Hollye. We don't know what's going on, and you're not returning our calls, so we're not sending any more payments until we hear from you." We get our return phone call that day. Mark tells us that he and Deanna are going through a messy divorce and custody battle over their infant son. He says all future payments should be sent to him directly at his new address. Later that day, Deanna calls, and basically tells us the same thing, and that all payments should be made to her directly.

Then Mark calls again and says that Deanna is on drugs.

And then Deanna calls and says Mark is a wifebeater.

Then we stop answering the phone.

I remember Mark showing us around the English garden, Deanna happily pregnant, serving us fresh baked cookies, drinking hot cider together at the kitchen table while we wrote up the paperwork for the Happy House. The thoughtful note Deanna had left us, "Welcome to your home." That was only two years ago. How can love unravel so quickly? Could this happen to us?

Troy and I call the bank to find out what's going on. Although we paid Mark and Deanna every month without fail, even when it meant our utilities were cut off, Mark and Deanna were not paying the mortgage—for almost a year. In addition to the rent we paid, we had already invested $14,000 into the down payment on the house. Where is our $14,000? What about our contract?

That week, we call every friend we know who has any kind of legal connection, and finally find an attorney willing to help us out pro bono. Her name is Wasserman. We fax our contract and all paperwork over to her. A few days later, Troy and I get on opposite extensions of the phone for our phone meeting.

Her voice on the phone is kind, but no-nonsense. "I've read your contract," she says.

"So we're protected then, right? I mean, it's a valid contract," I say.

"Yes, it is a valid contract that Mark and Deanna have violated. Unfortunately, your only recourse is to sue them, which will likely take years, and will definitely cost tens of thousands of dollars. And then, maybe you'll recover your money, and maybe not. Honestly, by the time you've paid your attorney fees, it won't be worth it."

"But how can we protect ourselves?" Troy asks. "We don't want to lose our house and our investment."

"You've already lost your investment. The only way to keep the house is if you buy it now before the bank seizes it."

Although Troy and I are in separate rooms on different extensions, I feel our hearts drop in unison. We are months out of a bankruptcy. We know damn well we can't buy the house.

"But in the meantime," she says, "do not pay them another dime. You stay there until the bank makes you leave, and save what you can. You'll need it to move."

Move? But we don't want to move. This is our Happy House. This is our home. There has to be another way. If bad things can randomly happen to us, then so can good things, right? Somehow, we will overcome this crazy situation we're in, and the house will be ours. Yes, think positive, think positive.

I sit outside in my garden, trying to write my way through this. The wind picks up, rattling the wind chimes, blowing my hair into my eyes. Even through all my positive thoughts, the truth seeps in. I've been so stressed at work lately that I'm constantly getting sick, but now there's no way I can quit. We need a stable income for our credit. We need the health insurance for our son's surgery.

It's very likely we're going to lose our house and all the money we put into it. The ground beneath me is no longer solid. No amount of positive thinking is going to stop that wind, nor stop fate from marching forward. The only choice I have is acceptance, come what may.

BEFORE DAWN, we walk through the entrance of the Jules Stein clinic at UCLA. I help Taylor change out of his clothes and into a medical gown as we prepare him, and ourselves, for his surgery. We took him to a myriad of specialists, and I, as always, asked a million questions and took notes. I could practically speak like a surgeon myself by the end of it all. I'm terrified, but glad he's having the surgery here, at one of the most advanced centers for eye care in the world. This is one of the only places that performs this particular corrective surgery for congenital nystagmus.

The surgeon comes into the room to speak to us, knowing how insistent I am about being given all information. He begins explaining what they are about to do, making a rough sketch on a piece of paper, "Now here's where we will make the incisions. We will have to take the eyes out of the orbital sockets before we can readjust the—"

"Stop!" I put my hand up, feeling woozy. "Don't explain it to me this time." I lower myself into a chair, "Just do what you have to do, and treat him as carefully as you would your own son. Please."

Troy takes the lead with the doctors, asking questions, listening to the plans for the surgery, letting me take on the mommy role at Taylor's bedside. He has a much stronger stomach for these things. When I had an emergency cesarean with Taylor, Troy watched the whole thing. He found it fascinating.

I hold Taylor in my lap facing me, his head against my shoulder as the anesthesiologist injects him. He begins to cry, and then his cry becomes gravelly and groggy. I feel that same panic I felt before the brain scan, watching him pass out in my arms as an infant. There is no more counterintuitive feeling in the world than to let someone drug your child and take him from your arms. They put him on a gurney and strap him down. Troy and I stand over him brushing his hair back from his face, kissing his cheeks. He is so perfect. I don't want them to change him. I love him exactly as he is.

"We have to take him now," the nurse says. Troy grips the side rail of the gurney with both hands, moving along with them.

"Sir? You have to let go," she says.

Troy and I watch them wheel him away through the double swinging doors, as we cling to each other, both wiping tears from our eyes.

We walk around the UCLA campus mindlessly while we

wait for the surgery to be over. I won't remember much about
the walking, or the scenery, only the helpless feeling I have.
We should eat, but neither of us is hungry. For hours, we
shuffle up and down the streets of Westwood, meandering
aimlessly, looking blindly into shop windows. With no feeling
or desire for them, I buy a pair of boots on markdown, and
then chide myself as I walk around carrying them. What kind
of a mother buys shoes while her child is in surgery? We
return at the scheduled time, and soon after, the surgeon
comes out to tell us it's done, it has gone successfully, and they
are expecting great results.

"He will be blind for the next few days," the surgeon tells
us. "He'll need you at his side night and day until he regains his
vision. We'll see him for a follow-up exam next week."

At home we put Taylor in our bed, where he sleeps
through the remainder of the day. I throw those stupid boots
in the back of my closet and never wear them or look at them
again.

The next morning we wake to Taylor crying. He can't
open his eyes. His thick long eyelashes are crusted shut with
blood. Tears run in red streaks down his face. I sit beside him,
putting a warm washcloth over his eyes to soften the scabs.
After soaking them for a while, I ask him to try to open his
eyes. When he does, I have to look away, grateful he can't see
my reaction. The entire whites of his eyes are blood red.

For the next several days, I guide him to the bathroom,
feed him, hold a water glass to his lips. I forget about life,
work, the house, and focus on nothing but my son. I keep my
thoughts on gratitude—this surgery will improve the quality of
my son's life, and we are so fortunate to have access to it. In
another country, or even in another state, we wouldn't have
been so lucky. If I didn't have my job, we wouldn't have had

the insurance. I feel blessed, thanking God, karma, Buddha, and whomever else was out there, while always holding onto the imaginary lucky rabbit's foot in my pocket.

A week after Taylor's surgery, we receive an eviction notice from the sheriff. We have ten days to get out of the Happy House.

IN A PANIC, we begin house hunting again. I make calls on rentals during my lunch hour, Troy makes calls from sessions, and every night we're out driving the neighborhoods until dark. We find a place we can settle on, and fill out the application. It's no Happy House, but it's a place to live, and that's what we need. But the landlord never calls us back. We apply to a couple more places but are turned down. It's near impossible for us to clear a rental agreement with a bankruptcy and an eviction on our credit report. We are rental lepers. It doesn't matter that we have paid on time every month for two years. There is no record of it anywhere, and we can't get a letter of recommendation from Mark and Deanna, who are both still calling us, each accusing the other of being on drugs and being at fault for this whole mess.

We drive by a place a few blocks away that has a *for lease* sign. Judging by the weeds growing around the base of the sign, it looks like it's been sitting empty for a while. We park the car and snoop around the perimeter, peeking in the windows. It doesn't have the charm of the Happy House, but it has almost twice the square footage and a lot of potential, from what we can tell. After leaving a few messages, the guy finally calls us back and agrees to show us the house. We meet him out front. Dunkelman is his name. He wears a beige polyester-blend business suit, his combover a muss. He reaches into his

pocket and hands us his business card: Dunkelman Investments. He ushers us inside, explaining that he owns a string of
houses as investments and tax shelters. The inside of the house
is filthy, but we aren't in a position to be picky. We have a
matter of days before we are physically kicked out of the
Happy House. Dunkelman isn't "hands on." He certainly isn't
going to be a Mr. Roper type of landlord stopping by to fix the
leaky pipes, but we don't care. We tell him if he'll lower the
move-in rate, we'll clean and paint the place ourselves. He
agrees. We then explained our whole situation to him: the
bankruptcy, Mark and Deanna.

He shrugs, "Eh, stuff happens."

We start packing.

WE TAKE EVERYTHING FROM the Happy House that isn't
cemented down; the ceiling fans, window treatments, towel
racks, toilet paper holders, and the twelve-seat Jacuzzi. It costs
us five hundred dollars to hire a crane to move that
monstrosity just two blocks away, but it's worth it. We had
sunk $14,000 into the down payment on that house, and now
the bank is walking away with it? Not with our Jacuzzi, they
aren't.

For the kids' sake, we make a big deal of the crane and
moving day, again trying to turn a crappy situation into an
adventure. The crane operator gives Taylor a ride, lets him sit
on top of the giant hook, lifting him straight up as Taylor
squeals with laughter and I cover my eyes. Troy and Taylor
drive slowly behind the crane to the new place where they lift
the beast fifty feet into the air, over the house and electrical
wires, finally lowering it into the backyard.

Donna, Cissy, and even Taylor don rubber gloves and help

me scrub down the new house. Troy's dad Dennis shows up with his truck. Dennis is great at managing things. Even for family vacations, he makes Excel spreadsheets listing the activities, sleeping arrangements, food, directions, etc. He shows Troy how to shut off valves, explains the physics of the angles of gas lines, but neither of them ever talk about what is happening to us. But by God if you need a truck, or someone to come over in fishing boots and a shovel to dig through ashes, Dennis is your guy.

Fourth of July weekend, the kids stay with my mom, while Troy and I paint the interior of the new house. We are exhausted and sweaty as the skies darken that day, barely noticing the boom and hiss of fireworks exploding nearby. We're intent on rebuilding, no matter how many times life tears us down. We're going to show our kids that life is what you make it. I tell them, "This house is even better than the Happy House! Aren't we lucky?"

We paint Taylor's room a pale teal and put up a cute and cheerful Looney Tunes border. Cissy gets the pink princess room with windows looking out onto the backyard. I hang white lace curtains and drape white netting over her bed.

The house is big enough that both Troy and I get our own offices. Troy is anxious to turn his into a makeshift recording studio, so happy to finally have a space of his own again, and I set up my easels and sketch pads in the small coat room off the front entry.

Troy adds the final touch by making a tree swing from lumber and rope, and hanging it from the thirty-foot elm in the front yard. The kids will fight over that swing every single day. Driving them home from school, as we round the corner toward the house they yell, "I call the swing!" Each of them jump out the car before I even set the brake, pushing and shoving for their place. I issue warnings and time outs but the power struggle continues. That swing is a symbol of home they both need to claim.

Two weeks after we move in, it's Taylor's sixth birthday. He's healed beautifully from the surgery, and for the first time in his life can make direct eye contact with us. The whites of his eyes are once again white, his eyes somehow a more vibrant blue green than before. The surgery was a great success. He can now read, watch TV, and see the chalkboard without having to turn his head, and his eyes hold steady when he looks at us.

We throw a party for his birthday that weekend. We order in pizza and cake, and Troy hangs a piñata from the elm in the front yard. The boys chase each other through the yard in a spirited game of freeze tag, with our new dog, Sky, chasing after them. It's so nice to have enough room for a bunch of rowdy six-year-old boys to play without knocking anything over, and enough room for Sky to romp and run. It's a good place for us. Maybe this happened for a reason. Troy had no room of his own at the Happy House, but now he is able to rebuild a studio. We all have the space to thrive and grow, and it feels luxurious. A blessing in disguise, I think. A nice name for the new house.

C'MON, GET HAPPY

❦ ❦ ❦

Between Taylor's surgery, losing our home, and spending the fourth of July cleaning and painting, it's shaping up to be a totally sucky summer. We know before long our kids will be returning to school and during their first week, just like every year, their teacher will ask them to write a story about how they spent their summer vacation. Every year their more fortunate friends draw pictures of Disney cruise ships and sailboats in Cabo San Lucas. What will our kids write about this year? Surgery. Sheriffs wielding eviction notices. Scrubbing floors. So after settling into the new place, we plan a camping trip with Erin; Joy, and her husband, Aaron; and Bob, and his little daughter, Maddie.

We camp at a place inland from San Diego, next to a stream where rock formations form pools and natural water slides. During the day, we splash and play in the water with the kids, then bask in the sun on wide, flat rocks, warming ourselves like lizards. Completely unafraid of us, the squirrels are assertive by daylight. They hop up on the table and grab something to eat as though they were just one of our gang, joining us for lunch. One of them jumps into my lap and takes a piece of bread right out of my hand.

At night, Troy, Aaron, and Bob build a fire and we all make dinner together. Side by side, Joy, Erin, and I chop and prep and laugh. We wrap salmon steaks with veggies, onions, and garlic in tin foil packs then roast them over the open flames. I don't know if it's the phenomenal hunger we accumulated from swimming and hiking, but this dinner easily rivals expensive meals I've had in New York and Los Angeles.

After dinner, we gather our camp chairs around the fire and tell stories, while the kids roast marshmallows. We play a game we've made up—each of us calls out a line, and the rest have to guess the film it's in.

"You can't handle the truth!" Bob says.

We all groan, *Too easy!*

"Okay, how about this one," I say. "Every time a bell rings an angel gets its wings."

They all hem and haw (except for Troy who knows but lets the others guess).

I jab at them. "Oh come on you guys! Did you grow up in a cave? This is easy!"

Erin shrugs. No one seems to know the movie.

I shake my head in disbelief, "*It's a Wonderful Life!* It's all about believing in the goodness in our lives. You *must* see it."

"You're a hopeless optimist, Hollye," says Aaron.

"A hopeless optimist. Isn't that kind of like . . . a jumbo shrimp?" Bob teases.

"I've got one! The dingo ate mah baybee," Troy says in a perfect Australian accent.

"Oh, I know this!" Erin says, snapping her fingers, "It's that one with Meryl Streep where she has that awful Dorothy Hamill haircut."

"Yes!" I jump in, "I saw that. What was it called?"

"Let's see . . . what were some Meryl Streep movies?" Joy ponders, staring into the fire, chin in hand.

"How about that one with Dustin Hoffman, *Dingo vs. Dingo*," Troy laughs.

I get on board, "I'm telling you, she just shattered me in *Dingo's Choice!*"

Aaron is searching for the words, "Uh . . . dingo . . . dingo . . . oh and then there were the cops, the investigation . . ."

"*An Officer and a Dingo!*" Bob calls out, which brings howls of laughter.

"Okay—new game. Oscar-winning movies with the word dingo," I say.

Troy chimes in, "How about that long, boring English film that won all those awards—*The Remains of the Dingo*."

More fits of laughter.

"Wait, wait—how about the classic Hitchcock film, *The Dingo Who Knew Too Much*," Erin says.

"Or *Rear Dingo!*" Cissy shouts. (She's recently developed an obsession for Hitchcock movies.)

The game goes on with no one any closer to the actual title of that film where the dingo ate a baby, when a loud commotion startles us.

"What the hell was that?" Aaron says. Sky is barking like crazy. Outside of our fire circle, the rest of the camp is cloaked in darkness. Troy grabs Sky's leash and reins her in but she's lunging in the direction of our dinner table.

Joy gasps, "Is it a bear?" She scoots closer to Aaron.

"Maybe it's a dingo," Bob whispers, and we all laugh. But the racket gets louder.

"Anyone have a flashlight?" Erin asks.

Troy peers over his shoulder, "Yeah, right over there," he

points to the dark table, where all the noise is coming from.

Erin and I grab the kids and pull them into our laps. We huddle together, closer to the fire. Troy scavenges a dried-out branch from the ground and lights it on fire, holding it up in the direction of the noise, and that's when we see the culprit.

A skunk looks up casually from our dinner table, completely indifferent to us, then continues rooting through our food. He's having himself one hell of a feast, and we are helpless to stop it. We watch as he drags the remaining salmon steaks into the bushes, then the bag of marshmallows, then the box of graham crackers. He gorges himself for a good fifteen minutes, until finally, with a full belly, he waddles off into the woods.

We grab our flashlights and camp lanterns and sheepishly pack up what's left of the food, knowing what dumb-ass camping amateurs we are. We stuff the garbage into plastic bags, and lock everything in our cars overnight. Later, lying in our tents just feet apart, as everyone is falling asleep, Troy calls out in the silence, *"Ver-dingo!"* Bursts of laughter erupt from all over the campground.

The kids have drifted off to sleep, lulled by the sound of crickets and hoot owls, and Troy and I are just about to do the same when Sky jumps up, barking again. She's sleeping in the front half of our tent, her leash attached to the tent pole. The tent shakes as she lunges, growling, pulling the tent pole with her. All at once she bolts, and we hear a *ping*—the sound of the metal ring of her collar hitting the ground as she tears off through the mesh, the tent collapsing in on one side. The kids scream as Troy and I scramble to our feet in the pitch black, so dark we can't see our hands in front of our faces. We're stumbling, tripping over each other. I poke my head out the tent flap screaming Sky's name. Groggy voices call out in the darkness, "What's going on?" Troy gets on his hands and knees, feeling around for the flashlight. Finally he finds it, switches it on. Erin is soon right beside us. Erin, Troy, and I stand in the middle of the blackness, looking around hopelessly.

"Sky! Sky!" I call.

The kids poke their heads out of the tent flap. "Where's Sky, Mommy?" Cissy asks, frightened.

"Stay in the tent! We'll find her." The temperature has dropped dramatically. It must be in the low forties. Troy stands shivering in his underwear, the flashlight shaking so hard in his hand the forest looks like a disco. Erin and I can't help but laugh because, well, that's what we do when things are bad. We hear a loud rustling in the darkness, a growl, a squeal, and then a sound like a high-pressure hose. Troy swivels, aiming the flashlight at the sound. The bushes rustle, then Sky bursts through, trotting toward us with her tail wagging. Erin, Troy, and I exhale with relief, but within seconds we're buckled over, pulling our shirts over our faces. Our eyes and lungs burn like we've just been doused with pepper spray. We're coughing and gagging, as Sky comes nearer. She stops at our feet and sits, her tail thumping happily as she smiles the way Labs do. Her mouth is dripping with a rank yellow foam, which she seems to not be bothered by at all.

We gag and retch, running away from Sky, who chases after us wagging her tail. Soon, Bob, Joy, and Aaron are up and out of their tents. "What happened?" Joy asks, her hands over her mouth.

"Sky caught the skunk," I call, "and by the looks of it, she caught him by the ass-end."

Everyone turns away, their arms over their faces like vampires at dawn. The situation couldn't possibly be more ridiculous—Sky running around happily, dripping with skunk foam, Troy doubled over shivering in his underwear. Erin and I lose it, laughing so hard we can barely catch our breath.

"What do we do?" Erin says, barely able to get any words out through her laughter.

"I don't know! The only thing I know about skunks is what I saw on the Partridge Family when I was a kid," I say, wiping tears from my eyes.

"I remember that!" Joy says. "When Danny got sprayed by a skunk when they were on tour . . . and then, and then . . . what did they do?"

"They put him in a bathtub full of tomato juice," I answer.

"Huh. Good memory, Hollye," Bob observes.

"Thanks. A lot of good my pop-culture trivia will do me right now."

"Did anyone bring any tomato juice?" Troy asks.

"I think there's a V8 in the cooler," Erin says, "Would that work?"

"It's worth a try," he says.

So there in the pitch of night, shivering our asses off in the wilderness, we do the only thing we know to do in such dire circumstances—follow the plot of a 1970s sitcom. We rinse Sky's mouth out with water, then douse her with water bottles, then pour a can of V8 over her, then scrub her with mud, then sprinkle dirt over her, but nothing takes the god-awful smell away.

At daybreak, we hike Sky down to the river and give her a good bath while Troy heads off to the country store for more tomato juice. At midday, Bob and Aaron go fishing. Troy keeps a few beers at arm's length, cooling in the river as he lazes nearby doing crossword puzzles. We girls chat and sunbathe while the kids splash and swim and chase each other. It is a perfect day of sun-drenched happiness.

Driving home, I relive the weekend in my mind. The squirrels, the skunks, the laughter. It's no Disney cruise, no trip to Cabo, but my kids have plenty to write about when school starts. My kids were happy this weekend, and Troy and I aren't doing so bad either. The laughter was strong medicine. We arrive home feeling renewed. I feel grateful for these few days, and I begin to notice the pattern of happiness that follows gratitude.

SOON AFTER WE'RE BACK from our trip, my singer friend Donna calls with the news that she's marrying her girlfriend Tisha. It isn't legal for them to marry, but they've found an officiant to do it. She asks if we would host the reception at our new house. We are thrilled to do this—not only because we love Donna, but also because we'll be christening the new house with love and friendship.

The wedding is held in Topanga Canyon on a sunny, blue-sky September day. Donna and Tisha stand in the shade of an oak grove while Troy plays acoustic guitar and I sing. It's a sweet and short ceremony, and only about twenty minutes from our house. We moved our furniture out and put rented tables and chairs in the adjoined living and dining rooms. As the new house fills with people, somehow it seems like love pulls more light through the windows. The room is warmed with that soft early-fall light. All the windows are open, letting the breeze blow through. Outside, kids play on the tree swing and chase each other, playing tag. I feel blessed, safe, settled. Once again, we've captured the feeling of home.

Lying in bed that night, I take inventory of all we've come through, all we have survived. I'm feeling a bit giddy, my tank filled up on love from the day. I'm also thinking about the fact that in a couple months I'll be turning thirty-four, which means to me that I have exactly one child-bearing year left. Once I turn thirty-five, *BAM*. Shop closed. That's what they say. I feel like time has passed us by while we were treading water, trying to breathe. But here we are at yet another crossroads, another new beginning. Lying there in the dark, I ask Troy, "Have you ever thought of us having another baby?"

"Nope."

"Well, I guess I have my answer then," I laugh. "Okeydoke."

He rolls toward me, putting his arm around my waist, "Honey, I'm happy with our family the way it is."

I'm happy with our family, too. One girl, one boy. Both healthy, thank God. What more could I want? But still the thought nags at me. "Are you sure?" I ask. "Because this is it. If we were ever going to do it—it would be now." But I know Troy is worried about money, and of course, that is a logical concern.

"Honestly," he says, "I don't want to push our luck. We have two healthy kids. Let's quit while we're ahead."

I can't argue with him there. The scares in Cissy's and Taylor's infancies were enough to last a lifetime. I'm not heartbroken that he doesn't want another child. The truth is I don't really want a baby right now, either. The mere thought of it exhausts me. How would we afford it? How could I continue to work? I guess I just panic at the thought of losing the option because, how can I explain this—somehow I've always felt there is someone missing. I never planned to have more than two kids, but there is this feeling that someone else will join our family one day. It's one of those "feelings" I sometimes get.

And Now, Back to Our Previously Scheduled Avalanche

❦ ❦ ❦

Our second fall after the fire, we launch our "Borderspalooza" tour, playing acoustic concerts at the Borders and Barnes & Noble stores in Southern California. After getting home from my corporate job at 5 p.m., we pack up the guitars and kids, and go sing for people. Cissy and Taylor get goodies from the in-store café employees, and nestle into a chair with some books. Some nights they do their homework there. Troy and I play a forty-five minute acoustic set, followed by a meet and greet, where we sell and autograph CDs, and still have the kids home and in bed by 9 p.m. We meet a lot of nice people along the way, and these gigs lead to us getting hired for other gigs.

We've just finished a gig and are walking out with our kids, guitar, and music stands when a guy approaches us. "Hey, great set," he says, extending his hand. "I'm Mikey D. Have you ever thought about getting your songs on the radio?"

Mikey D. is a chubby, slightly disheveled music nerd—the kind of guy who could recite album liner notes verbatim. He says he's a radio promoter and it turns out he knows a lot of our musician friends. He also works as a journalist for *Music Connection* magazine in Los Angeles. He says he loves our album, and is sure he can get us on the radio. Do we want to try? The kids are sleepy, rubbing their eyes and anxious to get home. "Sounds great," I say. "Let us talk it over and we'll set up a time to meet."

Over the next few days I call a few friends around town for references. People seem to know him and think he's a good guy. I see his name in the credits of *Music Connection.* Seems legit to me. Troy and I talk about it late into the night. Working with him will cost some money. It will be a risk. But there is good risk and bad risk. Bad risk is drinking and gambling all night in a Vegas casino. Good risk is like learning how to pilot a plane—a risk that takes you somewhere better. Troy and I eventually conclude that this risk could take us somewhere better. The music business is a grind, especially in L.A.with everyone grasping for the same brass ring. But all you need is one hit song. Just one.

Troy toured Japan with Stephen Bishop a few years earlier. Stephen was still living off the royalties from his couple of hits in the '70s: "On and On" and "It Might Be You" (the theme song from *Tootsie*). That's all you need. Just one hit.

Later that week, Mikey D. comes to our home for a meeting. He's on his way to San Francisco on a promotional tour. He'll be hitting all the radio stations in San Francisco and surrounding areas with a few other CDs he's repping, and for a thousand bucks he's sure he can get ours on the radio, too. Troy and I talk it over. We're both in our mid-thirties. Time is not on our side. Our recent, unexpected move set us back financially, but we decide to take the money out of my 401(k). We write Mikey D. a check.

That night we lie in bed, musing about the possibilities.

"It's kinda scary, but also kind of exhilirating. Anything could happen," I say.

"Something good is going to happen for us, baby," Troy says. "It's time."

It is time. Even if we're just people with "bad karma," as some had insensitively said, we've surely burned through it by now, right? Now is the time for something new and bright and positive to happen for us.

But it doesn't.

Mikey D. skips town with our money, and we never hear from him again. I call *Music Connection* magazine to ask if they know where he is. They say he disappeared, just no-showed at work. They have no idea what's up with him, but they suspect something shady. Drugs, probably. Later that year, Troy will spot Mikey D. walking through Topanga Canyon, looking unkempt and slovenly, muttering to himself.

After the kids are in bed, Troy and I sit on our front porch sharing a bottle of wine. Moths flutter above our heads and crickets chirps steadily, and that soothes me somehow.

"We just can't get ourselves out of this downward spiral. I mean, how many times are we going to be ripped off by scumbags like this?" I say.

"I dunno, babe. I'm kicking myself. I shouldn't have trusted that guy."

"But, we checked the guy's references. We made the best decision based on what we knew."

Troy shakes his head, "I should have known better." He's always quick to blame himself in situations like this.

"What's the lesson here? I mean, there has to be a reason, right?"

"There's no reason. Some people are just assholes," he says.

"Should we just not trust people anymore? Should we never try, never take risks again?"

He doesn't answer. The fact is, we have no idea why we've been so unlucky. We head back into the house and get ready for bed, where I do not sleep, but lie awake with my mind buzzing, like so many other nights. Life sucker punched us again. Maybe God is still punishing us for some unknown offense. Maybe it's just that we've been dog paddling in a tsunami of fear and defensiveness for so long that it's broken us, the cracks in our armor laying us bare to predatory people.

Maybe we're just suckers. Or we're just being toughened up for something else? Is this a message that we are on the wrong path? They say that when one door closes, another opens. Where is our open door?

BY MID-OCTOBER, the harsh glare of summer fades to a soft autumn light, the sun waning earlier every day. I'm outside hanging Halloween decorations, busying myself, attempting not to notice that it's fall, not to feel the second anniversary of our fire, not to think about the fact that we've lost two homes in two years.

It's a beautiful crisp day. It's been windy, so the air feels clean, but the lawn is a mess of orange-brown leaves. Cissy and Taylor are fighting over who gets the tree swing, who had it first and for how long. I'm taking a moment to appreciate the light, the colors, thinking I could probably train myself to like fall, maybe even love the unique beauty in it. That's when the mail comes. I wave at the mailman as he walks away. I finish hanging the skeleton on the front porch and pick up the bundle of mail, leafing through it slowly as I walk toward the front door. I stop. Letter after letter addressed to Dunkelman. I know this type of mail. The foreclosure vultures are swarming. *Just breathe . . . just breathe.* We have only been living here four months. This can't be happening again. No way.

I run inside and find Troy in his new makeshift recording studio, where he is engrossed behind the keyboard with headphones on. I tap him on the shoulder. I'm sure he sees the distress in my face as I hand him the mail.

"This can't be happening. This isn't happening, right?"

Troy looks through the stack of mail. He becomes quiet. With Troy, quiet means angry.

Troy calls Dunkelman and leaves a strong message, telling him we need to hear from him immediately. An hour passes and no return call. Troy calls again. And again. And then Troy calls the bank. The house is in foreclosure.

We'll soon find out that Dunkelman hasn't made a mortgage payment for almost a year. He knowingly allowed us to move into a house that was in foreclosure. He pocketed our money from day one, knowing we would be evicted. We were an easy mark. Just how many more sleazeballs would life be throwing in our path? I believed that lightning couldn't strike twice, but that was naivete. Now I know better. Lightning can strike repeatedly, and at this time in our lives, we seem to be a lightning rod.

I don't want to fight. I don't want to see Dunkelman and his cheesy beige suit. I don't want to wait until the Sheriff comes. I want out. Now. I want security for my family. I want a home that won't be ripped out from under us at any moment. We don't have a dime to move, Mikey D. saw to that. But we'll work extra shifts. We'll manage.

We have now lost three homes in two years.

Like nomads, we start searching for a new home the next day.

LOVE VERSUS FEAR

❦ ❦ ❦

In November, we move into the new(est) house. Jerry has owned the house for over twenty-five years, as well as several other houses in the neighborhood (a fact we verify this time) and the gas station at the corner. He meets with us, dressed in white workers' pants and a T-shirt splattered with paint and cement. He's the Mr. Fixit type. Now that he's retired, he spends his days going from property to property seeing what he can take a wrench to. He seems like a safe bet. We explain our whole situation before he has a chance to run our credit.

"I've been in the landlord business a long time," he says. "Either you'll screw me, or you won't. I go with my gut. I trust you guys."

We hire the crane, once again, to haul our enormous twelve-seat Jacuzzi. It's the one thing we own that no one has stolen from us. We aren't letting it go.

The house has a wide green lawn, and a lattice-covered patio overgrown with honeysuckle vines where Troy and I will share our morning cup of coffee, or a glass of wine in the evenings, trying to figure out what the hell is happening to us. I plunge headfirst into nesting. I want to get my house in order, on every level. When I get home from work each night, I focus on organizing. My mission is to have the place feeling like home before the holidays. I put my music career entirely on hold—no gigs, no writing. I work at my job obsessively, trying to earn a decent holiday bonus to help with the costs of moving twice in six months. I focus on nothing but the kids and our home. I am in my own world, and can't even poke my turtle head out long enough to see where Troy is. Inside I feel numb, like a callous is growing over my heart.

On top of losing our third home, Troy also gets the news that Doug's studio, where he's been working on a daily basis, is going to be closed down for repairs, for an indefinite amount of time. Troy is completely unmoored. He wanders around the house, depressed, directionless, not sure what to do with himself. He gets on the phone and tries to scare up some gigs. There is no space for him to work in this new house. He crams a desk and computer into a corner of the living room, and sets us up on this brand new invention called the Internet.

While I work during the day, he calls every connection he has. Troy is well liked and respected in the industry, but there just isn't much work available. He begins to feel desperate, and is sure others can sense it, so he pulls back. He loses himself, and he ponders quitting music, but he never tells me any of this.

We are both in survival mode again, dog paddling to stay afloat, neither able to help the other. Every man for himself.

I SIT AT MY DESK in my new(est) house. Markers, colored pencils, and brushes are scattered about my desktop. I wish I were more organized, but I can only seem to be creative in the middle of a mess. There's a life metaphor for you.

My journal sits before me, pen poised. Jealousy is a map. That's what Julia Cameron says in *The Artist's Way*. It is a map that will lead you to your heart's deepest desire. I'm working on this jealousy map exercise, as Joy, Bob, and I will be discussing it and comparing notes at our artists' breakfast on Sunday. We are to make a list of the people in life we're jealous of, even celebrities or people we don't know, and then in a separate column write what it is they have that we want. That's what jealousy boils down to: wanting something so badly for ourselves, but believing we can't have it.

At first I think I have nothing to write about. I don't consider myself a jealous person, per se. I'm happy for my friends when they have success. The way I see it, they are paving the way, showing the rest of us what's possible, so why should I resent their happiness? But the deeper I delve into it, I realize, I do feel envy. I feel envy when I'm struggling and I see others whose lives seem so damned breezy.

I write about this woman I've watched from afar. Our boys go to the same school and play baseball together. Her husband is a musician, on the road a lot. We have those things in common.

Here's what we don't have in common:

+ While my husband is being beat down by life, her husband is at the height of his career.

+ While I am stressed out, ragged, still dressing in donated hand-me-downs, she is elegant, easygoing, and wears beautiful, stylish boutique clothing.

+ While I spend my days working at a corporate job that's stressing me out, she is a stay-at-home mom. (I imagine her getting pedicures and eating bonbons while the kids are at school, of course.)

✦   And this, most of all: she is glowingly pregnant with
     her third child.

A little voice whispers in my head: *she's everything you're
not.* Every day when I see her walking her kids home from
school, that fact chafes against me until it rubs me raw. And
here's the kicker. Her name, I kid you not, is "Bane." From afar,
Bane and her husband seem like a better version of us—the
version of us I wanted to be. The reality is I don't know them
except for their casual smiles and waves on the school yard.
Their lives could be a living hell for all I know. But still, I envy
her.

In writing out my jealousy map and honing down my
specific points of jealousy, here's what I discover about myself.
I envy Bane for the ease of her life. The way she saunters back
and forth to school, never seems crazed or late to punch a time
clock. I envy her because her life centers around her family. I
envy the better versions of us that Bane and her husband
represent.

I find my answer in my jealousy map. What I really want
is inner peace, a secure home, a happy family—to be a better
us. So why am I working so hard at everything else? I spend all
my energy working my ass off at Aware, trying to be top
earner, and booking gigs every weekend, sometimes several a
week, promoting my album, when none of these things move
me closer to my heart's deepest desire. In fact, they take me
further away from what I really want.

Five hand-scrawled pages lie on my desk—it seems I had
much more to say than I realized. On page six, I begin to write
a plan for how to get myself on track with what I want. The
first step is to stop booking gigs. I thought a music career was
my only possible escape from the corporate world. But after

my bad experience with Mikey D., I'm not sure I want to be in the music business. Anyway, even if I "made it" and "got my big break," I'd never want to tour and be away from my kids. That would make me miserable. So why am I doing this? I sit in silence, stunned by the realization that I am slogging down the wrong path toward a destination that isn't right for me.

I decide to take a break from gigging (except for the well-paid corporate gigs—I need those). The very thought of this feels luxurious. I expand into the free space, exhaling. I remember a conversation I had with Erin, where I was whining about my life, "I'm trying so hard, trying so damn hard."

She replied, "Then why don't you stop trying?" and I was speechless because I didn't even know what that meant. I had tried all my life. Tried, tried, tried.

A yoga teacher reiterated this one day when he said, "Don't try hard. Try easy." So this is my new challenge: to try *easy*.

Instead of afternoons on the phone with club promoters and booking agents, and mailing promotional fliers at the post office, I'll be present with my kids, helping with homework, sitting in the stands at their baseball games. Instead of weekends rushing off to gigs, we'll go for family walks, take Sky to the park, to the beach, on day trips. Like Bane, I'll saunter a little more, instead of rushing. I set my pen down. I feel happier.

It's that simple. Now that I am clear with what I want, I can take the blame for my misery off Bane and take responsibility for my own happiness.

The next afternoon, I park my car and habitually rush toward the playground to pick Taylor up from school. I've just come from work, it's hot and I'm sweating in my dress slacks and blouse, swooping my hair up into a ponytail as I walk. That's when I notice Bane sauntering across the school yard with her compact baby bump, two beautiful blond children in tow.

For the first time, I don't feel that familiar pang when I see her. I know I am moving toward my own happiness. I slow my pace, wave and saunter with her.

ON CHRISTMAS MORNING IN our new(est) home, the living room is festive, twinkling with lights and snowflakes we've hung from the ceiling. The kids can't come in until they hear Andy Williams singing "It's the Most Wonderful Time of the Year." We cue the music, and they rush in together holding hands and giggling. Cissy has graduated from Polly Pocket dolls to boy bands, Taylor from LEGOs to baseball, but on Christmas morning they are still little kids.

I earned my bonus, and with it, I was able to buy Troy a fine Italian leather coat. After years of wearing donated clothing and never asking for more, he deserves something nice of his own. I won't know until years later that this deeply hurt his pride. Through fall and winter, while I felt far away from Troy, I worked every week at Phyllis's studio on his portrait, pouring all my love for him into fine sable brushes, tweaking, transforming, until I captured his essence. I studied the photo clipped above my easel—one that was taken when we performed at The Roxy in Hollywood. His face is passionate, eyes closed. He is playing his favorite Telecaster, taking a solo—you can tell from his expression that it's a good one. I did the painting in black and white, except for the twinges of red on his guitar.

When he opens it, he is quiet.

"Do you like it, honey?" I ask.

His eyes are full of tears. I'm beaming, so glad I could make him happy. But what I don't know is that his tears aren't from happiness, but more a feeling of helplessness. He wants to be the one to bring our family back from the brink. He wants to be the one to save us.

About an hour into our morning, my mom and Eric arrive to watch the kids open their gifts. I put on coffee and get breakfast started. As I'm scrambling eggs, my mom steps into the kitchen and says, "Kyle's going to stop by with his girlfriend." I stop scrambling and give her a wary look. "He's sober. He's doing great," she says, "and you'll really like his girlfriend, Genesis."

"Genesis? Let me guess. He met her in rehab."

"Well, yes. But she's really great. She's good for him."

And just as I'm about to get snarky and mention the fact that one of the first rules of rehab is not to get involved with someone in rehab, which is what my brother does every time, I decide to zip it. It's Christmas. Genesis. I wonder if she's anything like the stripper in Vegas my brother married on a whim then divorced months later.

Kyle and Genesis arrive within the hour, and this year he is sober. He is fun Uncle Kyle when he's not on drugs. He gives piggyback rides and plays with the kids. He's charming and funny. And Genesis seems nice, although I don't get attached. Kyle is a chick magnet: six foot two and Abercrombie-model handsome, plus he has that ability to turn on the charm and the Tom Cruise megawatt smile, but this relationship will eventually implode, like all the rest. Nevertheless this is the first Christmas in a long time that he has been present and sober, and for this I am grateful. Maybe there is hope for my brother. Maybe he's outgrown his addictions and is ready to face his demons, as I am facing mine.

I put breakfast on the table while my Mom and Eric help the kids assemble their new toys. The kids' big gift this year is a tiny, orange fluff-ball kitten that we adopted last week. We named her Noel. Everyone takes turns holding and snuggling her. At one point during breakfast Cissy can't find her. A few minutes later, we all gasp as Sky casually walks past with Noel in her mouth. Noel appears undisturbed, though covered in slobber. Sky gently places Noel in her dog bed, and this is where they both will sleep together from this day on, with Noel often kicking Sky out of her own bed.

As the day wraps up, the kids are taking inventory of their new stuff, Troy is on the phone with his family, and I'm loading dishes in the dishwasher, taking inventory of my own stuff. We made it through winter. Though stress has built a wall between us, we managed to be our best on Christmas. Maybe now that we're settled in the new house and the holiday is over, we can get back to each other. Maybe today is our new beginning.

But Troy is visibly upset when he gets off the phone.

"Everything okay?" I ask.

He's rubbing his forehead and has a pained look on his face. "Yeah . . . it's just. I had a really upsetting conversation with my mom."

I dry my hands on a dish towel, fold my arms across my chest, and steel myself.

"What happened?"

"She was just . . . really emotional and angry and . . . I don't know why you got dragged into the conversation, but . . ."

At this point the blood is rushing to my face, the muscles in my neck and shoulders tightening.

"She was saying you control me. And she said that all my family can see it, but I can't. So I said, Mom, I'm a grown man. I make my own decisions. No one is controlling me."

"And what did she say?"

"She said, 'Oh come on. That woman can bring you to your knees with one look across a room and you know it.'"

That woman. That's it. The trigger. The last straw. It isn't the fact that she accused me of controlling him. I already know she says that about me. It's those two words.

That woman.

The other.

The outsider.

The one who is not one of us.

Fury builds inside me. *"That woman? I am the mother of your children!"*

"I know, I know," he says.

"And what did you say?"

"I don't know . . . I was just . . . shocked. I didn't know what to say."

He didn't defend me. He didn't say, *"That woman* is my wife —I love *that woman."* Deer in headlights. He allowed her to make me the other, as he has for years.

I throw the dish towel down and storm out of the room. Troy can tell I am in no mood for conversation. He learned from therapy to just walk away when either of us is triggered like this. So he leaves and takes a walk, and I hole up in our bedroom, stewing.

After I fantasize about the many comeback lines I could have delivered, I realize this isn't about her, or what she said. It's about us. If our marriage was strong, nothing and no one could infiltrate it. But our marriage is not strong right now, and neither are we. We've been taking life's punches for two solid years. We are hanging by a thread. This negativity seeps in through all the places we are broken, infecting us.

When Troy returns, he appears numb, which makes me crazy. I have reached a breaking point. Life has triggered all my fault lines. The negativity tape runs in my head: *you're not supposed to be here—you weren't even supposed to be born.* I tell Troy I need my husband to claim me—to take me back from those words: *that woman.* I need him to embrace me, his wife, not just in private and in front of our friends, but in front of his family, in front of the world. But he doesn't, which makes me feel like a mistress who should be kept hidden.

Over the next few days, things escalate between us. He's raw. I'm raw. Our wounds are so wide-open that even the slightest breeze blowing on us can make us howl.

His sister Valerie recently sent him a letter saying she had things she needed to settle with him. Maybe we would finally know what all that drama at our wedding was about. But he ignored it. All through out December, I was a myna bird, repeating the same phrases over and over: *respond to your sister's letter. Call your grandmother. Call your mother.* He was the wide-eyed, emotionless robot. *We don't talk about those things.* Between Christmas and New Year's, we fight and I cry and we circle the issue in futility. Adulthood means dealing with the unfinished business of your childhood. I am hanging from an emotional cliff by my fingernails, and I can't be married to a child. I tell him if he doesn't respond to Valerie in the next couple days, I can't do this anymore.

He does not call her.

Feeling hopeless, I take a long walk alone. I wander into a wide-open field, with yellow mustard flowers growing waist high. At the center of it I plunk down, where no one can see or hear me, and I wail with grief. I let go all the rage and frustration of the past two years, the grief of being discarded by his family, our friends, all the way back to my own father. The shame I carry from my family, the bullshit I can never talk about with my mother, all of it. I wail at God over the injustice of our lives, the losses, the betrayals. "I don't care about your justice or your bullshit karma. We don't deserve this! We did nothing to deserve any of it!" I cry myself into a state of exhaustion.

When I am calm, I come to the sad realization that I couldn't change my ex-husband Gary, and I'm not going to change Troy. So where does that leave me? I finally have my head on straight. I fought so hard to bring myself back from the ledge. I'm no longer jumping out of cars or even thinking about it—and I can't go back. I will not, cannot, live another day being *that woman*. If I stay married to a man who doesn't honor me—it will send me reeling back to that place of worthlessness, and that's too dangerous a place for me. I have to take a stand for my own self-preservation. I have to be strong for my kids.

I know Troy doesn't want to hurt me. He just doesn't know how to stop it. Sometimes life asks us to give something we were never given. Troy is brave when it comes to riding motorcycles or standing up to a charging pitbull, but he was never given a chance to develop emotional courage. And now, I need something from him that he simply can't produce.

I feel all the color drain from my face and from my life as I come to the realization that my marriage is failing. Since I'm already on my knees, with nothing else to lose, I pray. I pray for help. I pray for strength, I pray for a miracle. And although my faith is practically nonexistent, I remember this small thing from my childhood when my babysitter took me to church every week: *if you have faith like a grain of mustard seed, you will say to this mountain, "Move from here to there," and it will move, and nothing will be impossible for you.* I am not oblivious to the fact that I'm literally kneeling in the middle of a mustard field.

By day four of our fighting, we've reached a breaking point. We've cried, yelled, and railed against what is, but nothing is changing. We are tired. Beat down. There is nothing else to do but walk away. He doesn't even fight it; he just starts packing.

We take Cissy and Taylor out to lunch at Red Robin to break the news to them. They are competitively playing word search on the back of the kid's menu. We buy them hamburgers and french fries and even chocolate shakes and then we blurt it out. "Mommy and Daddy are going to live apart for a while. We have some problems we have to work out alone." Cissy cries. Taylor is stone-faced. I am nauseated, so depressed I can hardly put one foot in front of the other. I have failed my children. In spite of all my efforts the last couple years, I have not made their world safe. I can't bear for them to look at me. This is an awful day. Awful.

At home, a black cloud hangs over us as Troy packs his things in the car. The air is thick, barely breathable. When the final moment comes for Troy to get in the car and drive away, neither of us moves. We stand awkwardly in the driveway, arms crossed, looking away from one another. After all we've come through, surviving fire and devastation and betrayal and homelessness together, this is how the story ends? If I were watching a movie I'd want my money back. My face is a mess of tears, but I turn away, masking my vulnerability with anger and bitterness. His face is blank, and that's what tortures me. He doesn't seem to care if he loses me, the kids, or his home. How can that be? Pictures flash through my mind of Troy catching Taylor the night of the fire, carrying Cissy on his shoulders at Disneyland, holding Taylor so tenderly after he was born, teaching them to ride their bikes, running alongside to catch them if they fell. I think of our wedding day, and jumping off cliffs in Jamaica, climbing mountains with him in Alaska, waking up in his arms. Feeling so loved. So in love. But it's unbearable to stay with him. And it will be unbearable to live without him.

He stands mute, shoulders slumped, by the door of his car. The keys are in his hand. Some people search for a soul mate all their lives. I found mine, and he is leaving me. Not knowing when I'll have another chance, I say, "I love you." And this is the first time he cries. He presses a thumb and forefinger against his forehead, as if he could squeeze the pain out. I look away. He walks over and grabs my hand with urgency. My hand hangs limp, but I don't pull away.

"I love you, Hollye. Don't you know that? Don't you fucking know that yet?" Huge, uncontrollable, unflattering sobs burst out of me. He wraps his arms around me tight, to stop me from shaking, "Can we *please* talk? Calmly?"

We set the kids up with a video in the living room, tell them Mommy and Daddy need to talk. Behind the closed door of our bedroom, over the next four hours we finally let our defenses down. Troy paces back and forth, one hand pinching his forehead. I sit on the edge of the bed, doing my best to talk through hiccupy sobs, "These last few years I've stood by helpless as everything was stripped from me. I had no power . . . and now I'm losing you."

"You haven't lost me. I love you."

"But I don't know that love is enough. All the love in the world didn't stop the house from burning or the bank from taking our house or your parents from hating me. And love didn't stop you from packing the car."

"Look at me, Hollye," he gets right up in my face. "This is

the one place we do have power. We can choose not to lose this time. We can choose love."

We can choose love.

For the next three hours we cry and talk and talk and cry, but instead of proving our points, this time, we listen to each other. And we try to understand. We both know, no matter how much we are hurting, we can't live without each other. We don't want to live without each other. We are going to have to find a way to grow up and get over these emotional challenges. We're going to have to be stronger and more resilient than we thought we could be. And the most amazing thing he says to me that day, the thing that changes everything, "When things are bad, we have to turn toward each other, not against each other." Such a simple concept. Why hadn't we always done that? Why was it so easy to say *fuck you* to the person I love the most? I don't want to do that, not ever again. I want to be a better person. He wants to be a stronger man. He wants to face the emotional stuff, even though it's hard for him, and I want to let my guard down and risk my heart, even if it means being obliterated.

That night, we tell our very confused children that Mommy and Daddy are staying together. Cissy exhales a huge relieved sigh. Taylor is silent and looks lost. We tell them to get in the car, we're off for an adventure. We grab an overnight bag and hit the road. We need to drive away from the hurt and breathe new air.

We arrive in Palm Springs a couple hours later, and check into a hotel where we let the kids jump on the beds and order ice cream from room service. We watch pay-per-view movies and fall asleep together in one king bed.

The next day, we take a tram to the top of Mount San Jacinto, a purple-blue mountain towering over the sprawling metropolis of Palm Springs. At the base of the mountain, it is a balmy seventy-five degrees, but when we emerge on the mountaintop a mere ten minutes later, it is snowing like a Christmas miracle. The kids run and frolic, catching snowflakes on their tongues. We hike through the forest, and have snowball fights, then head into the lodge for hot chocolates. Troy and I hold hands and hug each other all day, constant reassurance that we are still here, still together. I know the road ahead isn't going to be easy, but I signed up to take it on, and so has he.

Driving home the next night, the kids are fast asleep in the backseat and Troy and I are quiet. I'm processing all that has happened in the last week. I imagine he is too. I prayed for help, prayed for understanding, and suddenly the pieces are shifting to form a picture I can understand. Something clicks. I remember that Deepak Chopra said in his books, "If you want love, be love. If you want change, be change." I can't wait for Troy to save me. I can't wait for my real father to miraculously show up to claim me. I have to find the things I need in myself. I have to claim *myself.* For years I wanted Troy to love me so I'd know I was lovable. I wanted him to be proud of me so I'd know I was worthy. I wanted his family to accept me so I'd know I was acceptable. But have I ever truly accepted my *self?* No longer can I wait for him, or anyone, to make me feel valuable. I have to see my own value, just the way I am, with all my imperfections and fractures. I have to take my self back from the words—*that woman.*

I am that woman, and she is enough.

WHEN WE GET HOME, I write a long letter to his parents. I can't expect them to respect my boundaries if I haven't made them clear. I tell them I fully support Troy's and the kids' relationship with them, but I am removing myself from the crossfire. I feel like I am on fire, in a good way. My senses are revitalized, every nerve in my body alert. The sleeping giant in me has awakened.

After receiving the letter, Dennis calls and asks if we can meet to talk things through, and I am relieved. I want to clear up all the misunderstandings and start fresh. We've tumbled down the mountain as far as we could. There is nothing left to lose. Maybe now is our new beginning.

They arrive at our house on a winter afternoon. Dennis hugs me tight, his voice choked with emotion. "It's good to see you guys."

Shelby gives me a brief hug and presses something into my hands. "This belongs to you," she says. I look down to find the letter I had sent them. I don't know what this means, but it doesn't matter. I said what I needed to say, and now I'm letting it go. Dennis does most of the talking. There are minor offenses mentioned, over whether I had sent a thank-you card or not for a birthday gift ten years before, or who had been late to what event. We dance around the wall that's stood between us for years, never breaking through, until Troy brings up the fire. "You guys really weren't present for us after the fire. You never mentioned it. You never asked how we were doing, and that hurt," he said. "We almost died that night."

Dennis's face registers his grief. "We didn't know what to do," he says, his voice cracking. Dennis drops his head into his hands, and breaks into tears, his shoulders heaving.

The room goes quiet. No one reacts. I poke Troy in the side, hard, and whisper to him, "Go hug your dad!" He looks surprised, as though it hadn't occurred to him. I remember another time when his grandfather broke down and cried at a family event, how everyone got up and left the room. I'm confused by this. Troy is the most loving, affectionate person with me. He is always the first to wrap his arms around me and the kids when we're sad. I can't understand why he isn't that way with his family, when I know how much he loves them. It's as though there are gigantic fireballs of love trapped inside each of them, which become twisted, transforming into something confusing and paralyzing. When I am in the middle of their fireball storm, I become an easy excuse for the ways they aren't communicating. After writing my letter, I step back. It's up to them now to heal their relationships. And just that one small shift changes everything for me. It was like running into a wall for years and someone comes along and simply opens the door. I am free.

After several hours of talking, the conversation slows. We still have no answers as to what the problem was but we agree to check in with each other in the future if there are issues, and to try our best to accept each other as we are. I am ready to wipe the slate clean and start over. As we walk Shelby and Dennis to the door, Shelby gives me a brief hug and says in my ear, "Sorry. Okay?" She pats my shoulder and walks out the door.

IN JANUARY, we rent a cabin in Big Bear with the camping gang: Erin, Joy and Aaron, and Bob and little Maddie, hoping to soften the blunt trauma of the Christmas that almost obliterated our family. On our first night there, a snowstorm hits, with nickel-sized snowflakes falling in droves. Cissy stands at the window with Maddie on her hip, Maddie's pudgy little fingers pressed up against the glass. Taylor's eyes are wide with wonder. In the morning we wake to trees sparkling blue white, glistening icicles hanging from the eaves. Our cars have disappeared, and in their place are soft mountains of snow. We are snowed in, couldn't leave if we tried, and this makes me giddy. We bundle the kids up for a day of sledding, snowball fights, and building snowmen—and snowwomen.

The next day, still snowed in, we take the kids for their first ski lesson. Troy and I watch from the deck of the ski lodge as Cissy and Taylor wobbily snowplow down bunny hills. They fall, get frustrated, get back up again. We watch our babies face challenges and build courage in their young selves, hoping they'll never need it in the ways we have.

We meet back at the cabin, the kids gather around the fire with hot chocolate, while Aaron and Joy play cards at the table, and Erin listens to her walkman. Troy and I take the opportunity to slip away for a walk. All else is quiet under the hush of snowfall at dusk, except for the steady rhythm of snow and pine needles being crunched flat beneath our boots. We spent years in recording studios and sound booths, but never experienced a silence like this. It is almost holy. We walk hand in hand, breathing in the fresh, chill mountain air, feeling connected to everything. I feel a presence . . . something in that forest. Something good.

There is a newly kindled passion between us. It's exciting to feel so bonded, to know we are committed to facing everything together, come what may. Although we made promises to do just that on our wedding day, we didn't know then what those words really meant. Now, after walking through actual and metaphoric fire, we know. But now I sense the flames are dying down. Spring is around the corner, and just as new life is taking root under the cold, frozen earth, love is taking root underground, growing bigger than fear and faithlessness. And this is where it all begins to turn around.

❦ ❦ ❦

IN FEBRUARY, Troy receives a call that his good friend
Claude, from music school, has died of a heart attack. Claude
was in his early thirties, healthy, fit, successful, happy. He was
living his dreams. My God—we had just gone to see him
perform at the Greek Theatre in Los Angeles a few months
before, and he looked tan and beaming. This is incom-
prehensible. Troy sits down and, through his grief, composes a
song in Claude's memory. The chords he plays, so yearning,
pull me to him. I curl up in his lap and we hold each other for a
long time. I know that wherever Claude is, he can surely hear
this music.

Days later, we attend Claude's funeral. It is overcast and
chilly as the procession of friends and colleagues mount the
steps to the chapel, their jackets pulled tight around them. An
endless sea of people stream in from the parking lot. There is
no doubt that Claude was beloved. Troy runs into old friends
on the church steps, falling into long, silent embraces with
many of them. It is impossible to comprehend how a person so
full of life is not alive. There are no words to wrap around it.
The church is packed to standing room only—a fitting final
tribute to a performing musician. Everyone who speaks that
day, including producer David Foster, whom Claude had been
working with, says that though Claude's life was short, he lived
more than most of us. He did everything he wanted to do. He
went after his dreams without fear or insecurity, and
consequently, his dreams became his reality. He lived in
possibility, and in his realm of possibility, failure was not a
concern. He left behind no regrets, nothing undone. His life
was a profound lesson for us all.

Driving home, I feel different, all the way to a cellular
level. Something happened to me in that chapel. Like the

music that filled Claude's life even at his funeral, a note of truth was struck inside me. I study Troy as he drives us home in silence. He looks older. Wiser. He too has been changed, and not only by the loss of his friend. He has been shaken wide-awake. We've had some tough challenges, for sure, but we are alive.

We. Are. Alive.

Life is ours to live. Dreams are ours to dream. But we had forgotten for so long. We had forgotten how to dream.

UNDER THE FROZEN GROUND

❦ ❦ ❦

Troy and I sit outside on our patio, amidst willows and eucalyptus trees. I'm writing in my journal, and he's working on his goals in his calendar. I breathe in the sweet scent of blooming jasmine that surrounds our home, relaxing back into my chair. The skies are blue and cloudless. Sparrows perched on telephone wires take their fledglings out for solo flights. The world is in bloom. And me? My head is a jumbled mess of pestering thoughts; I hate the pettiness and hierarchy at my corporate job, but I am still one of the lost seagulls of Chatsworth. I'm still metaphorically crouched in a defensive posture, no idea what life will throw at me next. I am still insecure about my marriage, still wobbly on my faith, and if there is a God, I still think he's pretty sketchy.

Yet, everything really is okay. Troy and I love each other; the kids are doing great; I'm making money at my job; Troy is back working at Doug's studio. And it's fucking spring and I should be happy but here's the deal: I don't trust happiness. You never know when it's going to suddenly appear, and when it does, you never know when it's going to leave you high and dry. It's elusive. It isn't practical or logical. Happiness is a sneaky motherfucker.

You can line up your life just so: husband, 2.4 kids, family dog, house, job—and still be miserable. And then, you can be depressed and suicidal, and your kids do some silly thing and say, "I love you, Mommy," and all of a sudden you're a happy, grinning fool. But tragedy, despair, depression? I grew up with that. I know how to navigate it. I know to stay alert and ready for it. I'm programmed that way.

I want to change. I want to get comfortable with happiness. To appreciate it for what it is, to enjoy it when I have it. I want to live my life without regret, like Claude did. A heart attack might take me at thirty-four. I don't want to be on the lookout, preparing myself for it. I want to find my faith again. I want to have dreams, and I want to live them.

"We need something to look forward to," I say.

Troy leans back in his chair smoking a cigar, his feet propped up. "Yeah, we do."

"I'm tired of feeling beat down and sad. I want to be excited about something."

"What have you got in mind?" he asks.

"Ever since Alaska, you and I have been talking about how much we want the kids to experience a cruise."

"It would be great if I could get another cruise gig," he says, wistfully.

"I don't want to wait for life to happen. I'm so close to making another quarterly bonus at work. Let's just do it. Let's book a cruise."

He doesn't say anything. He's worried about money.

"Look, it's been a tough year. You and I survived a lot. Look what happened to Claude. We don't ever really know how much time we've got on this Earth, right? We need to celebrate life."

He nods, "Okay. We can look into it."

Troy and I do our research and find the best deal on a cruise through the Mexican Riviera—seven days on the Pacific, with stops in Mazatlan, Puerto Vallarta, and Cabo San Lucas. It would be during the week of Troy's birthday (if we actually go through with it, and nothing bad happens between now and then). I'm not sitting around waiting for the other shoe to drop. At my funeral one day, I want people to say I lived a full and happy life, with no regrets. We put our deposit down.

Next on my list is to find my faith again. I searched the outer reaches of my life, looking for signs. But I'm learning that faith cannot be manufactured, or gleaned from books or scriptures. It's something I can only find for myself. It is a long and difficult journey, and hard earned. Intuitively I know I have to journey deep within to find it, all the way to the dark places where my deepest fear resides, and then I'm going to have to walk right through it. So I get my background check, have my fingerprints run, and am cleared to work with foster kids at Kalliope House. Here I will come face to face with my shadow—the unwanted child.

Working with foster children has always been a yearning for me, as long as I can remember. Though Kalliope House is nothing like the dream vacation I planned, it will bring me a different kind of happiness—the happiness that purpose brings.

SIX KIDS LIVE AT Kalliope House, ranging from five to eight years old. They live in a house in a residential neighborhood, tended to by staff that are paid minimum wage to shuffle them between school and weekly appointments with psychologists and social workers, where they are constantly being assessed. Some weekends, those who are eligible are taken to an adoption fair, where potential parents can check them out and "kick the tires," so to speak. I see the sadness in their eyes when they come back to the group home, knowing they were not chosen.

Corey.

Joel.

Deon.

Brandon.

Stephanie.

Sonny.

Those are their names. Each child's story is sadder than the next.

Joel is a severely autistic seven-year-old boy whose family didn't want him. He doesn't speak at all. He still wears diapers. You can't touch him or talk to him—he's shut everyone out. I know that Joel will never be adopted, and will most likely live in an institution for the rest of his life.

Deon is only five. She is funny and smart with a sparkling smile—an exuberant and joyful child. She can also hurl a chair through a window when pain and confusion overwhelms her. Deon was dropped off at the Department of Children and Family Services a couple years earlier. She was clean, nicely dressed, hair braided, carrying nothing but a backpack with a few items of clothing, and a document signed by her grandmother, relinquishing custody. It was her third birthday. No one from her family ever came to see her again.

On my first visit to Kalliope House, Deon wraps her arms around me and calls me mommy, but for months, she won't remember my name. None of the kids will. To them, grown ups are just a rotating cast of characters who will one day disappear, so why bother with remembering them? I'm just a nice lady from whom they will one day be taken with no explanation, if I don't flake out on them first.

I go to Kalliope House in the evenings after work, or on weekends. I help them with homework, teach them songs, how to braid hair—little things a mom would do or should do. Not everyone can work with these kids. They are wounded. They have emotional outbursts. Their life stories are too sad to bear. My friends and coworkers are always happy to donate and support my work with the kids, but they can't show up in the way I can. For most it's too painful a reality to confront. But I understand how it feels to be lost and untethered in the world, to know that you were a mistake, and no one was expecting or hoping for you. I have the demeanor for this work. I am tougher than I thought. I can face what others can't, and I'm good at it.

One of my self-appointed jobs at Kalliope is to tuck the kids in at night. It seems like a small thing, but I feel it is my most important work. These are our quiet moments, when they each have my undivided attention. I make up bedtime stories where Deon is the hero. I tell Brandon I'm proud of him for how well he's doing in school. I tell Stephanie, who at five years old sometimes comes back with bruised arms after weekend visits with her father, that she will grow up and marry a wonderful, kind prince who will love her and never, ever hurt her. I tell all the kids that I love them, and that their lives are going to turn out beautiful. Their eyes shine with hope (they are too young yet to be cynical). I rub their backs, give them goodnight hugs and kisses, and pray for them after I leave—pray that I wasn't lying when I said their lives would be beautiful.

Months later, on an average weeknight, I'm helping to get dinner on the table at Kalliope House. Because I continue to show up and never break my word, the kids have finally remembered my name. That alone is a small victory. We're all sitting around the table, eating the cupcakes I brought, when Joel gets out of his chair and stands with his back to me. He slowly backs up, pressing his body into mine. He stands like that for a while. I relax and soften my posture as Joel, the boy who never let anyone touch him, sidles into my lap and pulls his legs up. I put my arms around him and he doesn't push me away. Instead he leans back, resting his head on my shoulder, and lets me rock him. At the end of my life, when I look back on my most worthy moments, this will be one.

I am now the only person who can hold Joel, and he will climb into my lap on every visit. I wish I could adopt every one of these kids. Of course I do. But with everything Cissy and Taylor have already been through, it wouldn't be fair to bring home six wounded children who need all my attention. If nothing else, I can be one person who shows up and gives these children love. I can be one person who lets them know they matter. And I hope maybe one day they will remember that kindness if they are ever standing on a metaphoric ledge.

One night, after tucking in the last child and turning out the light, it hits me that this is not just a volunteer job. This is my calling. My story, my childhood, everything that happened up to this moment—even the homelessness—was necessary for me to become who I am. My experiences made me a person who can reach out to foster kids and not turn away. I was not a mistake. I am not a mistake. Just like everyone else, I have a reason to occupy space on the Earth.

I often take Cissy and Taylor with me to Kalliope. Others had been there for us in our time of need, and it is now our turn to give back. Both our kids go to good schools where their peers are more or less living pampered lifestyles. Their friends have every latest toy—all the newest, coolest technology and video games. No one goes without. I want our family to be of service, and want my children to see another side of life.

On our way home from Kalliope one night, Cissy asks me, "Why are their lives like that, Mom? They're only little kids."

I stumble for an answer to the question I wrestle with myself. If there were a God, how could He allow children to live in a world so cruel, so hopeless? Were all our lives just hanging by a thread? "I don't know why, honey. I wish I did. All we can do is try to make it better."

"But . . . ," she has tears in her eyes, "why is my life so good, when theirs is so bad?"

I feel pressure on my chest, an invisible someone putting a heavy hand on my heart. "I don't know, love. But be grateful. Stay grateful for all you have."

Cissy is quiet for the rest of the ride home, and so am I. I wish I had better answers for her, but I don't. A wave of sadness and gratitude moves through my body. Gratitude that after all we've lost, Cissy considers herself the fortunate one. Sad that I can't give her the answer that will make it okay.

CISSY SOON DEVELOPS AN interest in making short movies. She writes scripts, and then finagles Taylor and his best friend Michael into dressing up in costumes and playing the characters she's dreamed up. Many of them are spoofs of videos and shows on MTV. Cissy has a keen sense of humor, and writes sharp, witty scripts. She does a *Behind the Music* spoof on Britney Spears's humble beginnings and rise to fame. Erin is cast as the agent. Cissy, playing a young, very "country" Brittney, looks like she just stepped out of a baby beauty pageant in her short shorts, high heels, feather boa, and pigtails. Taylor (eight years old) plays her pimped-out, backwoods manager. He wears a fedora hat, plaid shorts, sunglasses, and a big gold medallion around his neck. In one scene, Cissy plops down into Taylor's lap and we all about hemorrhage laughing.

Cissy becomes obsessed with making these films. Every weekend it's a full production. Scripts, costumes, actors—all the neighborhood kids are roped in. And then there's the premiere. Sometimes she'll catch us having an artist's meeting or a barbeque and she gets a full house of our friends for her audience. Her face lights up as we erupt into riotous laughter. I think that she, like me, discovers that art connects you to the world, and nothing unites people like laughter. Cissy learns that when you are creating, you aren't waiting on any God to hand you your fate. You write the script, you direct the action, you create the happy ending. It is perhaps the only place in life where we measly humans have any real control, and Cissy has learned how to take the wheel.

FREE FALLING

✿ ✿ ✿

I t's already hot this morning in Malibu Canyon, the sun burning through the marine layer at 9 a.m. The Pacific Ocean breeze sweeps through tall eucalyptus trees, offering some relief. I hold hands with Troy as we walk across the lawn at Calamigos Ranch—the place where we had married nine years earlier, and over the bridge, the place where I'd almost passed out on my way to the altar. Ducks glide along the surface of the glassy lake, rippling the reflection of the former bride and groom, now banged up and bruised inside, walking along the water's edge.

Erin, Donna, and her wife, Tisha, walk ahead of us, talking. Donna works for a company that runs ropes courses for corporate team building. Today, she arranged a private session for her close friends and family—about a dozen of us altogether. Donna has never been able to forgive herself for leaving our house that night of the fire. She felt something was wrong but didn't know what to do about it. "I should have stayed," she's said to me countless times. Today is her do over, her chance to save us, figuratively.

Donna and Cindy, our team leaders, carry huge packs with harnesses, helmets, grappling hooks, and cables. We gather around them, waiting for instructions.

"Okay guys, you ready to face your fears?" Cindy asks.

Yes! is the fist-pumping, enthusiastic cry from our group, myself not included. Yes, I want to do this, but fear is something I've been trying to distance myself from. I'm not sure I want to revisit it just yet.

Our first exercise is a trust fall, but not your average falling-backward-into-a-partner's-arms drill. We are instructed to climb up a ladder and fall backward into a human net of twenty-four arms. Then we are to let them "cradle" us in silence for a full minute. The idea is to allow yourself to feel supported. As my turn comes nearer, my body tenses, my stomach tightens. I have no reason to think these people, most of whom I don't know, will not catch me, but neither do I have reason to believe they will. I've learned that people are unpredictable. Troy is the only person I can trust-fall with. He's the one who caught Taylor falling from a window, the only one who's ever been there to catch me.

I climb atop the five-foot ladder, close my eyes, and fall backward clumsily. Twenty-four arms catch me, hold me, faces up close, twenty-four eyes looking into mine. I hear their breathing, feel the warmth emanating from their bodies. I have never been this intimately close with so many people at once, and doubt I ever will again, outside of the New York subway. After the exercise, we gather in a circle cross-legged to talk about feelings that came up. Many express fear of surrender. For me, it comes down to the fear that I will do it wrong—that I will somehow screw it up. Our group leader Cindy suggests, "Maybe it isn't that you don't trust others, but more that you don't trust yourself. How can you build trust in relationships," she asks, "if you don't trust yourself?"

Zing.

For the next exercise, we march along behind Donna and

Cindy toward a thirty-foot-high telephone pole. Donna climbs a few feet up and rattles the pole back and forth with her body, showing that the pole is designed to be loose (part of the exercise) but it will not fall. Everyone is outfitted in harnesses and attached to belay lines by giant grappling hooks. Donna adjusts my harnesses so they are snug, "Geez, look at you. You're so tiny," she says. It's true—I have withered down to a wisp of a girl.

"Small but mighty," I say, unconvincingly.

"You feelin' mighty, girl?" she says, enthusiastically.

"Not really," I murmer.

She shoves a helmet over my head. "You can do this!"

I nod, eyeing the dizzying height of the pole I'm about to climb. I have been afraid of heights my whole life. So has Troy. And jumping out the windows of a house on fire didn't help.

Erin goes first. Troy, Donna, and I hold her belay line. If she were to fall, Donna explains, we pull the line tight, suspending her in midair. But I know Erin would never fall. She is too together and dependable and strong. Not to mention she is a naturally gifted athlete. I watch her climb that pole straight up like it's nothing. Our group hoots and hollers encouragement, "*Go, girl! Woo hoo!*"

She scrambles onto the flat top of the pole, gets her balance, then stands up with her arms outstretched. "*YEAH!*" everyone cheers. "We've got you, Erin!" She makes it look so easy. For kicks, she wobbles the pole back and forth with her feet, then jumps. Donna, Troy, and I quickly pull back on her belay line, then let her down slowly. She sways back and forth, like a leaf floating on a wind current. It is beautiful to watch.

We watch several more team members accomplish the exercise with relative ease, and soon it is my turn.

Everyone whoops it up, shouting terms of encouragement. Maybe they sense it is going to be tough for me. I am small, delicate, and not particularly athletic. But Erin, Donna, and Troy know the deeper fears I am confronting.

Troy hugs me, "You can do it, baby."

I approach the pole and give it a good once-over, assessing where the metal rungs are, mapping out a plan (giving me the illusion of control). Troy, Erin, and Donna are behind me, holding my belay line. I take a deep breath, put my foot on the first rung and haul myself up. My crew behind me is clapping. "Alright! On your way!" Holding tight to the metal rungs with my hands, I feel around the side of the pole with my foot for the next rung. I make it about halfway up and then I freeze. Oh God, I know this feeling—dry mouth, heart pounding, lungs collapsing. I look down, the ground below me looks swimmy. My brain short circuits like scrambled images on a television.

I am hanging my child out the window by his fingertips and can feel the cold hard stucco scrape against my arms.

My body trembles uncontrollably. I'm crying, clutching the pole in a death grip.

The stench of electrical fire overwhelms me. My eyes burn. I can't breathe.

Troy's voice wafts up from below, "We've got you, baby! You're okay!"

Holding Taylor by his fingertips. I can't let go.

Donna and Erin shout, "You got this, Hollye! We've got you!"

The sound of Troy's body hitting the ground . . . bones against cement.

The distant sounds of cheering below, "You're strong! You can do it!"

The sirens, the whir of helicopters, the roar of fire . . .

Troy's voice breaks through, "You want me to come up and get you, honey?"

"No!" With trembling limbs, I squeeze my eyes shut and reach blindly for the next rung. Deafening cheers come from below. Tears stream down my face. I pull myself up another rung, and another.

"Yes! You're almost there, honey!"

"We've got your back, girl. Keep going!"

With wobbly legs I push myself up until I can feel the top of the pole with my hands. Unlike Erin, I'm not going to be performing any acts of bravery.

"That's as far as I'm going!" I shout, clutching the pole.

"That's okay, you did it! You made it!"

"We've got you—just let go."

Those words. Just let go. Just let go.

Taylor's tiny hands in mine . . .

Just let go.

I can't let him go. I have to let him go . . .

Just let go. Troy calls out, "I've got you!"

Troy catching him midair.

I let go.

Free-falling backward, landing smack against the pavement, flames raging around me, running barefoot through shattered glass.

I free-fall backwards, my belay line snaps tight, swooping me back up into the air.

Troy, Erin, and Donna lower me down. Slowly I drift. My feet touch the grass. Faces crowd around me, cheering, hugging me, "You did it!"

Troy holding Taylor in his arms, "I've got him."

Troy drops my belay line and runs to me. He hugs me, lifting me off my feet. "I got you, baby. I'd never let you fall." I bury my face in his shoulder, my body trembling, my tears soaking his T-shirt.

Troy is next to climb. Erin, Donna, and I hold his belay lines. He approaches cautiously. Once he is off the ground, like me, he seems to lose his sense of being. He doesn't reach for the metal rungs. Instead he wraps his arms and legs around the pole and climbs it like a koala, splinters wedging their way into his thighs and palms.

"Grab the rungs, honey!" I shout.

He doesn't.

"You have resources, Troy. Use them," Donna calls up to him.

He doesn't.

He continues his clutching, tortured climb, hurting himself with every move.

"Stop fighting the pole, Troy!" Cindy calls.

He doesn't. He fights the pole all the way to the top. I imagine he is reliving his own nightmare.

He heard me screaming.

He called out, "Hold on, I'm gonna jump!"

He climbed over the balcony outside our bedroom. Holding on to the railing and leaning backward, he was thinking about the best way to fall when the railing gave way.

He tumbled backward, landing on his back.

He couldn't answer when I called out—the wind was knocked out of him.

He got up and ran to me.

He saw only a storm of black smoke rushing out the children's bedroom window.

He didn't know if he was too late.

He saw the bottoms of two tiny feet in the center of the smoke cloud, dangling, then plummeting toward him.

He held out his arms.

Troy makes it to the top, puts one knee on the surface, then the other. He plants one foot and tries to stand up when the pole wobbles, and just like the night of the fire, he tumbles backward.

This time, we have his belay pulled tight.

I run up to embrace him with the same enthusiasm he'd shown me. But he is disappointed in how he faced the challenge, frustrated with himself. Instead of the exercise being a breakthrough, it leads to a sort of breakdown. His experience will manifest very differently than mine.

The ropes course turns Troy into a Mr. Magoo kind of wrecking ball. It seems to have knocked something loose in him, rattling him to his core. He becomes accident-prone. He accidentally breaks the window in our kitchen door. He leaves the ceiling heater on all day in our bathroom, causing the drywall to smolder. The fire department comes with their hoses and axes and tears the ceiling and heater out. He drives away from a gas station with the nozzle still in the tank, ripping the hose out in the process. We have to pay for all of these things. It seems it is Troy's turn to fall apart.

Years later, in therapy with him, I'll learn that when he becomes stressed he leaves his body, in a way, his head literally in the clouds. He stands blocking doorways, bumps into people, knocks things over. I don't yet know that my husband caves inward when he is in pain. He doesn't appear sad. He appears emotionless. Robotic. Spaced out. I could have been more supportive, had I known. I only know he is acting crazy and it's costing us money, which scares me. My response is to work like hell, so that we don't end up playing camping charades with our kids again. The more I work, the sadder Troy becomes. He doesn't want me to work. He wants to be the one to save us. But he is still fighting the pole.

AN UNPLANNED MEETING HAS just been called at work. A last-minute meeting usually means bad news. I sit in my grey cubicle watching the clock until it's time. I shuffle to the meeting room and see a posted sign, "Meeting in Warehouse." *That's odd.* In the warehouse, a large crowd is gathered, some of us in suits, some in lab coats and hairnets. I sidle in next to Erin. My boss, Kevin, stands on a makeshift stage of wooden crates stacked in front of a huge steel vat brewing shampoo. A banner draped behind him reads, "Aware Products Employee of the Year." I'm mumbling to Erin as Kevin begins his speech, "What is this? We've never had an employee of the year before, have we? This is so weird . . . ," and just then, Erin nudges me. Did I just hear my name? *Hollye Dexter*—Employee of the Year. No one is more shocked than I am. Shocked doesn't even cover it. There are days I yell at Kevin, then he yells at me, then I threaten to quit and then somehow make it to punch-out time without getting canned. Hardly what you'd consider Employee of the Year material, but nonetheless, I'm their top salesperson for the year, so there I stand, stunned, shaking Kevin's hand in front of the entire company, accepting my framed certificate and a $1,000 bonus. And then it dawns on me—we set our intention, we made the plans, and now we are actually going to be able to take our kids on that cruise.

TROY AND I HOLD hands on the ship's top deck, watching the sun set in dramatic fiery hues over the Pacific. The air is cool and balmy against my skin. We laze in lounge chairs with festive umbrella drinks, while our kids sit nearby playing cards with my Mom and Eric, who decided to join us on the trip at the last minute. Eric is grinning like the Cheshire cat, having just won nine hundred dollars on the ship's casino.

Today is Troy's thirty-seventh birthday. We are happily exhausted from spending the day at a local beach in Puerto

Vallarta. Troy rented a car and took us on a forty-minute ride from where our ship was docked, to a beach where only the locals went—a place he'd been in his younger, single-guy years. From the looks of it, we were the only tourists there, and that's just how we like it. We sat under thatched roof huts and drank cold beer with the locals. We ate grilled fish on a stick. We swam in the ocean and built sandcastles. A beautiful, young Mexican girl with dark, round eyes braided Cissy's blond hair.

Tonight on deck, a mariachi band plays sweet, sultry love songs as darkness creeps up and over the sky. We just finished a gourmet lobster dinner and birthday cake. Our bellies are full, our skin sun kissed and warm. My husband looks so handsome, tan and relaxed, lying back with a cigar and a good after-dinner scotch. Cissy, now thirteen, made friends with a group of kids her age who run around the ship like a gangly pack of puppies. Taylor is happily worn out, snuggled next to me in my lounge chair. He lays his head against my shoulder and falls asleep, one arm draped over me.

Troy smiles at me, a soft look in his eyes.

"We did this," I say. "We made a dream come true."

He smiles, leans forward, and we click our wedding rings together, "Shazam!"

I take in the smell of the salty sea air, the warm tropical breeze, my son's sleepy head nestled against me. I feel absolutely safe. I have never been so happy in my life. I want to trust this feeling.

The next day in Mazatlan, we rent kayaks and snorkeling gear, then paddle to an island where we snorkel in a shallow cove offshore. I surrender to the beautiful feeling of floating while holding hands with my kids, schools of silvery fish move around our bodies like one entity, forming the shape of us. Later we hike through the jungle where we encounter a ring-tailed coati—a rare species in Central America—that eats Cheetos out of Cissy's hand. As we paddle back to Mazatlan beach and are dragging our kayaks ashore, we see people parasailing over the ocean.

"I wanna do that, I wanna do that!" Taylor jumps up and down excitedly.

I shake my head, "No way, that's too dangerous."

"That's not fair!" Taylor protests. "You always tell me to go for my dreams. I dream about flying. Let me fly, Mom!"

I look at Troy. The profundity of Taylor's statement is not lost on either of us. Let me fly, Mom. Somehow I know that will not be the last time I'll hear those words. So we let him fly. And Cissy decides to go, too, even though she is nervous, vacillating back and forth. We watch our children lift off from the beach under rainbow-hued parachutes, soaring into the sky without us until they are nothing more than a small dot against the bright blue. I pace the beach back and forth, wrecked with anxiety. *I just let my children disappear into the sky in a third-world country. What have I done?* But as they eventually drift back down to Earth, exhilarated, their faces flushed, I know we've done the right thing. I'm glad we gave our children this opportunity, to show them we trust them to soar on their own.

AFTER THE CRUISE, I start writing the first rough sketches of my childhood memoir. This kicks up a yearning in me, awakening things I don't want to feel. I am compelled with thoughts of my biological father. My mother won't talk about him, nor will my aunts. No pictures exist of him. My mother once told me my dad looked like one of the Everly brothers. So I start searching record stores for old Everly Brothers albums, and wonder which one looks like him. The blond, I imagine. I also wonder if my mother just made that up. My father's name and all information about him has been so shrouded in shame and secrecy, I've always feared I was a product of rape, or worse, incest. Who am I? I sign up for one of those 1-800-US-SEARCH things, but never get any conclusive results for my membership fees. I never tell my mother.

The small sketches I write unleash a torrent of vivid memories, more than I can handle. I stuff my notes away in a drawer and abandon them. But what has been unleashed will not rest. After this, I can't bear to see my mother. I tell her, on the phone, that I need some time to myself. She doesn't ask why.

Months later, in an attempt to be brave, I go to her house to try to talk to her. It goes something like this.

We sit down in her living room, on her floral chintz sofa, the one that matches the drapes and the throw pillows. I tell her I've been writing about my life. She sits back, then forward. She adjusts the pillows behind her back. Crosses her legs, then uncrosses them.

"You never talk about my real father, Ted. I don't know anything about him."

"You don't want to know anything about him. He was a heroin addict and a thief. He OD'd years ago. He's dead."

This instantly makes me feel small and ashamed, so I drop it.

"There are so many other things that happened . . . and we never talk about it."

"Why do we need to talk about things from the past? It's over."

"We've never talked about Gene leaving, and how that affected me."

"You were fine. He was Kyle's dad, it was Kyle who had the problems."

"I wasn't fine, Mom."

"You seemed fine. I never had to worry about you. But your brother . . ."

"I wasn't fine. *I tried to commit suicide, Mom.*"

"That was just one incident. You were fine after that. And anyway, you know how kids are. You were probably doing it for attention at that age."

"But you sent me away to live with Aunt Laura for a year."

"I didn't send you away. I thought you'd like the school there. It was brand new, state of the art . . ."

My brain bashes itself against the sides of my skull, trying to flee. The blood is rushing to my face as my breathing becomes shallow.

"We've also never talked about the day Kyle was shot."

She sighs heavily and sinks back against the couch. "Why do you want to bring that up now?"

"Because you and Kyle weren't the only ones affected."

Her lips become a pursed, straight line.

"Mom . . . I held him in my arms in the backseat while he bled! You were yelling at me to help you, he was begging me not to let him die. I was fourteen, Mom. I didn't know what to do." I am becoming worked up.

"Well, I needed you to help me. I didn't have anybody else."

"I know that, but you never asked me how I was, after the fact. I slept nights in the hospital, and you never checked on me."

"I had Kyle to worry about. And if there was a problem, you certainly never said anything."

"I needed *you* to be the adult."

She paused, looking irritated. "Well, how was I supposed to know anything was wrong?"

"Because I'd just held my brother with a bullet in his head! I was covered in blood."

She was quiet for a moment, slumped. Then straightened up, "There's nothing we can do to change the past. We just have to move on. You can't hold onto things. It will just bring you down."

She pats my knee, looking at me sympathetically, "How's your therapy going, by the way? Are you getting the help you need?"

I shut down. She shuts down.

We never talk about it again.

PAYING IT FORWARD

❦ ❦ ❦

Troy and I pack up the kids and a guitar, and head off for Kalliope House on Christmas morning. We have a big sack with gifts for all of them—some are from us, some donated by friends. I'm excited to play Santa this time, to repay the charity that had been given us just a few years before.

Deon, Brandon, Corey, and Joel are at the group home—no home visits for them. No home to visit. Stephanie is with her dad. I pray she won't return with bruises. Sonny is with a foster mom who has kept him on and off for the past few years. Cissy and Taylor sit on the floor with the kids, helping them set up their new toys: train sets, matchbox cars, and for Deon, I bought a beautiful porcelain doll like I've always bought for Cissy. I'm glad that the owner of Kalliope House, a very kind woman, has seen to it that Santa delivered a new bike to each of the kids. There is not much else in life to put their faith in, but at least the kids believe in Santa. For now.

Troy gets his guitar out and we all sing Christmas carols. Deon climbs into my lap, and Joel pushes against her for his coveted spot. The kids are silly and loud, dancing around shaking tambourines. We're having a great time until we hear screaming in the front yard. Thelma, a full-time staffer at Kalliope, opens the front door to find Sonny being dragged across the lawn by his foster mother. He's crying, "No Momma, I don't wanna go! Please!"

She yanks his skinny little arm, "You been working my last nerve, boy. You don't deserve nothin'!"

Another little boy about eight years old and a girl about six, follow slowly behind her, looking rumpled and dirty, their faces so sad it pains me to look.

Thelma steps out onto the front porch, "It's okay Sonny. Come on now, honey. Just calm down."

The woman pushes Sonny toward Thelma, "You take him. I can't handle him no more. He's no good."

I have never known Sonny to be anything but good.

The two other children stand behind the ranting woman, pale and silent little ghosts with big, sad eyes. Thelma takes Sonny by the hand as the woman turns her back and walks away, her back fat hanging over her spandex snakeskin pants, her wig askew. Sonny cries and struggles to break free, screaming, "Momma! Momma! Please don't leave me! I'll be good! Momma!" Thelma picks him up. He is hysterical, sobbing and grasping at the air. "Momma! Momma!"

The ghost children stand silent and unmoving by the front porch. The woman shouts back at them, "Don't just stand there like a coupla idiots. Get yo asses to the car now before I send y'all back, too."

They linger a moment longer, staring up at us, waiting. Maybe hoping one of us will do something. This situation is wrong and we all know it, but what can we do? Kidnap them? They are legally entrusted by the state to this awful woman. So there we stand, Troy, Thelma, and I, witnessing this horrific scene, doing nothing. It is all I can do to not tear my hair out as the grief and hopelessness twists my insides. I want to kneel down and say something to them, anything that will make it better. But there is nothing I can say. In my dreams, I will clearly see those two children, their little dirty faces, unbrushed hair, and haunted, hopeless eyes, as they slowly turned to follow her, getting into to her beat-up Camaro with rusted fenders. No seat belts, no child safety seats. Christmas day.

I run to the bathroom and crumple against the closed door, clapping my hand over my mouth to stifle the sobs that come against my will. What I just witnessed was inhuman. I can think of no other way to describe it, for surely this woman has been emptied of her soul. It breaks me that a child in his desperation would pin his hopes to such a worthless human being, simply because it's all he's ever known. I put a towel over my face and let it all out, and when I'm calmer, I pull myself back together, blowing my nose, splashing my face with cold water over the sink. I have to get back out there and be someone to Sonny. If I do nothing, a scene like this will destroy his faith in the world, and mine, too. So I breathe, center myself, and step out with a smile on my face.

Sonny is sitting on Thelma's lap, sniffling, gasping, hiccuping.

"Okay now," Thelma says. "Just calm yourself, child."

I look at Thelma, questions in my eyes.

"Oh, this ain't the first time," she says. "We been through this before. These kids ain't nothin' but a meal ticket for her."

I kneel down to Sonny's level, patting his back, wiping the tears from his cheeks, "Sonny, sweetheart, Santa came last night, and brought something very special for you." I say, "Would you like to see what it is?"

He sniffs and nods his head.

Troy and I take his hands and lead him to the backyard

where his new bike and helmet await him. He jumps right on, a small smile on his lips. Children can be so resilient in the moment, but I know that scene in the front yard will shape him for the rest of his life. In her one cold action, that trashy woman has impressed on this child forever that he is easily thrown away.

Troy and I spend the day teaching the kids to ride their new bikes, singing songs, and just basically being someone who cares. If nothing else, if I can't save each and every child, at least they will have a memory (I hope) of a kind family who once showed them love. At least they will know it's possible. Years later, one of my teen students, whose own crack-whore mother turned her out onto the street at fourteen years old, will tell me, "I never knew there were people like you and Troy."

"What do you mean? Creative people?"

"No, I mean, people who are kind."

Because she'd only ever been exposed to hustlers and dealers and prostitutes and pimps, she simply didn't know other people existed.

Kindness isn't enough to save anyone, but it's something. Kindness and empathy are things we now have in large currency. I am determined to use it—to make a difference in the lives of children who are thrown away.

Start Again, Again

❦ ❦ ❦

My family is still asleep as daylight seeps through the curtains. I sit by the window, writing. I have a new habit of journaling in the quiet of the mornings, centering myself before I leave for work. It is important for me to remember the dreams of my heart, rather than just being pushed along with the tide every day. Each morning I get clear with my intention for the day as I take account of where we are and how far we've come.

Life is coming back into balance. The home we are now living in feels stable and secure. Our children are thriving. Cissy is making her movies, taking piano lessons, doing great in school. Taylor is playing Little League, has become obsessed with the sport in fact, and has a bit of a crush on his fourth-grade teacher, who inspires him to write short stories. Even though I'm plotting my escape, I am making good money at my job, and Troy's work is really picking up, lifting his spirits as well. He started coaching Taylor's Little League team, which is sort of his own "Kalliope House" experience. Being able to mentor the kids brings a comforting sense of purpose to his life. No longer is he breaking windows and walking into walls. He is calm and centered. He is fun again.

It has been four years since the fire, and we are settling into the new selves we've become. Our home is once again full with material things. It seems impossible that just four years ago we had nothing, and now we are making seasonal trips to the Goodwill to donate unwanted stuff. It's amazing how quickly things accumulate.

I close my journal and put on my tennis shoes, setting off for my daily morning walk. This is my meditative time to let thoughts surface. At the top of the steep hill I climb each day is a well-kept neighborhood with an eclectic mix of houses. One house in particular always catches my eye. It is a two-story home with big, open windows, shaded by trees on all sides. I fantasize about living in that house.

One day, there is a For Sale sign in front.

For days and weeks I pass that For Sale sign, wistful. Our credit is destroyed and it will most likely be a decade before we can think about buying a house. But I keep dreaming, writing about it in my journal, what it would be like. I believe it will be possible. Someday.

April 21, 1999

This is my dream: our home is a rustic two-story house, nestled in the mountains. It is surrounded by trees with large open wilderness where we can hike with Sky. There is a shaded deck with a beautiful view, where Troy and I can share our morning coffee and write, and where we can gather at the end of the day with a glass of wine. It has a fireplace for cozy winter evenings and Christmas mornings. It has lots and lots of large open windows that let the light in, and space for Troy to build his own recording studio. We love our home. We are happy there. This is what I envision. Anything is possible.

ONE MORNING, I stop in front of the house, staring at the sign. *I'm going to call that realtor.* I know we have a recent bankruptcy, and not a dime of savings for a down payment. But there's no harm in calling.

After I get home from work that afternoon, I call and leave a message. Within minutes, the realtor, David, calls back full of enthusiasm. I tell him I just want to know what's involved in the purchase of a home like that, and, if it doesn't sell, maybe they would be interested in renting it, or offering a lease option?

David calls the owners and checks into it, but says they are set on selling.

"I figured. Oh well, it was worth a try."

"Wait a minute," he says. "Why don't we see if you can buy it?"

I laugh, and tell him our situation. He is strangely undeterred. He convinces me to give him all our financial info, fill out some forms, and he'll see if he can get us prequalified.

"I mean, okay, but I don't want to waste your time," I say. "I can't see how we'd qualify."

"Don't be so sure," he says. "Anything is possible."

A day after sending in all our paperwork, David calls to tell us we don't qualify to buy that house, but we are qualified to buy a home at a lesser price. "How soon can you start shopping?" he asks.

"How can that be, I mean, with our situation?"

He says, "There's a government program that can get you into a home with no money down, and we can work around the bankruptcy."

I'm amazed. Skeptical.

"So?" he asks.

I figure there's no harm in looking. It will help me to

finalize my dreams, and get a clearer picture, like practicing for when the real thing comes along.

"Why not?" I say.

HOME

❦ ❦ ❦

Since dreaming is free, Troy and I take ourselves "dream shopping." The houses David sends us to see are longtime rentals that have been neglected. The cottage cheese ceilings have cracks and water stains, the windows are painted shut, the carpets dingy and threadbare. And the neighborhoods are, well, a domestic cookie-cutter existence and we are anything but.

We tell David we're looking for something nontraditional. We are artists, musicians. We need the space to create. We want our home to feel like a refuge, a place where we can find inspiration. We know we're asking too much, but we're only dreaming, so why not ask for everything we want.

The next day, David calls to say he has a perfect neighborhood in mind, but it's in a canyon on the far northern edge of the Valley, away from Woodland Hills and our kids' schools. With nothing to lose, we decide to check it out.

We travel north, driving until the structured roads become narrow and winding. We pass a gated wildlife preserve with rolling meadows, a hidden lake, a little white chapel on a dirt road, a log cabin mercantile. I had grown up my whole life in the San Fernando Valley and never knew this place existed.

Troy slows the car to avoid a rogue chicken, scratching

and pecking the dirt along the roadside. "Wow," he says, "well, we did say *nontraditional*."

"Where are we? I feel like I just traveled back in time," I say.

The directions lead us into a small community nestled in the side of a red rock mountain. As we turn down the one-lane road where the house is listed, I roll down the window. Even the air smells different here. The late-morning sun filters through pepper-tree branches arched over the street, creating a canope of shade. We have to stop our car to let three peacocks meander across the road.

I look at Troy, "Are you kidding me?"

When we come to the house at the very end of the street, our jaws drop. Literally.

I double-check the paperwork, "Wait, is this the right address?"

"It's got to be a mistake," Troy says, shaking his head.

We stare up at the two-story redwood house with modern angles and a wraparound deck, and I immediately flash on what I'd written in my journal: *Our home is a rustic two-story house, nestled in the mountains.* The entire upper level seems to be made of glass. Windows stretch upward. Two chimneys jut up to the sky: *it has a fireplace for cozy winter evenings and Christmas mornings.* Pine and pepper trees shade the yard. Impatiens bloom along the side of the driveway. It looks like a cabin you'd see in a mountain resort town, not a house in the Valley.

I look at Troy in disbelief, "This house can't be in our price range."

Troy shrugs, "Well, we're here. Might as well take a look, right?"

Just then, a woman peers over the second-floor deck. She waves at us, "Come on up!" she says invitingly.

She greets us at the front door, very pregnant. (What is it with houses and pregnant women?) Her name is Hope. "Sorry my husband isn't here," she says. "He's a minister, and had some work to take care of at the church."

We follow her inside, and just like that, I am smitten. The hallway has scrubbed pine floors and textured walls. Dark wood beams run thoughout the house. Even the baseboards are a rich, polished mahogany. On the ground floor are two good-sized bedrooms and a full bath. Hope leads us downstairs into the fully finished basement—a huge, open, carpeted room: *a place where Troy can build a recording studio.*

She takes us upstairs to the top floor of the house, and that's when I begin to feel my whole body vibrate. I remember stories Troy's grandad told about water-witching back on the farm in Kansas. A person with "the gift" would carry a witching stick, and as they approached a source of under-ground water, the stick would begin to tremble. That's where they would build their well. As I reach the top step, I am trembling. I am the witching stick that has found my well. I grab Troy's arm. This is not just any house. This is the house I journaled about all year. The wild thumping in my chest and ears is so loud I wonder if others can hear it.

The top level is an open floor plan comprised of the living room, dining room, and kitchen. No walls between. Three sets of double glass doors surround the living area, flooding the room with morning sun: *it has lots and lots of large open windows that let the light in.* They open to a wraparound deck, where a long outdoor dining table sits: *the place where Troy and I can share our coffee and talk about our dreams.* The living room has a stone fireplace in the center, and pine cathedral ceilings with skylights. Troy nudges me and points at the ceiling. There are automatic fire sprinklers in every room. I have never seen that in a house before. We look at each other, stunned.

Above the living room is a loft with a wooden ladder that I climb immediately, feeling the need to explore every inch of this dream place, to see if it indeed matches my intentions. It does. The loft is all windows. From it you can see the lake, the wildlife preserve, and acres of wilderness: *the place where we can hike with Sky.* The kitchen is open with a place to set bar stools at the counter. I see myself cooking in that kitchen, while my kids and friends visit with me. It's such a clear vision.

Overwhelmed with emotion, I lean into him. "This is my house," I whisper. And even as I say it the words catch in my throat, because I know we're only "dream shopping."

Our realtor David arrives shortly afterward, caffeinated and upbeat. Another realtor sits at the table on the deck with a young couple, filling out paperwork. David consults with the seller, comes back and tells us the other couple made an offer. The minister has been transferred to another parish and they have to move right away, before the baby comes. They are motivated to sell.

David asks, "Do you want the house?

"Of course we want the house, but how?" I say.

"If you want it, I'll make it happen," he says.

"And the price on the paperwork was correct? What's the catch?" Troy asks.

"No catch," David responds. "People just won't pay as much to live out here. You're on the edge of wilderness. There are no streetlights or sidewalks. You've got a propane tank for gas. No sewer lines, just a septic system. But if that doesn't bother you . . ."

Troy and I look at each other and share a private laugh. We've camped in the yard, bailed water from the Jacuzzi, eaten pancakes for breakfast. What he describes as inconveniences for others are nothing to us. He looks at us with his high energy, go-go-go personality. "Well? You ready to make an offer?"

Without even discussing it we both say, "Yes."

Driving home, for the first few minutes we're quiet. I have a moment of doubt. My God, what did we just get ourselves into? But then, I start to laugh. Within seconds Troy joins me.

"I can not believe we just did that!" I shout, giddy and almost delirious.

We come to a stop sign. He looks at me and says, "Stick with me, baby. I can't promise you it will always be easy, but it will be one hell of a ride."

"I'm in," I say.

He lifts his wedding ring hand, "Shazam, right? We're doing this?"

I clink my band against his, "Shazam."

It turns out dreams are a powerful thing. Within twenty-four hours, our offer is accepted. We are in escrow.

IN AUGUST, as we nervously await our thirty-day escrow, our tenth wedding anniversary is upon us. After almost separating the prior year, this is a huge deal. We made it to hell and back, and now it's time to re-up our contract. On our actual ten-year anniversary, we invite our immediate family and closest friends to join us for the weekend as we renew our vows at a guest ranch in the mountains above Santa Barbara. Unlike our wedding day, I'm not nervous or passing out with fear of the unknown. I know now what can happen, and that I will stand with Troy come what may.

Our very casual ceremony is about to begin when we are told we have a phone call. Troy hustles into the restaurant kitchen and picks up the extension. I stand behind him, listening in. Shelby and Dennis are caught in traffic and are worried they may not make it. They apologize profusely. What none of us bring up, but we are all surely thinking, is the fact that our whole relationship went south over what was perceived as our lateness that first Christmas. Today is our day to start over, and we're all standing on this new and shaky foundation.

I wave it off, saying to Troy, "Tell them it's no problem. We'll see them whenever they get here." Troy tells them not to stress, just to drive carefully. We tell him we can push back the ceremony but Dennis says, "Please don't change anything on our account." Troy assures them everything is absolutely fine, on every level.

We gather with our family and friends in the shade of two mighty oaks, their branches intertwined above us, which is fitting as the oak is one of the only trees that will stand strong through fire. Charred black, its trunk will bear scars, but in time its leaves will bloom again. Its seeds, burst open by the blaze, will take root, bringing new life to the world.

Joy and Aaron perform a song they wrote for us as we take our place, holding hands under the shelter of the trees. Joy's voice belts out clear and strong, over the mountains, along the top of the Pacific Ocean, around the world . . .

They have each other to cling to in darkness
Surrounded by angels their souls sleep tight
There have been battles, hearts broken and mended
Fires raging by morning light . . . .

I close my eyes and let her song move through me, receiving the blessing of our friends ushering us into the next phase of our journey together. When I open my eyes I see

Shelby and Dennis have made it. They are taking their seats in the front, and everything is as it should be.

Troy and I wrote new vows, with new understanding for what they really meant. We hold hands and lock eyes.

I speak first: "Ten years ago, I stood at the alter and I thanked you. I said, 'Thank you for yesterday, and today, and for the privilege of sharing your tomorrows.' And what a privilege it has been."

"Above all else, I thank you now for the ten most incredible years of my life.

You have enriched my life and soul beyond words. You have brought love, laughter, music, joy, comfort, challenges, and sometimes heartache. We have walked through fire together, and I would do it all again to be by your side. All the challenges we have faced have made me a better person, and made my love for you even stronger."

"Ten years ago, I thought I understood what those marriage vows meant.

But now, with the wisdom that only comes from experience, I can say these words to you from my heart, well knowing what they mean."

"For better or for worse, I will be by your side."

"In sickness and in health, my love for you will never falter."

"For richer or for poorer, I will stand tall beside you, for I will always feel rich in my heart."

"I will love you, respect you, support you, believe in you, be your best friend always."

"I won't say till death do us part—because even then you will be with me."

"You will always be part of me, as I will always be part of you."

"We're soul mates . . . Our bond is forever."

Our friends snap pictures, and a few blow their noses while Troy composes himself to speak. He pulls me closer to him, reminding me of our first gentle kiss, when he pulled me close and stepped on both my feet. He doesn't have to step on my feet this time. I'm not going to run away. He holds his vows and prepares to read. His hands are steady and strong.

These are the words my husband reads to me: "I, in return, thank you for loving me, standing by me, and for always believing in the 'me' that you married ten years ago. Thank you for believing in our tomorrows and for the privilege of sharing them. Thank you for lighting the path to growth when I needed to walk it, and for coming to me, putting your head to my chest, and trusting in me when you didn't feel strong and needed comfort."

"You are my best friend. More with you than anyone, I love to love, and to laugh, and I hurt when you hurt. I will always be there with you and for you to work on bringing us back to what we have both come to know as the good place."

"I will do everything I know to support and facilitate your dreams, and to help you soar. I will hold your lifeline as you stand atop the tall, skinny, unstable poles of life."

"I will strive to give you security and stability that you and our beautiful children so richly deserve. I will continue to stand by you, respect you, be strong, and grow stronger with you. I will hold your hand as we brave the road ahead, be a worthy friend, a sensitive lover, and an equal partner on our wonderful journey."

"I love you Hollye Dexter, and right here and now, as I have done in my heart every single moment that we have shared together, I renew my commitment, and my faith in you and me, forever."

We take a moment to let the promises we've made settle into our bones. Then we kiss, and everyone applauds. Aaron strums his guitar as we embrace our friends and family: Joy, Erin, Kelly, Tara, Stephen La-dee-dah, my mother and Eric, Dennis and Shelby, and even my brother Kyle. But the guests of honor today are the ones who had a backstage pass to it all— all the pain and suffering and drama: Cissy and Taylor.

We host everyone to a ranch-style lunch on long picnic tables covered with red-and-white checkered tablecloths. Troy and I first toast our family and friends, then Cissy and Taylor get up to read a speech they prepared together. She has just turned fourteen, and Taylor, nine. Cissy stands tall, heart-shaped barrettes pinning back her blond hair. She wears a patterned dress with a matching cardigan. Smiling wide, her mouth full of braces, she begins her speech. "Hollye and Troy Dexter are not only good parents, a happy couple, and wonderful providers, but they are also our good friends. They are the most caring and generous parents a child could ever ask for. They teach us lessons that we will hold close to our heart through our life—even if it is extremely hard to learn them. They give us the love we need and so much more."

She elbows Taylor, who takes the paper from her hands, scanning it for his part.

He reads, "My dad taught me all I need to know about baseball, and other sports. Mom was always there for me when there was food on my face and it needed cleaning."

The audience laughs. "They help me be the best boy I can be."

After lunch, Troy's parents get up to say their good-byes. I give Shelby a hug. "I really appreciate that you came. It means a lot," I say.

"Of course. It was so nice. Thank you for inviting us," she

says. The hug feels different this time, like a new beginning, a chance for us to hopefully get it right. Troy walks them to their car. I watch him wave as they pull away from the ranch.

The rest of us are staying for the weekend. As day turns to evening, we gather with friends around the campfire, where Troy plays guitar and we all sing. We conjure up every nostalgic song we can think of, dubbing Troy the "Human Jukebox." We sing like Jamaicans, with all the joy that is in us. We gawk at the stars speckled across the black velvet sky. We laugh as we share stories of our wild and crazy journeys. We marvel at the miracles of love we have all been lucky enough to experience.

A few weeks later, I get this letter in the mail from our friend Stephen La-dee-da, the one who'd picked us up when we were abandoned on the side of a freeway, the one who'd backed the production of our album, and loaned us money when we were desperate. Stephen, my practical, no-nonsense friend, wrote this:

I remember coming to visit you some years ago, when you were sure the relationship with Troy was over. Your face was swollen from crying. Troy had just left for a three-month tour. You relayed to me that it had been a repeated experience in your life that a man leaves and doesn't come back. I well remember giving you my opinion that in Troy you had found the perfect match. My faith in your selection of Troy has proven to be well placed. It has been my experience over the years that the majority of marriages (mine included) are doomed to failure. But if I had been asked at anytime to pick a single marriage that I thought could overcome those odds and endure, it would have been no contest. Your marriage to Troy has been a source of inspiration to the romantic within me. I go to see romantic movies all the time, but if I did not have you and Troy for friends it would be very easy for me to write all of these off as examples of Hollywood make-believe.

THE NEXT DAY A group of us head up into the mountains. We hike to a waterfall, and through meadows, along jagged paths to the very top. Troy and I stand atop the mountain, looking down on the Pacific Ocean that stretches like a forever blue sky. I take his hand. "We made it." He squeezes back and smiles. "The avalanche is behind us now."

When we return home, David calls to tell us the good news: escrow has closed. The house is ours. On a hot August day, exactly twelve years to the day from our first date, David delivers the keys to us. I think about that drunk psychic at the bar who said we'd be together forever. Troy puts the keys in my hand. "It's your house, baby." He hugs me so tight, "Just like you dreamed. It's yours," he whispers.

We call the crane operator and make an appointment to move our beast of a Jacuzzi—one last time.

REDEMPTION

❦ ❦ ❦

Nine years after the fire, I am driving through Laurel Canyon, my Aunt Diane in the passenger seat beside me. She and I have embarked on a genealogy project together, both looking to prove our Native American ancestry. We hope it might help us to get college grants for both my Cissy, now headed to college, and her granddaughter Nicole. We have photos of my great-grandmother Annie, a Cherokee, but she doesn't exist on any official records as she, ironically, wasn't considered an American citizen. Aunt Diane tells me the Mormons keep records of everyone's family history in a bomb shelter beneath their temple on Santa Monica Boulevard, a fact that I find both helpful and a little creepy. We are on our way to check it out.

I've always felt close to my Aunt Diane. I lived with her and my uncle and cousins Tracey and Tammey for a while when I was a kid, when my mom couldn't get her life together. We have an easy relationship. Even if we don't get any college money from all this, the journey is fun, and a chance for us to bond.

"I'm really glad we're doing this together," I say.

"Me, too," she says.

My mother isn't with us. She and I are once again estranged. Kyle's addictions escalated to the point where he put my children at risk and that was when I had to draw a hard boundary. My mother is outraged that I'd turn my back on my own flesh and blood, even though she's done it to me throughout my life. This time when our relationship crashed and burned, I didn't fall apart. Nor did I tuck my tail and slither back apologizing. Standing in my truth is the right thing for my family and for myself. I hope eventually my mother and I will find our way back to each other.

Aunt Diane and I walk through the side entrance of the Mormon temple, and take an elevator to the underground Hall of Records where a genealogist named John, who makes sure to inform us that he is not a Mormon, just a genealogist, helps us to access the archives. There we find birth and death certificates, and obituaries that provide clues to our family's history. Aunt Diane and I put our heads together, like private eyes solving a case. With her, I broach a subject I never could with my mom.

"With all these birth and death records, I'm kind of curious to find out when my biological dad died, and where he's buried."

"Who, Ted?"

"You knew him?"

"Of course I knew him! He was a sweet guy."

"Really? That's not what my mom said."

"Well, he did drugs, and that was early in the sixties when no one did drugs. But your mom was crazy about him."

A sweet guy? My mom was crazy about him? All I'd ever heard about him was that he was a bad man and he was dead. Somehow the estrangement from my mother gives me the courage to pierce the veil of secrecy around him.

"What did he look like?"

"For heaven's sake, your mom never showed you a picture?"

"Never."

"Well, he looked kind of like you. You have his blond hair, for sure. And maybe his heart. He was a gentle soul."

A gentle soul? That thought never occurred to me before. My mother's reaction any time I would dare to bring him up made me afraid to know anything more. Driving home, I am quiet in the car. Now that there is the possibility of my father actually being a decent guy, I wonder about him. Incessantly.

Shortly after moving into our mountain home four years ago, Troy's career took off, and I quit the corporate world. His work was enough to support us while I launched a nonprofit arts program for foster kids. But the stillness of being unemployed gave me time to feel everything that wasn't resolved from my past. The main questions that lingered in my soul were: Who am I? Who is my father? Am I the product of hate, of rape, incest? Is that why no one will talk about him? Although I found my home on a physical plane, I am still searching for my place internally. I'm not sure how I fit in the world. My unraveling process had only just begun in 1994, and apparently, nine years later it isn't over.

Troy encourages me, almost to the point of loving harassment, to find my father. He says it will bring peace to know the truth. But knowing my father had been an addict and in prison was enough grief for me. Troy persists, reminding me that I'll never fully know who I am if I don't know who I came from. His words sting, because there is truth in them. I don't know whose child I am, what genetic traits I carry and pass on to my own children, as well as unresolved spiritual issues I might have inherited from him.

❦ ❦ ❦

ON OUR SECOND VISIT to the Mormon bomb shelter, Aunt Diane and I spy John the genealogist sitting at a table, studiously writing. He looks like every high school history teacher I ever had: he has short blond hair combed to the side, a moustache neatly trimmed, wire-rimmed glasses, and pens in his shirt pocket.

This time I bring my birth certificate. The only information I have is my father's full name, age (seventeen at the time), and his birthplace of Texas. I hand my birth certificate to John, and ask if he can help me find my father's death certificate. We search through all the death records in the United States with no results.

"You sure he's dead?" John asks.

"That's what I've been told."

"Hmmm . . ."

"What is it?"

"Well, it's just that I get these hunches, and something tells me your dad isn't dead. It's just a feeling. Do you mind indulging me for a minute?"

"Not at all."

So we begin our daunting search amongst the hundreds of living men in California who share my father's name— thousands nationally. One by one, we look up the Teds in California, but there is always something that doesn't match up —either middle name or age.

"Your father was born in Texas, right?"

"Well, that's what my birth certificate says. No one in my family ever told me anything about him, so I don't know."

"I bet he went back to Texas. Let's look there."

I shrug, "Sure."

In Texas, there are hundreds more men matching my

father's information, but John whittles it down to the ones he gets "hunches" about. He writes a list for me, containing about twenty Teds. There are three listings in a small town called Galena Park. He puts an asterisk next to those.

"Call these first," he says. "I've got a hunch about these."

"Okay I will," I smile.

"I know it sounds kooky," he says, hesitantly.

"Nothing sounds kooky to me, believe me."

"I'm not religious or anything, but since I've been working here, these people have been helping me," he says.

"The Mormons?"

"No, these people," he points to the air above him, "the ancestors."

I've been witness to enough odd things in my life that this doesn't faze me at all. Besides, what more perfect place for a bunch of ghosts to hang out than the Mormon basement bomb shelter?

He gives me a half-apologetic look. "I know it sounds weird, but . . . they want people to reunite with their families. When you go home tonight, just pray to your ancestors to bring your father to you."

"Okay, I will."

"Seriously, I'm telling you it works."

I nod, "I promise I will."

That night, before bed, I keep my promise to John. I sit in my darkened bedroom and meditate for a few minutes, and then I pray to the mystery ancestors on my father's side, whoever they may be, to help me find him. In the darkness behind my closed eyes, it's as if a video montage begins to play. Faces appear, one morphing into the next, clear and vivid, their features defined. These aren't memories I am conjuring up. These are faces I have never seen before. I'm a bit shaken, but then shrug it off, figuring the mind can play strange tricks on you sometimes.

The next day, I busy myself, trying not to notice the three-by-five index card with the twenty names and three asterisks. It sits on the corner of my desk as I breeze past it countless times, always aware of it. I feel it in the room: the deed undone, the call unmade.

That night, as I'm about to head out to celebrate one of my foster student's birthdays, I grab the card. If I don't call right now, the sun will set on this day and I'll know I chickened out. I decide to make just one call before I leave, figuring I'll still be out the door in five minutes because I certainly won't find my father on the first try. One call a day. That's what I decide.

I choose one of the listings with an asterisk. My hands tremble as I punch in the numbers. The phone rings twice, then a woman with a strong Southern accent answers, "Hello!"

John told me not to say who I am when I first make the calls, just keep it simple.

I quickly blurt out, "Hello, is this the Fisher residence?"

"Yes, it is."

"Does a Ted Fisher live there?"

"Yes."

"I'm sorry to disturb you. I'm doing a family tree research project, and I think we may possibly be related. Did Ted ever live in California?"

"Yes, he did. Hold on a minute—I think you found who you're looking for," she says, with no element of surprise. She must have mistaken me for someone else.

Troy walks in the room and sees my glazed, tense expression, "What? Who is it?" he asks. I put my finger up, signaling for him to give me a minute.

"Hello?" This voice resonates in a deep place inside, a place I didn't know existed.

I clear my throat and compose myself, "Hello . . . is this . . . Ted?"

"Yes." He pauses, "Is this . . . *Hollye?*"

My knees are rubber. "Yes," I barely whisper, my eyes stinging with tears.

The man's voice wails, "I can't believe this! We were just talking about you *last night!* I've been praying to find you!"

And so begins my first conversation with my father. He tells me I'd spent weekends with him when I was young, but after I turned three, he was locked up. He was a heroin addict, a Haight-Ashbury dropout who spent my entire childhood in prison, mostly for repeated petty theft. The judges got sick and tired of him so they finally put him in San Quentin to teach him a lesson. During that time, his sister, my aunt Marti who used to babysit me, was searching for me. Because my mother had changed my name, Marti hadn't been able to find me. My father tells me Marti passed away the year before. He says he's sorry she isn't here to see this day, but then again, maybe she is.

He says he's always remembered my birthday, circling it on the calendar and thinking of me every year. He remembers the unique spelling of my name, the honey color of my hair, just like his.

I find out, and here is the greatest miracle, that I have three younger brothers, all loving, good men who will become an integral part of my life. I also discover that all three addresses John the genealogist had asterisked are my relatives. My father, grandfather, and two of my brothers share the same name.

I learn that I am, in some ways, very much like my father. He is an oil painter, an avid reader, and at times, a lost soul—

although he is an ordained Baptist preacher—a spiritual seeker, just like me. He's got a dry, sarcastic wit, like me. Unlike me, I will later find out that my father still struggles with addiction, though it is medication prescribed by his doctors after three failed back surgeries. He will from time to time go into detox to clean up, and then will fall back to that familiar numb place. When he is addicted he will not preach, and will look away from God, because otherwise, he says, it's "like offering God sideways prayers." *Hell is the place where God can't hear you.*

Two weeks after that phone call, Aunt Diane and I return to the Mormon bomb shelter to share my news with John the genealogist. We find him thumbing through records, the ghosts no doubt hovering over his shoulders helping another lost soul find his way back home.

He looks up, "Oh. Hi ladies. I'll be right with you."

Diane and I sit at a long table, where John joins us moments later, and I tell him the whole story. He is smiling, but quiet. I show him photos my father sent me, including pictures of my aunts, uncles, grandparents, and my three brothers. And a photo of my father's great-grandmother, also a full-blood Cherokee.

"This is great," he says, "really great." He gets teary and looks away.

Aunt Diane purses her lips, making a sympathetic face.

"I do this work," John says, his voice breaking, "because I want other families to reunite. My daughters are estranged from me, and have been for years. I write them letters every single day, but they've never responded." He takes off his glasses and wipes his eyes. "This gives me hope."

I put a hand on his back, not knowing exactly what to say. "Just keep loving them," I say, "and don't give up."

He sniffs and rubs his face vigorously, taking a deep

breath. "Hey, let's see those ancestry records of yours. Where did we leave off?"

I open my file with the records I copied on our last visit, "This is what we've got so far."

He studies our census reports, many of them over a hundred years old, stopping to take a closer look at one of them, "Wow, that's odd. Your family name is Kindred?" he asks.

Aunt Diane nods, "Yeah, Scottish, I think."

"I have Kindreds in my family, too," he says, "but they couldn't be the same ones. Mine are from a really small town in Illinois—population of about four thousand."

"Wait a minute. Are you talking about Atlanta, Illinois?' I ask, hesitantly. "Our ancestors built that town."

He looks at me, stunned, "Are you kidding me?"

John, Aunt Diane, and I dig furiously through records, tracing both his ancestry and ours, eventually finding the place where we connect. We are distant cousins.

Imagine the probability of this: from a small Illinois town of four thousand people, we end up in Los Angeles, a city of over three million, and the three of us, all non-Mormons, meet in the bomb shelter of a Mormon church. Now I have no choice but to believe in the power of the ancestors. There is a reason I was led here, and a reason my father and I were brought back together. And perhaps, like Troy and so many others said after the fire, there is a reason for everything that happened.

THE REUNION WITH MY FATHER, like life, isn't perfect. For two months, he and I talk on the phone every day and I am floating on air with my Pollyanna happy-ever-after ending. I finally fly out to meet him on Thanksgiving, and that's when I witness the trembling hands, the sweating, the beast of his addiction. He cleans up for good a few years later, after a failed suicide attempt. (The apple doesn't fall far from the tree.) Over the years, I'll make an annual trip to Texas, and become closely bonded to my brothers. We are like any other family. At times we are close and loving, but we are all walking wounded, a little bruised and banged up by life. Our relationships are wobbly at times, but when we're together, we're still standing like a three-legged table.

Troy champions this journey for me, always in the background with the video camera running. Cissy and Taylor are ambivalent about it. Taylor is happy for me, but personally unaffected. The idea that I have a father, that this person is his grandfather, is abstract to him. Cissy is wary and skeptical, especially after becoming aware of his addictions. She's seen enough with Kyle. She doesn't let my father become someone important to her.

I try to let my father become someone important to me on this long, confusing journey as I discover the lineage I descend from, and what that means.

MY FORTY-FIRST BIRTHDAY is the worst. Cissy is away at college. My friends flake out on me. And Troy, who was always so good about birthdays in the past, completely fails at this one. But the worst of it is that neither my mother nor my father call. I am estranged from both sides of my family, which reactivates those broken-record feelings of not being wanted— feelings I thought I had left far behind.

Only a year after our happy reunion, my father has evaporated from my life again as though he'd only ever been a mirage to begin with. He is submerged in prescription drug addiction, has stopped preaching, stopped returning calls. And my estrangement from my mother is well into its second year, but even still, she'd never blown off my birthday before.

I wake up the day after my birthday feeling so depressed I can't get out of bed. I know Troy and my friends love me, even if none of them made my birthday a priority this year, but the fact that my own parents didn't acknowledge the day I was born is tough to bear. I am the orphan of two living parents.

I lie in bed all day, weepy, playing a CD of songs about angels while repeating this prayer, "God, send me an angel to help me believe in the goodness of the world again."

And God, the trickster that S/He is, answers.

A month later, I become physically exhausted. If I sit in a chair I fall instantly to sleep, and can barely keep my eyes open past 8:30 p.m. I worry I am sick with some awful terminal disease. Being in my forties now—maybe I'm just not as strong as I used to be. Maybe this is the hormone imbalance you hear women talking about. A week later, I realize I missed my period, but I'm too old to be pregnant, and besides we use birth control, so that's off the table. Just to rule it out, I take a home pregnancy test, and before I even finish peeing on the stick a bright blue plus sign appears. I'm pregnant.

I convince myself it's a mistake. This was something I thought about years ago—but now I'm older, at high risk for complications, and my immediate worry: although the rest of my family is covered, I have no health insurance. Little did I know all those years ago, at the moment I admitted suicidal thoughts to my therapist, it went on record and I became un-insurable. Although I've been out of therapy for years, my prior anxiety and depression are considered a preexisting condition.

What will I do if I really am pregnant? How will we pay

for the hospital bills and prenatal care? I imagine myself giving birth at home, *Little House on the Prairie*–style. We're going to need lots of towels and boiling water. *That's ridiculous, I'm not pregnant.* Just to set my mind at ease, I take a second pregnancy test. I hold it in my hand, eyes closed, and say a prayer, "Whatever way this goes I will accept it as a blessing."

Yep. I'm pregnant.

I sit on the edge of the tub, breathless.

How can a baby be anything but good?

But I'm older. *What if something goes wrong?*

What will Troy think?

Troy made it clear years ago that he didn't want to have more kids. Cissy has already gone off to college in Santa Barbara, and Taylor is in high school. We are long past the years of cribs and baby strollers.

I walk out of the bathroom. Troy is sitting at the dining room table on a business call. I walk back into the bathroom. What do I do? I have to tell him. I reemerge, standing outside the bathroom door. I don't know how to begin. I pace, shaky, unsure of myself.

He stops talking mid-sentence when he sees me, then makes an excuse to get off the call. He sets the phone down, "What's going on?" he asks. I stand frozen to my spot, across the room, not sure what to say. "Sweetie, you're freaking me out—what's wrong?"

"I'm pregnant," I say, my voice barely above a whisper.

"You are?"

I nod, tentatively, my stomach tight with a mix of giddy elation and terror.

"You *are?*" he repeats, with what I hope is a look of wonder, not nausea.

"Yes," I smile warily, wringing my hands, "I am. I know this is nuts. Are you . . . happy?"

He rushes over and swoops me up in his arms. "Yes!"

I burst out in relieved tears. He hugs me tight and says, "I'm happy! I'm so happy!"

As close as we can tell, the baby was conceived on Christmas Eve—my time of hope, and just weeks after I said that prayer: *Send me an angel to help me believe in the goodness of the world again.*

I love being pregnant. I have no morning sickness this time. I hike and do yoga throughout. I lie in bed in the mornings, present to the baby's rhythms. He wakes at the crack of dawn and starts kicking (which he still does), and I sing to him. I know this is my last hurrah so I am present for every moment, appreciating the miracle for all it is.

I go into labor late in September, just as a freak electrical storm hits California. Thunder and lightning and contractions, oh my. Cissy and Taylor ride with us to the hospital as I breathe through contractions, and are the first to hold Evan when he is born (at the crack of dawn). Shortly after, the nurse brings him to my room. He is quiet but wide-awake.

"It's remarkable how alert he is for a newborn," she says, adding, "I mean, it's almost disconcerting."

It's true. His dark grey-blue eyes are enormous and round, and he stares directly into mine, unblinking, for long stretches of time. His eyes appear all-knowing, as if he is solving all the problems in the universe. And every time his little baby lips stretch into an "O," I half expect him to spill the secrets.

I'll tell Evan he rode into the world on a lightning bolt, because that child is electrified, and as Troy says, he's got stray voltage. At eighteen months old, he is reciting the alphabet. At nineteen months he recites it backward. At twenty months, he becomes obsessed with Maya Angelou's books. No others will do. He finds them on my bookshelf, drops them in my lap (before he even has the power of speech) and points. I'll pull him into my lap and read to him, tracing each word with my finger. Evan begins reading at two years old. At three he begs me each night to read him the world atlas, though I try unsuccessfully to sway him toward Dr. Seuss. He memorizes all the countries of the world in alphabetical order, and loves to recite them while jumping on a trampoline. I still cannot remember the countries of the world even though I'm the one who reads him the atlas each night. He has perfect pitch, and when the doorbell or phone rings he will tell you it's a B flat or a G. Troy will run to the piano to check, and Evan is always right. We start him at piano lessons at four. He still wakes every day at the crack of dawn. I hear his thundering footsteps moving across the wood floors, coming my way, and I smile. My miracle child never would have existed if I had checked out of this world back in 1995. This is why I know now we must always, always hold on, no matter how dark and hopeless it all seems. We can't even imagine the astounding riches life has in store for us.

Evan is the one I had always felt was missing from our family. He's the one I had that "feeling" about. Now we are complete. All members present and accounted for.

ON A HOT SUMMER day nearly thirteen years after the fire, I'm standing in Tower Records with Taylor, who has now grown to be a tall, muscular seventeen-year-old with shaggy blond hair that falls over his face. We're thumbing through newly released CDs, bobbing our heads to the music. Taylor wanders down another aisle and I'm lost in my own world when he heads back toward me.

"Mom," he says under his breath, "look who's here."

I look up at the same moment Sarah does, and we lock eyes. Very surprised eyes. Kayla stands behind her, tall and willowy, with long strawberry-blond curls to her waist. Taylor and Kayla used to take baths together when they were toddlers. Now they stand across from each other as a young man and woman, eyeing each other with vague recognition.

"Hollye!" Sarah moves toward me with a wide smile and open arms. I am stunned motionless. She hugs me with real feeling, takes a step back, her hands gripping my arms, "Wow, it is so good to see you!"

I force a smile but feel removed. Mostly it is very strange to see her. But there is no rush of adrenaline, no butterflies in the stomach.

"How are you?" she asks, looking me in the eye.

"I'm good," I say, so glad that it's finally true.

I hesitate to ask how she is in return, because I already know what happened. Troy and I ran into Sarah's parents a few years before, and they invited us to their house for lunch. They told us then that Sarah and Scott had cut them out of their lives, and they didn't know why. A year later, they called to tell us that Sarah's marriage with Scott was over—it turned out that Scott was gay, which we had always suspected. He loved Sarah but couldn't live a lie any longer. He now lived happily with his boyfriend, and Sarah was remarried, to another guy named Scott. Sarah's picture-perfect life, like mine, had shattered to pieces. She lost her marriage, her business, her self. Sarah and Scott—the perfect couple with all those ducks in a row, always doing the right thing, all the proper insurance policies to boot, and none of it was enough to protect them from the messy business of living.

I study her face for traces of the girl I used to know. She looks a little less precisely coiffed than when she was with

Scott. She is wearing workout clothes—she always was an exercise enthusiast. Her curls are loose, hair slightly disheveled, no makeup. She looks healthy. She looks a little more herself.

"Maybe you heard, Scott and I divorced."

"I did hear," I say, "I'm really sorry."

"No, don't be sorry," she waves her hand, "We're still best friends. We spend all our holidays together with the girls. Our relationship is actually better *now.*" She smiles wistfully. "You and Troy are still together, I hope?"

"Yes," I say. If only she knew how hard we'd worked to keep it that way, "and we had another child. A little boy named Evan."

She gasps, "You're kidding! Congratulations! How old is he?"

"He's almost two now. He's just a blessing in our lives. A real character," I say, smiling genuinely now. The thought of Evan trumps everything else, bringing a warmth to my solar plexus.

"I want to meet him!" she says with an enthusiasm I can't match. I am finally over her, over the whole thing, and while I wish her and Scott well, I have no desire to revisit the past. I change the subject, "Yeah, he's very cute. He really keeps us on our toes."

She looks me in the eye, and with sincerity, says, "I really want to talk to you. I mean, really talk."

I'm thinking, what would be the point?

She continues, "I have some things I need to tell you. Will you give me a chance?" She keeps eye contact with me, something she never used to do.

"Sure," I say.

I leave the record store feeling shaken, but not stirred.

"Wow. That was weird," Taylor says.

"Yeah," I say, starting the car.

"How do you feel, Mom?"

"Strange. Kind of in shock, really. How about you?"

"I dunno. Kinda awkward," he says, wrestling to get the wrapper off his new Deftones CD.

"Do you remember much from that time, Tay?"

"I pretty much remember everything," he says, and that makes me sad.

Everything. The memories filter back—me sobbing in the car, Cissy and Taylor's little hands on my shoulders, saying, "Don't cry, Mommy." The cards and pictures they drew to cheer me up, the ones I still keep in a chest by my bed, in case I ever forget what truly matters.

When I get home, Troy is working in the recording studio. Evan naps in his playpen beside him. This is my safe place. I plop into Troy's lap, my arms around his neck, "You are never going to believe what just happened."

SARAH AND I MEET at Starbucks a few days later. We hug and exchange some small talk. But as soon as we sit down, she takes my hand with both of hers, looks me in the eye, and says, "I love you."

This shocks me. She squeezes my hand hard, as pools gather against her bottom lashes, spilling over and rolling down her cheeks. She doesn't bother to wipe them away.

She looks up at the ceiling, takes a deep breath and continues, "and I have missed you in my life, so much." Her voice breaks, and I can't help but feel a connection, my eyes brimming up with hers. She continues, "I'm sorry for the way I treated you. I don't know why I acted that way back then, I guess I was afraid. Afraid of what was happening to you, and how it was affecting me. If you can forgive me, I really want another chance to be in your life—as the person I am now."

And just like that, there is a shift in my heart. It happens naturally, without my needing to think about it.

Forgiveness is not easy. I spent years trying to forgive Kyle, because people said it was the right thing to do. But forgiveness can't be planned. It's spontaneous, much like falling in love. I can't force it, no matter how I pray, or meditate or read books about it.

With Sarah, it is instant, because she opens the door. She lays herself bare, with no agenda. There is no lip service, no bullshit. Her remorse is palpable. I know her life was turned upside down. She and I are not so unalike. We were both stripped of everything we once were. She is no longer standing behind a kitchen chair like a lion tamer, keeping me away. Her heart has been broken open, and I am able to get in.

She tells me that after Scott came out, she spoke to no one about it. They lived together as roommates for two more stifling years, working together in their clothing business, shipping boxes side by side, she, occasionally, rushing to the bathroom to cry. She was estranged from us, estranged from her family, and suffered through it alone.

"Oh Sarah, the tragedy in all of this is that you pushed away the person you most needed to get through that. You know I would have been there for you, and for Scott. I would have loved you both without judgment. So would Troy."

"I know," she nods tearfully.

We talk for hours. Although neither of us have answers to the why or how of what happened, we recognize we were all broken in our own ways. The difference was, at that time she and Scott were working hard to deny it, while Troy and I had our guts spilled on the table, whether we liked it or not. Our reality was too ugly for them to confront.

"I have a strange question," she says. "Someone gave me a birthday gift years ago . . . a wish box. On the bottom, it said 'One of a Kind' and I swear, I thought you made that box."

I laugh, "I did."

She shakes her head, "I knew it. It just looked like something beautiful you'd make."

"What's crazy is that I made that art to heal myself from the pain of losing you. I find it pretty amazing that your friend would buy it for you—that she unknowingly thought a piece of my soul was something you would love."

We are both quiet for a moment, letting that sink in. How incredible that as our friendship was falling apart, the universe would deliver a gift from me to her on her birthday.

There is still so much I don't understand about that time, but what is clear is this: I am no longer the wounded girl throwing herself from cars, and Sarah is no longer the girl who stood in the shadow of a truth she couldn't confront. Her experiences changed her, as did mine. She is attending college working toward her degree in psychology. Her goal now, like mine, is to help others heal. And one day in the future, I'll stand cheering for her as she walks across the stage in cap and gown, "Pomp and Circumstance" blasting across the college campus. I'll look over at Troy, Evan on my hip, and say, "Who'd have ever thought . . ."

That we can find forgiveness in the wake of all that happened is no small miracle. When all else has burned to the ground, hope finds a way to take root. This is a gift in my life, to which I can compare no other. If I hadn't had my heart completely shattered, the journey to forgiveness wouldn't have been as profound. Now I know what love is. It is the most powerful force in the universe. It prevails through fire, through fall, through the deep freeze of winter. It courses through all of us, connecting us, even when we don't see it. It doesn't need validation, or understanding or praise. But when we awaken, and realize that love is, and always has been at the core of everything, that's when it all changes.

EPILOGUE

✿ ✿ ✿

Troy and I sit in the darkened audience as my friend Lyena's one-woman play, *Caterpillar Soup*, begins. Lyena is the new writing teacher for Art and Soul, the nonprofit program Joy and I founded. We bring arts programs to teenagers living in foster care, teaching them how to release and channel their pain through art. Lyena is a huge inspiration to our students, and to me.

Lyena is seated center stage, in silhouette. She stretches her arms upward and sways against a violet backdrop, the image of a tall oak tree projected behind her. It was from an oak tree that this beautiful dancer fell, shattering her spine. She landed, eventually, in a wheelchair. Her fall was only the beginning of loss. But it was also the beginning of miraculous transformation.

Lyena explains the reason behind the title of her play. A caterpillar doesn't crawl into its chrysalis for a long hibernation, popping out weeks later a well-rested butterfly. The truth of what goes on inside that chrysalis is an ugly affair. The caterpillar liquefies, becoming, as she coins it, caterpillar soup. There is nothing left of what it once was, but something new begins to take hold. When the butterfly is fully formed, it will begin to emerge, struggling to make its way out of the chrysalis. If you cut the chrysalis open to release the butterfly, it will die. It is the struggle that gives the wings strength.

Troy and I sit mesmerized, awed by Lyena's courage and honesty as she details her road to recovery, and her metaphoric journey inside the chrysalis to her eventual release as the powerful woman she is today. As the play comes to a close, the audience leaps to their feet, giving Lyena a standing ovation. People hardly speak as they gather their things and filter out of the theatre, but I stay, frozen in my chair, the movie of my own life playing in my head.

As I lay in my burning house gasping for breath, losing consciousness, it was the butterflies plummeting from the ceiling, hitting my body like fat raindrops, that woke me up so I could grab my son and escape. Those butterflies are the most vivid image I retain from that night thirteen years ago. Like Lyena, my journey also began with a fall. I fell from a window, and though my back did not break, my spirit shattered on impact. I too had been liquefied. There is nothing left of who I once was. Tears roll down my face as the revelation hits me. How compassionate, the Creator of the universe, to allow me to liquefy, and then to struggle, so I could find my wings. Who would I be, I wonder, had I not lost everything?

FIRE CAN DESTROY, but it can also purify and reform. It can kill us, and it can keep us alive. A small flame will be extinguished with the slightest puff of air, but put wind to wildfire, and watch what happens. Tragedy was the wind that could have extinguished a smaller love, but like wind to wildfire, it made my love for Troy and our children grow more fierce. This love can never be taken from me. What a deep and rare gift to know this, to really *know* this.

I still struggle with my faith. The truth is, as long as I am alive, I will be questioning it. But I have learned to get comfortable living in the questions, trusting that answers come in their own time. I still don't know if there actually is a protective God watching over us who whispered in my ear that night, or if it was just my instinct of survival. On good days, I suspect the former. But I do know there is an order to everything, and that love is the force that generates it. And if God is love, then I can safely say I believe in God.

I've learned what it really means to be a family. There is no Brady Bunch. Sometimes we fail each other. Sometimes we step away and then, hopefully, come back again. Sometimes we hurt each other without ever meaning to. We're just a bunch of imperfect humans doing the best we can, trying to learn how to love each other, and that is enough.

I've learned to love the fall, the season that brought my father and brothers to me. The season that brought my Evan. Fall taught me not to be afraid of things dying and blowing away with the harsh winds. Life regenerates. Love regenerates. I get that now.

I've learned that everything *is* going to be okay, no matter what. Each time Troy told me that, I thought it naive, but he was speaking a deep truth. There are no guarantees, and no insurance policy to protect us from unexpected tragedy. Our possessions, job titles, our stations in life are fleeting, and even our relationships with those we most love can change. But our spirits have the ability to be shattered and made whole again. Our hearts can break but still love mightily. Everything is going to be okay. Everything *is* okay.

And here is what I absolutely know: every day that we are alive is our new beginning. Each challenge holds for us an opportunity to learn and grow, to find our strength and goodness in the midst of tragedy. And just like the forest after a wildfire, there is a seed of greatness in every one of us, waiting to break open. And it is never, ever too late to bloom.

WE STILL LIVE IN our beloved mountain home. Did I mention it is one block from the fire station?

GRATITUDE TO:

My husband Troy Dexter: the impetus for most every good thing that has happened to me. Choosing you was the best decision I've ever made.

My daughter Cristen, my sons Taylor and Evan, and my grandson Ayumu: you are my greatest gifts, my world, my heart.

Erin Doyle for being my rock. Like the Sting song says, "If I ever lose my faith in you, there'd be nothing left for me to do." And to her beautiful wife, Beth, and son, Benjamin, and to Dani Robinson, Hayden, and Carly. You all are the best family a girl could ever choose.

Amy Ferris for encouraging me to shine brighter than I knew I could, and giving me the courage to stand in my own truth.

Amy Friedman, my wise and beautiful friend who lovingly insisted I write this book so I could straighten my life out.

Barbara Radecki whose friendship, wisdom, insight, and excellent editing chops led to this book becoming so much better and so much more true.

Bernard Selling who first taught me how to write, and continued to provide excellent insight into my inner dynamics.

Joyce Maynard for taking both my hands, looking me in the eye and saying, "You are a writer"—a small, simple gesture that changed the trajectory of my life.

To my fabulous Facebook posse: friends from all over the country and world, who constantly chimed in on my blogs telling me to "write this book." Your encouragement made me strong through this process and I am forever grateful.

To my friends who read early drafts and provided invaluable feedback: Monica Holloway, Victoria Zackheim,

Laura Davis, Jesse Loren, Dani Robinson, Amy Ferris, Erin Doyle, Barbara Radecki, Diane Lindley, and Beverlee Peters— thank you.

To Brooke Warner for encouraging me and believing in me.

To the friends who got me though those difficult years after the fire: Diane Cyphers, whose letters and phone calls kept me sane. Kelly Rose, who called me every year on November 19 to tell me how glad she was that I was alive. Tara Donnelly, for music and song. Keri and Steven Mann, who made me laugh when I didn't think I could. Joy, Bob, and Donna for being my creative life raft. To those friends and family whose generosity got us through the worst of times: Julie Silver and family, Jon and Jerri Baker, Kevin Winard, Stephen Van Lydegraf, Velma Willard, and so many more that my mind just couldn't retain all these years later, but to whom I am so grateful.

My dad for showing up in my life, and for loving me.

My mom and Rick for their unwavering love and support during those dark years.

And finally to Troy's family for hanging in there and working through all the hard stuff with us until we got to a good place.

ABOUT THE AUTHOR

photo credit: Erin Doyle

HOLLYE DEXTER is the author of two memoirs and co-editor of *Dancing at the Shame Prom* (Seal Press), praised by best-selling author Gloria Feldt (former CEO of Planned Parenthood) as "a brilliant book that just might change your life." Her essays and articles about women's issues, activism, and politics have been widely published in anthologies, as well as in Maria Shriver's Architects of Change, Huffington Post, The Feminist Wire, and more. She teaches writing workshops internationally and for at-risk youth in LA, where she lives with her husband and a houseful of kids and pets. Learn more about Dexter at www.hollyedexter.net.

SELECTED TITLES FROM SHE WRITES PRESS

She Writes Press is an independent publishing company
founded to serve women writers everywhere.
Visit us at www.shewritespress.com.

Where Have I Been All My Life? A Journey Toward Love and Wholeness
by Cheryl Rice. $16.95, 978-1-63152-917-7. Rice's universally
relatable story of how her mother's sudden death launched her on a
journey into the deepest parts of grief—and, ultimately, toward love
and wholeness.

A Different Kind of Same: A Memoir by Kelley Clink. $16.95,
978-1-63152-999-3. Several years before Kelley Clink's brother
hanged himself, she attempted suicide by overdose. In the aftermath
of his death, she traces the evolution of both their illnesses, and
wonders: If he couldn't make it, what hope is there for her?

Breathe: A Memoir of Motherhood, Grief, and Family Conflict by Kelly
Kittel. $16.95, 978-1-938314-78-0. A mother's heartbreaking
account of losing two sons in the span of nine months—and learning,
despite all the obstacles in her way, to find joy in life again.

Splitting the Difference: A Heart-Shaped Memoir by Tré Miller-
Rodríguez. $19.95, 978-1-938314-20-9. When 34-year-old Tré
Miller-Rodríguez's husband dies suddenly from a heart attack, her
grief sends her on an unexpected journey that culminates in a
reunion with the biological daughter she gave up at 18.

Seeing Red: A Woman's Quest for Truth, Power, and the Sacred by Lone
Morch. $16.95, 978-1-938314-12-4. One woman's journey over inner
and outer mountains—a quest that takes her to the holy Mt. Kailas in
Tibet, through a seven-year marriage, and into the arms of the fierce
goddess Kali, where she discovers her powerful, feminine self.

Renewable: One Woman's Search for Simplicity, Faithfulness, and Hope by
Eileen Flanagan. $16.95, 978-1-63152-968-9. At age forty-nine,
Eileen Flanagan had an aching feeling that she wasn't living up to her
youthful ideals or potential, so she started trying to change the world
—and in doing so, she found the courage to change her life.